Culture and Customs
of the United States

Culture and Customs of the United States

Volume 2
Culture

EDITED BY BENJAMIN F. SHEARER

Culture and Customs of North America

GREENWOOD PRESS
Westport, Connecticut • London

Library of Congress Cataloging-in-Publication Data

Culture and customs of the United States / edited by Benjamin F. Shearer.
    p. cm.—(Culture and customs of North America, ISSN 1940–1132)
    Includes bibliographical references and index.
    ISBN 978–0–313–33875–5 (set : alk. paper)—ISBN 978–0–313–33876–2
(vol. 1 : alk. paper)—ISBN 978–0–313–33877–9 (vol. 2 : alk. paper)
    1. United States—Civilization.   2. United States—Social life and
customs.   3. United States—Social conditions.   I. Shearer, Benjamin F.
    E169.1.C843   2008
    973—dc22   2007039174

British Library Cataloguing in Publication Data is available.

Library of Congress Catalog Card Number: 2007039174
ISBN-13: 978–0–313–33875–5 (set)
        978–0–313–33876–2 (vol 1)
        978–0–313–33877–9 (vol 2)
ISSN: 1940–1132

First published in 2008

Greenwood Press, 88 Post Road West, Westport, CT 06881
An imprint of Greenwood Publishing Group, Inc.
www.greenwood.com

Printed in the United States of America

The paper used in this book complies with the
Permanent Paper Standard issued by the National
Information Standards Organization (Z39.48–1984).

10   9   8   7   6   5   4   3   2   1

Contents

5

Cuisine and Fashion

Benjamin F. Shearer

American Cuisine

> We are barely beginning to sift down our own cuisine.
>
> —Charles Beard

"Let's grab a bite to eat." This typical American expression suggests a host of unsavory connotations. Children are chastised for grabbing. There is a sense of lawlessness and a certain impropriety about grabbing things. Grabbing is not polite, but millions of Americans are grabbing a bite to eat every day. Grabbing is what is done on the run. There is a kind of national fast food cuisine to cater to all these people on the run, but fast food is just part of the story. Contrary to their portrayals in film, Americans are not always running. In fact, their expenditures on fast food are a relatively small portion of their total food expenditures.

The same transportation and food handling systems that helped to create a national fast food cuisine have also blurred the lines among regional cuisines. It is not at all unusual for Maine lobsters to be served in restaurants in California or Rhode Island quahogs to show up in chowder in Arizona. Traditional American cuisine is, however, regional, based on what is available. It is differentiated generally by method—frying in the South and boiling in New England—and by national origin. The Germans and the English had the biggest effect on the development of American cooking because they represented the largest groups of America's first immigrants. It should not be forgotten, however, that the United States began its existence as 13 English colonies inhabited mostly by English men and women who brought their taste for English cooking with them. The development of the jambalaya that became called American food can be seen, therefore, as a gradual liberation from simple English home cooking, decried by visitors to England for centuries as an abomination, a tradition kept alive today by French presidents. Midwest cuisine is based heavily on the movement and settlement first of Germans and then Scandinavians. Southern cuisine is inextricably mixed with the legacy of slavery, as black slaves over time turned high-table English plantation cooking into flavorful dishes no longer English or African, but completely American. Southwestern cuisine can no longer be broken down into its component native Indian, Mexican, Spanish, and Anglo components. California, with its incredible ethnic diversity, has developed a regional cuisine that is consciously based on fusing the culinary arts of various cultures with locally produced goods. The Pacific Northwest is a developing cuisine but is most certainly based on regionally available fresh food.

"That's American as apple pie." This often heard American expression is meant to refer to anything an American thinks is really American, like an old Ford truck or Bing Crosby singing "White Christmas." The fact is, of course, that apple pie is not American at all. Recipes for apple pies showed up in Elizabethan England and were even stowed away on the ships bringing the first colonists to American shores. Typically, apple pies became so ubiquitous that Americans appropriated them as their own. To most Americans, apple pie is a national emblem of American cuisine. Yet in spite of the American preoccupation with uniformity in food—a Big Mac is a Big Mac in Boston, Kansas City, and Los Angeles—even apple pies are susceptible to regional variation. Germans and Amish in Pennsylvania may toss in some sour cream and raisins or ice the top pastry layer. In Massachusetts, some cranberries may find themselves baked with the apples. Apple chiffon pie is popular in upstate New York. In Illinois, apples and pumpkin might be pureed together in a pie. An old California recipe cooked the apples first and laid them on a bed of caramel sauce before baking.

The case of the lowly bean illustrates even better the regional nature of American cuisine. Beans, no matter the variety, have always been a staple in American diets. Boston has proudly accepted the appellation "Bean Town" since the 1700s thanks to its great northern baked beans flavored with brown sugar and molasses. In south Texas, however, barbequed baked pink beans get spiced up with chilies. In Vermont, baked navy beans get a treatment of apples and maple syrup. Hoppin' John in the southern Low Country pairs rice with black-eyed peas and ham. In the Southwest, Pueblo Indians combined chorizos, a legacy of Spain, beef, hot peppers, cumin, corn, and tomatoes with Anasazi beans for a local delicacy.[1]

So what does it mean to have an American meal? There is no recipe for cooking the American way. American cooking, like American life, is an individual effort in which innovation and efficiency are prized. Quite simply, American food is what Americans cook and eat. It is food appropriated from the cultures of the people who lived or came there and, in most all cases, changed to fit local circumstance, taste, and the means of mass production.

Eating and Drinking in America

In 2002, each American ate (per capita consumption) 64.5 pounds of beef, 48.2 pounds of pork, 56.8 pounds of chicken, 15.6 pounds of fish and shellfish, 180 eggs, 885.3l pounds of dairy products, 30.5 pounds of cheese (topped by American at 12.8 pounds, followed by Italian at 12.4 pounds), 26.4 pounds of frozen dairy products, 191.3 pounds of flour and cereal products, 63.2 pounds of sugar, 125.6 pounds of fresh fruit and 146.0 pounds of processed fruit, 193.4 pounds of fresh vegetables (potatoes in first place at 45.0 pounds, and lettuce in second place at 22.4 pounds), and 208.6 pounds of processed vegetables. Americans also per capita drank 23.6 gallons of coffee, 7.8 gallons of tea, 21.9 gallons of milk, 8.0 gallons of fruit juice, 21.8 gallons of beer, 2.1 gallons of wine, and 1.3 gallons of distilled liquor.[2]

Food is big business in America, the birthplace of casual dining. In 2006, there were about 925,000 restaurants in the United States, which means there is roughly one restaurant for every 300 people, and 70 percent of them are single-restaurant small businesses. More than 50 percent of American adults have worked at one time in the restaurant industry. Estimates are that Americans spent $511 billion in these eating and drinking establishments, which have 12.5 million employees, thus making the restaurant industry second only to government in number of workers. On a given day, 130,000,000 Americans visit a restaurant for a meal or a snack, and they spend, on average, $2,434 per household, or $974 per person per year, eating out. Americans spent 47 percent of their total food money in restaurants in 2006, up dramatically from only 25 percent in 1955. Americans like to eat out. Sixty-six percent of them agree that they can get flavorful food eating out that cannot easily be duplicated at home.[3] Americans spend about $165 billion a year at full-service restaurants. Snack and nonalcoholic beverage bars pull in almost $17 billion, cafeterias and buffets, another $5.3 billion. Bars and taverns have annual revenues of more than $15.2 billion. Hotel restaurants bring in nearly $25 billion a year. Business and leisure travel help to fuel restaurant sales, as do major holidays. Mother's Day, for example, brings 62 percent of those celebrating the occasion with special meals into restaurants. Many will go out for more than one meal. Twenty-two percent go for breakfast, 51 percent for lunch or brunch, and 59 percent for dinner.

Fast-food eating places account for over $134 billion per year of Americans' food expenditures.[4]

All-you-can-eat restaurants and buffets are popular in America. Needless to say, Nouvelle cuisine, as it morphed into American cooking as the new American cuisine, was not a hit with the typical hungry American. The problem was not fresh ingredients, or even the lack of rich sauces (gravy to Americans), but the outrage that a speck of meat supporting an architecture of unknown and strangely cut vegetables amid dots of red or green stuff dropped strategically on the plate appeared to be an appetizer at a main course price.

Full-service restaurants, all characterized by a waitstaff serving sit-down meals in the establishments, run the gamut from tiny little independent neighborhood eating establishments to themed, casual dining chain restaurants like Chipotle Mexican Grill, Outback Steak House, Olive Garden, and Red Lobster, all the way to world-class restaurants that have won the coveted five stars from the *Mobil Travel Guide*. In 2006, only 15 restaurants in all the United States earned that distinction. New York City had four; the San Francisco area, three; Atlanta, two; Los Angeles, Chicago, and Philadelphia, one each. The others were located in Washington, Virginia, Summerville, South Carolina, and Kennebunkport, Maine. Another 122 restaurants earned four stars, led by New York City, with 14, and Chicago, with 9.[5] A meal at any of these restaurants would be beyond the means of most Americans, even for a special occasion, and even if they could get reservations.

What do ordinary Americans order when they go to restaurants on a typical day? The top 10 selections for men in descending order according to one survey were a hamburger, French fries, pizza, a breakfast sandwich, a side salad, eggs, doughnuts, hash brown potatoes, Chinese food, and a main salad. Women ordered French fries, a hamburger, pizza, a side salad, a chicken sandwich, a breakfast sandwich, a main salad, Chinese food, and rice.[6]

Hamburgers, sold in the billions each year from ubiquitous franchises (McDonald's, Burger King, and Wendy's are, in order, the largest), bars and taverns, and county and state fairs—anywhere there are Americans—are the quintessential American food. Hamburgers are also featured at most backyard cookouts, tailgate parties, picnics, and sports events. Most of the beef consumed in America is in the form of ground beef—hamburger. American ingenuity has elevated the simple hamburger to a gastronomic art form. The hamburger chains have attempted to brand their burgers by charbroiling them, flame-broiling them, steaming them with onions, and grilling them; by shaping them round, square, and triangular; and by heaping them with varieties of condiments including lettuce, tomatoes, mayonnaise, special sauces, secret sauces, salad dressings, onions, peppers, chilies, mustard, and ketchup, not to exhaust the list. Many a local restaurateur claims to have the best hamburger

in town. Indeed, the variations are endless. A hamburger steak, ground sir-
loin, may be at the pinnacle of the hamburger hierarchy, but the American
meatloaf (a baked loaf of ground beef and pork and spices of choice) is a basic
American concoction that has reached such gustatory heights that famous
American-born French chef Julia Child called it American pâté.

Ordering a hamburger and fries is like ordering ham and eggs or milk
and cookies—they just go together naturally in the American mind. French
fries, as the name implies, are not American in origin (they are Belgian, as
the name does not imply). Neither, of course, is pizza, which Americans
have transformed from a simple Italian tomato bread starter into a gigantic
complete meal. Bigger is always better; Americans eat around 100 acres of
pizza every day. Ninety-three percent of all Americans eat at least one pizza
a month; about 3 billion pizzas are sold every year. Like the hamburger, the
pizza has been subjected to American inventiveness. There are nearly 70,000
pizzerias in the United States, 64.3 percent of which are independents, but
they accounted for a bit fewer than 50 percent of total U.S. sales of almost
$31 billion. The top 25 pizzeria chains with nearly 25,000 stores account for
just over 50 percent of total U.S. sales. Pizza Hut, the largest chain, alone accounts for over 17 percent of all sales.[7] They, too, are round and square, small
and large, and can have just about anything on them. There are Hawaiian
pizzas (pineapple and ham), Mexican pizzas, barbeque pizzas, white pizzas
(no tomato sauce), fish pizzas, vegetable pizzas, Cajun pizzas, eggplant pizzas,
venison pizzas, duck pizzas, and even breakfast pizzas, with peanut butter and
jelly or bacon and eggs. Sixty-two percent of Americans want meat on their
pizza, and 36 percent of all pizzas ordered have pepperoni on them. Other
traditional favorite ingredients are mushrooms, extra cheese, sausage, green
peppers, and onions.[8]

There are about an equal number of Italian and Chinese full-service restaurants in America. Among limited service restaurants, mostly carryout establishments, Mexican restaurants outnumber Chinese restaurants seven to
five and Italian restaurants seven to two.[9] All together, there are more than
40,000 each of Mexican and Chinese restaurants in the United States. Italian,
Chinese, and Mexican cuisines have been completely incorporated into what
might be called the category of typical American food, what Americans like
to eat, and they eat a lot of it. Spaghetti and meatballs, egg rolls, and tacos are
standard fare eating out and at home. If college students can be thought of as
future trendsetters, there is no going back to old-time plain American cooking. When asked what their favorite cuisines were, 95 percent liked Italian;
90 percent liked Mexican; and 83 percent liked Chinese.[10]

Many have decried the fact that the traditional American sit-down family meal has gone the way of tintype and typewriters. Most parents work

outside the home, and kids have busy schedules filled with athletic activities, events, and other after-school obligations, to which they must be shuttled back and forth. Eating on the go is the new American meal tradition. There is little time for food preparation and precious little time to gulp it down. America has produced new generations for whom comfort food in later life is a box of macaroni and cheese, which they learned to make in a microwave at the age of five, mostly out of necessity. So what are Americans eating at home?

A trip to the grocery store, where shelf space is at a premium and grocers give space only to what sells fast, lends some understanding. Fresh fruit and vegetables get half an aisle, as do fresh meats (a lot of space for hamburger) and breads. Soft drinks (Coke, Pepsi, and tens of variations) and snacks (potato chips, tortilla chips, peanuts, etc.) get an entire aisle. Juices and various kinds of sport drinks have nearly half an aisle, and canned vegetables get half that. Soups, in cans, in ready-to-eat containers, and in boxes, get about a quarter aisle. Fruit, in cans, but mostly in ready-to-eat containers, get about a quarter of an aisle, but cookies and crackers get more space. There seems to be a lot of boxes: rows of cake mixes, bread mixes, muffin mixes, and cookie mixes. Cereal, the all-American breakfast food, gets a full side of an aisle. Even more impressive is the space given to boxes of rice, potatoes, and pasta. Boxes of potatoes may seem unnatural, but by just adding water, milk, and butter or margarine, and a few minutes of cooking, a variety of potato dishes can be created quickly. Rice gets some space, but not much in its pure form. Small boxes of rice with flavor packets tucked into the box get quite a bit of space. Nearly an entire row is filled with pasta in all its sizes and shapes, accompanied by jars of prepared spaghetti sauce, clam sauce, and Alfredo sauce. The Mexican food section is growing, but the Italian foods, as understood, coopted, and transformed by Americans, are the space winner. Busy American cooks can also go to another aisle to choose from nearly half a row of boxes of macaroni and cheese, pasta salad, and pasta dishes. In fact, in the continuing tribute to American food as the ultimate fusion cuisine, a chicken quesadilla flavor pasta is now available in a box. Those who find that to be too much fusion can always rely on Hamburger Helper available in several flavors. Just fry the hamburger, add the flavor packet and pasta and some water, and you have an American meal.

There are often two entire aisles of frozen food cases in grocery stores, which stands to reason because 94 percent of Americans sometimes buy frozen food on a typical trip to the grocery, and 30 percent always do. Six times a month, the typical American sits down to a heated up frozen meal.[11] In 2003, Americans spent over $6 billion on frozen dinners and entrees. In total, they spent $29.2 billion on frozen foods. Frozen vegetable sales of $2.8 billion,

A long grocery store aisle in one of America's large supermarkets. Corbis.

which included $858 million of frozen potatoes, nearly equaled frozen pizza sales of $2.74 billion. Sales of ice cream, which many Americans would consider a homegrown invention, came to $4.8 billion.[12]

Wine is sold in some 3,000 grocery stores as well as other stores across the nation. U.S. wine consumption has been increasing steadily since 1991 and across age and ethnic lines. Many Americans now consider wine to be a requirement of a good meal, especially in a good restaurant, but it is also served at home on special occasions. Wine is a staple at parties, often replacing hard liquor. In 2005, wine sales in the United States totaled 703 million gallons, valued at $26 billion. Table wines accounted for most of the sales at 619 million gallons; champagne and sparkling wines came to only 30 million gallons. The remainder was dessert wines. Amazingly, California wines took a 63 percent market share of all wines sold. California produced 532 million gallons of wine in 2005, of which 441 million gallons were sold in the United States. Premium wines, defined as $7 or more per bottle, were 66 percent of revenues, and everyday wines, below $7 per bottle, constituted the remainder. U.S. wine exports of 101 million gallons were 95 percent California wines. While wine is grown all across America, there can be little doubt that

California wines are the ones that have made American wines respectable around the globe.[13]

Americans like American beer. In fact, July is American beer month. Breweries were first licensed in New England in 1637. Beer is now an $83 billion business. In 2005, domestic beer sales of 178.8 million barrels (a barrel equals 31 U.S. gallons) dwarfed sales of 25.7 million barrels for imported beers. The large brewers, such as Anheuser Busch, with its flagship Budweiser brand, dominate the domestic beer market. That company alone accounts for around half of all domestic beer sales. The big brewers—also including Miller, Coors, and Pabst—have attempted to bolster their sales by catering to weight-conscious beer drinkers with light and low-carbohydrate brews, which are overtaking traditional lagers in sales. There is, however, another concurrent trend in American brewing filled by America's 1,415 craft breweries, which are turning out multiflavored and full-bodied 100 percent malt beers. These regional craft breweries, contract breweries, microbreweries, and brewpubs together are a $4.3 billion dollar business that produces about 7 million barrels annually and takes a 3.42 percent share of the American beer market. That is not much compared to the noncraft domestic brewers' 84.14 percent of the market or even imported beers' share of 12.43 percent, but craft brewers are providing Americans with an alternative to what critics have been known to call insipid American beer.[14]

America's original contribution to the family of distilled spirits was inspired by a Native American food staple combined with Scotch-Irish immigrant distilling know-how and then given a French name. It even caused a rebellion in 1794 in Pennsylvania that George Washington himself had to put down after the federal government tried to tax it. Bourbon whiskey, the old red eye, rotgut, and firewater of the Wild West, was distinguished from other whiskies by the use of corn in the mash. Corn was preferred in southern whiskey making, rather than the rye that was used prevalently in the North. Americans soon came to favor the smoothness of the corn-based whisky. By 1784, commercial distilleries were operating in Kentucky, and Bourbon County, Kentucky, named for the French royal family who supported American independence against the English, became the center of bourbon whiskey production in the United States, thus lending its name to the product. Today, regulations require that bourbon be at least 51 percent corn and aged for not less than two years in new charred barrels. Tennessee whiskey, a distinct classification from bourbon, has an additional requirement of being filtered through sugar maple charcoal. Moonshine, untaxed clear whiskey (the Civil War brought in the permanent taxation of whiskey) legendarily distilled in the hills of Kentucky and Tennessee by the light of the moon to avoid federal agents and aged in a glass jar, is the source of much

American humor and a stepping off point for story lines that celebrate individual freedom over government regulation.[15]

Alcoholic beverages made up only about 13 percent of each American's total consumption of 192 gallons of liquids in 2004. In the country that made Coke and Pepsi internationally known trademarks, combined diet and nondiet carbonated soft drinks alone counted for 28 percent of consumption. That is about 52 gallons a year for each American, for which Americans spent about $66 billion. Far behind in second place, bottled water was only 12.4 percent. Curiously, milk, coffee, beer, and all others (including tap water, vegetable juices, and sports drinks) each account for between 11 percent and 12 percent of liquid consumption per year. Fruit juices came in at 7.6 percent and tea at 4.4 percent. Americans have about 450 soft drinks from which to choose that are produced in around 400 plants. The most efficient plants can produce 2,000 cans of soda per minute per line to satisfy the demand for more than 68 billion cans a year. Only 23 percent of soft drinks are fountain dispensed, rather than packaged.[16]

Americans consume legumes in large amounts, and in the case of peanuts, without knowing they are eating them, since most think they are nuts like walnuts or pecans. Peanuts came to the United States via South America and are grown today mostly on small farms in the South that average 100 acres. Each American eats over six pounds of peanuts—a favorite snack food both roasted and salted and great with beer and cocktails—and products made from peanut butter a year. Most peanuts are used to make peanut butter, which was patented by Harvey Kellogg in 1895, who also brought corn flakes to the world, but it was first sold at the 1904 St. Louis World's Fair. By 1908, it was being produced commercially. The annual consumption of peanut butter, on which Americans spend $800 million a year, is enough to make 10 billion peanut butter and jelly sandwiches (PB&Js). Peanut butter and jelly sandwiches—soft white bread, peanut butter, and Concord grape (preferably) jelly—have a place in every young student's lunch pail. The typical young American will have eaten 1,500 PB&Js before graduating from high school.[17]

In America's schizophrenic lifestyle, there is one thing that brings families together: the backyard cookout, which usually takes place on weekends with family and friends. For Americans in New England and the Midwest, it is a celebration of the outdoors after being shut in the house all winter and liberation from the kitchen. Most families have outdoor grills—some cheap and serviceable charcoal grills, others gas-fired and quite elaborate. Grilling the meat—spareribs, steaks, hamburgers, hot dogs, pork chops—is typically the man's job for some primordial reason. Back in the kitchen, the woman prepares (or opens the containers of) the staples of the cookout: coleslaw (a gift to America from early Dutch settlers), macaroni salad, and baked beans. The red ketchup and yellow mustard, the jar of pickles, and some sliced onions and tomatoes are placed on the backyard picnic table with the hotdog and hamburger buns, the beer and soft drinks are in the cooler, and the party is under way. Ice cream, brownies, and watermelon are for dessert.

Regional Cuisines

The East

American cuisine began, of course, in New England, where English cooking and ingredients fused with native Indian cooking and local ingredients. Indian succotash, or mixed vegetables (green beans, lima beans, and corn), is still the most eaten vegetable in the United States. A cookout or picnic anywhere in America probably includes Boston baked beans, for which there are innumerable recipes. Cranberries in one form or another and Vermont maple syrup are available in every big grocery store in the country. Pumpkin pie is a required Thanksgiving dessert. Indian pudding, made with molasses, yellow cornmeal, and brown sugar, is a fusion of English pudding making with native corn. Rhode Island Johnny Cakes are popular pancakes made with white cornmeal. Boston brown bread is also made with cornmeal.

The coasts off New England make seafood a basic staple of the New England diet. Massachusetts even named the cod its state fish. Baked cod, codfish pie, and cod balls remain popular dishes. Rhode Island is famous for its clam cakes. If there were a state soup in Massachusetts, it would be creamy white New England clam chowder. The New York version, called Manhattan clam chowder, has tomatoes that redden the broth. The New England clambake and Maine lobster bake are, however, the region's premier outdoor eating events. Quahogs are hard-shelled clams that can be found up and down the eastern coast but are most prevalent between New Jersey and Cape Cod, where environmental conditions favor them. In order of smallest to largest size, quahogs are also known as little necks, cherrystones, and chowders. Native Americans used the shells as money, and they were also the probable source of this cooking technique. The clambake, in its elemental form, takes place in a pit on a beach, in which rocks have been placed and a fire lit. The heated rocks steam the clams, unhusked corn, and potatoes, which have been layered in seaweed, when the pit is covered. The Maine lobster bake employs the same cooking technique and uses the same ingredients, to which lobster and mussels are added. Melted butter is a must with the lobster.

On down the coast, every cuisine in the world is available in New York City's 17,300 restaurants, including the best Jewish delicatessen food anywhere. Coney Island hotdogs, which also made their way to Cincinnati via an impressed immigrant restaurateur, are a local specialty. In upstate New York, around Endicott, spiedies, chunks of meat marinated in vinegar, oil, oregano, and other spices, then skewered, cooked, and usually placed on a bun, were the creation of Italian immigrants. Buffalo helped to make chicken wings dipped in various sauces a national food, but its beef on weck (Kummelweck, a potato, caraway, and salted roll) of German origin remains a local specialty.

Turtle soup, rich, thick, and often flavored with sherry, are specialties in Maryland and Philadelphia. Meat from terrapins is used in Maryland, snapper meat in Philadelphia. Crab cakes can be found all along the Maryland coast, but the Chesapeake Bay crab cakes on Maryland's Eastern Shore are legendary.

In Philadelphia are those foot-long submarine sandwiches called *hoagies*. In Connecticut, they are called *grinders*. The Italian hoagie is made of salami, capicola, and provolone, with optional lettuce, tomatoes, red peppers, onions, vinegar and oil, and oregano. Meatball hoagies, drenched in a tomato sauce, are also available. The Philly cheesesteak, however, is Philadelphia's best-known sandwich. Fresh, thinly sliced beef is grilled, and American cheese (sometimes provolone) or a processed cheese spread is placed on the

A fresh Maine lobster satisfies the taste buds of many New Englanders during the summertime. Getty Images/PhotoDisc.

beef in a long roll. Peppers, onions, and other toppings may be added, but if the cheesesteak is not dripping and nearly impossible to eat politely, it is not a real Philly cheesesteak. Cheese fries, French fried potatoes topped with cheese, can usually be purchased wherever cheesesteaks are sold. Philadelphia and the region north and west of the city are famous for soft pretzels, a gift of the heavy German immigration there. In Philadelphia, soft pretzels are eaten with mustard. It is worth a trip out of Philadelphia to Amish country around Bird-in-Hand, Intercourse, and Lancaster to satisfy a sweet tooth with local specialties. Shoofly pie is an incredibly sweet molasses and sugar pie. Whoopie pies are two cookies, usually chocolate, but oatmeal cookies can also be found, that are sandwiched together by a cream filling. It seems clear how shoofly pie was named, and apparently, whoopie pies make one yell whoopie! at first bite.

The South

Fried chicken is the South's primary contribution to a national cuisine, but in fact, many southern dishes have crept far beyond their original boundaries. Soul food as well as Cajun and Creole cuisines are subsets of southern cooking. They are popular and available everywhere. Georgia pecan pie and Florida key lime pie, buttermilk biscuits and corn bread, hush puppies and salt-cured Virginia country ham are not just southern anymore. Traditionally, southerners prefer rice to potatoes and pork to beef; they like their meats fried or barbequed, their iced tea sweet, and grits for breakfast with ham, biscuits, and red-eye gravy.

Rice has long been grown in the Carolina lowlands and finds its way into numerous traditional southern dishes. (Potatoes do not grow well in the hot southern climate.) Savannah red rice, kin to Louisiana red beans and rice, mixes rice with bacon, peppers, onions, spices, tomatoes, Tabasco sauce, and optional shrimp or sausage. Florida's yellow rice, colored with saffron, is a gift from Spanish colonizers. Rice pilau, also called purloo, is thought to have been brought into the port of Charleston by trading ships in early colonial times. There are many recipes for pilau, a dirty rice dish that may contain bacon fat, okra, red peppers, onions, seafood, and country ham. Rice pudding is also an old southern dish, but fresh Georgia and South Carolina peaches make an even better dessert.

The pit barbeque probably originated with blacks in the Carolinas, and pork was the meat of choice, doused with a somewhat vinegary sauce. Chickens, too, were barbequed. Today, any kind of barbeque, including beef, is popular in the South. Along the coasts of southern states, seafood is abundant. Fried fish is a favorite, but crabs offer special treats. Around Mobile, Alabama, crabs from Mobile Bay are the basis for the local specialty, West

Indies salad: fresh crabmeat and diced onions in a marinade of vinegar and oil, eaten with crackers. Soft-shell crabs, when in season, might be found in spider burgers. Stone crabs in south Florida are a very special delight. In Virginia and parts of Maryland, Crab Norfolk is a specialty that combines lump crabmeat, tarragon, rice, cream, country ham, and butter for a uniquely southern taste.

The submarine sandwich, made with various cold cuts and lettuce, tomatoes, onions, and so on, as optional toppings, is available all over the South. Around New Orleans, however, the East Coast grinder, hero, or hoagie morphs into a po'boy. Po'boys can have about anything in them—oysters, ham, beef, shrimp, sausage, lunchmeat, chicken, hamburger—but the French bread makes them distinctive, and eating a po'boy with mayonnaise, ketchup, and gravy calls for an immediate change of clothing. New Orleans also has a distinctive local sandwich of Sicilian origin, the muffuletta, which is also difficult to eat daintily. This large round sandwich is filled with cold cuts and cheese, over which is spread an olive salad flavored with garlic, peppers, capers, celery, and oregano. The South also has its own version of the midwestern White Castle slyder, the Krystal. Only true gourmands can distinguish between a slyder and a Krystal because in America, a hamburger is a hamburger.

Soul food originated from slaves imported primarily from West Africa before 1808, when the external slave trade was ended by law. They brought with them various cultural cooking habits, which were once isolated to southern plantations but moved throughout the country, especially after World War II, to northern urban areas as African Americans sought employment there in a tremendous northern migration. Soul food developed from these West African cultures as they were homogenized on plantations, and blacks used the new foods available to them. African cooking influenced both Creole and southern cooking. Soul food is characterized by the use of pork fat, usually bacon fat, as a substitute for palm oil used in Africa, the use of sauces and spices (often pepper), beans, mustard and turnip greens, okra, yams, bananas, and melons. Pork and chicken are the preferred meats, and Africans ate the whole animal. Bread is a staple. Corn is used to make cornmeal, hominy, grits, and bread. Barbeque is a specialty. Typical dishes include black-eyed pea soup, fried pork chops, chitterlings, fried chicken, fried fish, collard greens, and mixed greens. Gullah rice (rice, nuts, butter, and celery) is a specialty of African Americans isolated on islands off the Carolinas and Georgia who maintained old traditions.[18]

The Creole and Cajun cuisines of south Louisiana around New Orleans are often spoken and thought of together, but they have separate origins, even though time has obscured differences. Creoles were the first born-in-America children of the mix of Europeans (Germans, Italians, French, English, Spanish), Africans, and Native Americans who settled the Gulf Coast from Mobile, Alabama, to New Orleans early in the eighteenth century. Creole cooking developed in New Orleans from the contributions of all these groups. Spanish paella became jambalaya. French bouillabaisse became gumbo, flavored with okra from Africans and filé powder (ground sassafras leaves) from natives. German sausage makers contributed their knowledge to help create Creole hot sausages and chaurice. Acadians (Cajuns), French Canadian settlers forcibly cast out from Nova Scotia by the British, began reassembling in south Louisiana in the 1750s. Already with over 100 years of pioneering experience, these were hard-scrapple people accustomed to living off what the land provided them. More isolated than the Creoles, Cajuns nevertheless came into contact with the Creole culture that surrounded them. The three classic dishes of New Orleans—gumbo, bisque, and étouffée—are built on a roux, which is flour browned in oil. Onions, bell peppers, celery, and garlic usually are added, along with a variety of seafood choices. Chicken can also be used, and spicy sausages like andouille and tasso give added flavor to these one-pot stews, which are usually served over rice.[19]

Cajuns also were known to cook anything that swam or slithered or crawled or flew through the swamps they inhabited. The Cajun crawfish boil remains a celebratory event. Anything could end up in a 20-gallon pot over a propane burner filled with salted and spiced water or beer. Most often, it is crawfish, but shrimp and crabs are popular, too. The seafood boil includes potatoes, ears of corn, and onion, like its northern cousins, but garlic, vinegar, lemons, and zesty spices may be added, too, which gives this boil a special flavor. Beer is the preferred beverage, and Dixie is the preferred beer.

The Midwest

Traditional midwestern cooking is quite plain and, to many tastes, quite bland. Salt and pepper in moderation are the spices of choice. The English and German habits of overcooking meat and vegetables survive in this basic meat and potatoes fare, where a beef roast, mashed potatoes, corn on the cob, green beans, and apple pie make up a fancy dinner. The hearty homemade farm meals of the past—chicken noodles, pork with dumplings—have given way to hasty box-top recipes that reflect the fact that farm families, like most American families, need two incomes to survive, and time is at a premium. Quantity is often more prized than quality—witness Chicago's contribution to pizza, turning it from a delicate crust with a dash of tomato sauce, cheese, and pepper flakes into a deep-dish thick crust to contain all the cheeses and meats available in the Midwest.

The potluck dinner is the most radically democratic of American culinary experiences. There are no rules; no one is in charge. All it takes is one person with the nerve to invite several friends over for a party with the instruction that they have to bring something and bring their own beverages. (The fomenter of the event usually supplies plastic glasses, plastic silverware, and paper or plastic plates, and, with luck, iced-down coolers.) Potlucks are, clearly, not upscale social events, or they would be catered at the expense of the host. Potlucks can be found in homes, offices, and church basements. They can be found all over the country, but they are a favorite in the Midwest. Those who accept an invitation to a potluck may compare notes about who is bringing what, but it is a fact that potlucks always seem to work out—there is never all appetizers, all main dishes, all vegetables, all salads, or all desserts, and these are the only five choices.

Potlucks bring out foods familiar to midwesterners, in part owing to the cook's need for adulation, and in part owing to the cook's desire to fix something everyone will like. Typical appetizers might include deviled eggs, a tray of cheese and crackers, little hot dogs enveloped in a crust (often called pigs in a blanket), cut fresh vegetables (carrots and celery are the most popular) with a dipping sauce, and guacamole with tortilla chips.

Casseroles are popular at potlucks. Main courses seem to always include macaroni and cheese, tuna noodle casserole (canned tuna and store-bought noodles baked in canned cream of mushroom or celery soup, topped with potato chips, sometimes with peas), and chili-mac (a concoction of hamburger and onion, noodles, tomatoes, and some chili powder, with cheese on top, with or without red kidney beans). Salads can range from a simple shredded lettuce and cheese tossed with ranch dressing to taco salad, carrot salad (shredded carrots with mayonnaise, raisins, and nuts), three-bean salad (green and yellow beans with kidney beans and onion in vinegar and oil), and fruit salads (canned fruit encased in flavored gelatin). Vegetable selections might include creamed corn, scalloped potatoes, a sweet potato casserole sweetened with brown sugar and a topping of marshmallows, a broccoli and cheese casserole, and a green bean casserole (canned green beans in canned mushroom soup with fried onion rings on top). Desserts are often spectacular because the real cooks like to show them off. There are apple pies and cherry pies with golden peaked crusts, chocolate meringue pies, lemon meringue pies, and butterscotch meringue pies. Creative mixtures of cherry or raspberry gelatin and Cool Whip (a fake whipped cream purchased already whipped in a frozen container) can also be found. Every potluck has a least two pans of brownies, cut into squares, from which to choose. The chocolate-frosted ones go first, but all of those moist chocolate little cakes quickly disappear.

The big American breakfast still survives in the Midwest, if not at home, in the diners and little restaurants that cover the countryside. Eggs—scrambled or fried, over easy or sunny side up—with bacon, ham, or sausage, buttered toast with jelly or jam, a side order of pancakes with butter and syrup, or maybe some French toast or hash brown potatoes, and as much coffee as you can drink are expected. Ham and eggs as a breakfast duo is believed to be an American innovation, but the American breakfast is of certain English origin.

The Midwest is not without interesting or unique foods. Wild rice, which is actually a large-grained grass, grows naturally in lakes, rivers and streams around the Great Lakes area. Native Americans, particularly the Ojibway and Menominee, harvested it from canoes by flailing the grains off the plants into the canoes. Also called water oats, squaw rice, and marsh oats, wild rice (genus *Zizania*) was a staple to Natives and European adventurers in the North Country. Today, it is often mixed with long-grained rice as a side dish, but it is also cooked alone. It was not until 1950 in Minnesota that wild rice began to be grown in flooded fields surrounded by dikes. Minnesota remains the largest producer, followed by California.[20]

The Germans certainly left their mark to the extent that native midwesterners think that goetta, leberwurst, bratwurst, weisswurst, and blutwurst are American foods that could be found everywhere. The Germans, of course, also brought beer to the Midwest to drink with the sausages, centering brewing empires in St. Louis and Milwaukee as well as Cincinnati. Sauerkraut is a frequently served side dish and a requirement with a pork roast. Zwieback is often fed to teething children. Pretzels and potato salad are ubiquitous. Rye and pumpernickel breads, Danish coffee cakes, and pastries are typically available.

The Poles who migrated to Pennsylvania, many to work in coal mines, gave Pittsburgh one of its culinary claims to fame: pierogies. Pittsburgh prizes pierogies whether fried, baked, or boiled. They are circles of dough pinched together in a half-circle with any assortment of fillings, including, but not limited to, mashed potatoes and cheddar cheese, sauerkraut, cabbage, cottage cheese, or hamburger. They are perhaps best fried in butter and onions. They can be a meal or a side dish, and since they can be filled with anything, they can be subject to complete transformation in the American kitchen, but most pierogie aficionados want them the way grandma used to make them.

The Norwegians who settled in Wisconsin and Minnesota remember their North Atlantic heritage around Thanksgiving and Christmastime by enjoying a feast of lutefisk. Not unlike the New England baked cod dinner, this is served with potatoes, peas, and bread, which in this case is lefse. However, the cod is neither fresh nor restored salt cod, but marinated and preserved in lye. The vapors from lutefisk, which translates as "lye fish," is said to have the power to peel paint from walls, bring tears to the eyes, and buckle the knees of a latter-day Viking. Lutefisk, after several water baths, is simply salted and peppered, baked, and served with melted butter. Gently put, a lutefisk dinner is an unforgettable experience.

Wisconsin is the biggest cheese-producing state in the United States, accounting for 2.4 billion pounds (26.4%) of America's total cheese production of 9.13 billion pounds in 2005. There are 115 plants making cheese in Wisconsin, and where cheese is being made, cheese curds, the local specialty that does not keep over a day or so or travel well, are available.[21] Cheese curds result from the cheese-making process, and they are plucked from vats before the cheese is blocked and aged. They may come from any cheese, but American-type cheese (a cheddar) is the favorite and the most produced in Wisconsin. Cheese curds are a slightly salty snacking treat with the consistency of a pencil eraser, and they emit squeaks against the teeth as if they were polishing the teeth squeaky clean.

The stockyards of Kansas City and Omaha, on the edge of the Great Plains, were the last stop for millions of animals on the way to slaughter. Omaha is so proud of its beef that they named a local football team the Omaha Beef. There could be no greater honor. The city is famous for its steaks. Kansas City even has a cut of steak named after it, but the city is perhaps more famed for its barbeque, both beef and pork. Kansas City barbeque is defined by the use of hickory in the fire for a special flavor and a sauce that is, in midwestern tradition, neither too spicy like Carolina sauces nor too hot like Texas sauces. Molasses helps to thicken the tomato-based sauce and lend it a certain sweetness. A dry rub is used to flavor the meat before cooking. Kansas City is filled with barbeque joints.[22]

What barbeque is to Kansas City, chili is to Cincinnati, a city with a old German heritage. A Texan, however, would find Cincinnati chili to be something other than chili, if not a bit of a joke. There are more than 180 chili parlors (it is not clear why a chili restaurant is called a parlor) in Cincinnati, serving a chili that was created by a Greek immigrant restaurateur of the 1920s who had trouble selling Greek food to Germans. He invented what he called a chili out of a Greek dish, substituting ground beef for lamb, adding some chili powder, but keeping spices like cinnamon, allspice, and cloves in the dish. In this great fusion of cuisines, he also decided to serve his chili over spaghetti. Today, this is known a two-way chili. Add grated cheese and it is three-way chili; add onions and it is four-way; add kidney beans and it is five-way. Coneys are hot dogs with mustard, chili, and grated cheese.[23]

For folks who live around the upper Great Lakes in Michigan, Wisconsin, and Minnesota, the fish boil is a Nordic right of summer and fall. Unlike the New England clambakes and lobster bakes, this is not a celebration of seafood, but rather a celebration of lake food—freshwater fish like lake trout and whitefish. The fish boil is an outdoor event. A raging fire is stoked under a large kettle or pot filled with salted water, seasoned with bay leaves, peppercorns, and allspice. First, a wire basket of potatoes is lowered into the boiling water. Then onions are placed in the wire basket to boil with the potatoes. Then the cleaned fish are lowered into the kettle in a separate basket to cook for about 10 minutes. A pint or so of kerosene is then thrown on the fire to produce an overboil. After the pyrotechnics, the meal is ready. The fish, onions, and potatoes are usually accompanied by bread and coleslaw, butter, and lemons.[24] Beer is the preferred beverage for adults.

There are two foods born in the Midwest that are still largely available only in the Midwest. Long before there was a McDonald's, a Wendy's, or a Burger King, the Midwest had White Castles and Maid-Rites. The first White Castle restaurant opened in Wichita, Kansas, in 1921, selling hamburgers for a nickel. Now with 380 locations, many of those in Ohio, Illinois, Michigan, Indiana, and around St. Louis, Missouri, White Castle sold around 500 million burgers, affectionately called slyders, in 2005, and claims to be the first hamburger chain to sell 1 billion hamburgers. Slyders are three-and-a-half-inch square, very thin, salted and peppered hamburgers with five holes punched through them that are steamed with dehydrated onions, and then the bun is placed on top of them so that it absorbs the flavor of the process. A slice of dill pickle is placed on the meat, and the sandwich is placed in a box. A sack of slyders is six burgers (mustard and ketchup separately packaged) and a little bit of heaven. White Castle considers its product so unique that they have based their advertising on craving slyders, a message not lost on midwestern college students with the munchies in the early morning.[25]

In 1926, a butcher in Muscatine, Iowa, combined "a special cut and grind of meat with a selected set of spices" and the Maid-Rite sandwich was born, when an unknown patron declared on tasting the sandwich that it was "just made right." There are now more than 70 Maid-Rite restaurants branching out from Iowa and declaring to be "America's #1 Favorite Made to Order Loose Meat Sandwich." The special seasoning remains a secret, but is thought to contain garlic, onion, tomato juice, brown sugar, Worcestershire sauce, and seasoned salt. Maid-Rite claims to have invented casual dining and prides itself on providing an atmosphere of gracious, hometown hospitality. In addition to the Maid-Rite sandwich, the menu also includes a pork tenderloin sandwich, greatly favored in the Midwest, and, in deference to the Midwest's changing taste, a Taco-Rite. The restaurants also serve shakes, malts, and ice cream cones.[26]

The Southwest and West

In the Southwest and on into the southern West Coast, Spanish influence, mixed with native and Mexican, has created a special regional cuisine. Southwestern cuisine's basic ingredients are corn, chiles, beans, and squashes. Tamales are cornmeal flour, masa, stuffed with meat or Spanish rice and steamed in cornhusks. Tacos are soft or fried corn tortillas stuffed with meat and covered with salsa and lettuce, tomatoes, and cheese. Enchiladas are corn tortillas fried and stuffed and dipped in chili sauce. Chiles rellenos are deep-fried mild chiles stuffed with cheese and served as an accompaniment to meals. Some main ingredients are chayotes, pear-shaped squashes; chiles—Anaheims, Chiles del Arbol, chimayos, jalapeños, poblanos, and serranos; and dried corn in the form of cornmeal, posole, and tortillas. Blue cornmeal is especially flavorful. Posole is the hominy of the Southwest, produced by treating dried kernels of corn with lime. It is cooked before use and often eaten as a side dish and sometimes alone. Jicama is often used for salads and side dishes. Nopales (cactus pears) are eaten as vegetable or in salads. Piñones, pine nuts, are used in cuisine, too. Tomatillos, related to tomatoes but staying green when ripe, are used in salads, soups, and sauces. Burritos and chimichangas are southwestern

A giant enchilada is cut into many pieces to be distributed to visitors at the Whole Enchilada Fiesta in New Mexico. © AP Photo/The Las Cruces Sun-News, Norm Dettlaff.

U.S. adaptations of old Mexican foods. Modern southwestern cuisine fuses various other cuisines with traditional southwestern ingredients to create new flavors. Thus one might find escargot enchiladas with Madeira sauce and endive or a cassolette of sweetbreads and pinto beans on the menu.[27]

Tex-Mex cuisine can be considered a Texan take on Mexican food, and since Texas is cattle country, adding beef to the Mexican dishes was only natural. Chili, once simply beans in a tomato sauce, became chili con carne, or chili with meat. Texas red chili is not imaginable without beef. Chili lends itself to personal innovation and the addition of secret ingredients, especially spices and chiles. Chili cook-offs are frequent and popular events. Fajitos, wheat tortillas filled with marinated skirt steak, are, like red chili, a pure Tex-Mex creation. What passes for Mexican food in most of America's Mexican restaurants is, in fact, an American adaptation, like Tex-Mex of true Mexican food.[28] The frequent use of chiles also distinguishes Texas barbeque, which was traditionally beef. The sauces used in and on barbeque tend to be hot and spicy, as opposed to the vinegary Carolina sauces and sweet Kansas City sauces.

New Mexico green chili is often just a hot wedding of pinto beans with green chiles flavored with salt pork. Green chile stew adds pork to the pot. Another popular New Mexico dish is *calabacitas,* a mixture of green chiles, squash, corn, and cream or cheese. In northern New Mexico, dried and roasted corn kernels called *chicos* are cooked with red chiles, spices, and pork to make a favorite dish, also called *chicos.* Sopaipillas, triangle-shaped deep-fried pastry with honey, for dessert can help take the sting out of the chiles.

The birth of California cuisine is generally traced back to Alice Waters in the early 1970s and her restaurant Chez Panisse. Waters introduced the idea of using natural, locally grown fresh ingredients to produce her dishes. California cuisine is, therefore, not any one thing, neither a method of cooking nor any group of particular ingredients—it is local, based like most traditional regional cooking on available ingredients, including abundant seafood. Fresh vegetables, lightly cooked, and fresh fruits, berries, and herbs characterize the cuisine generally, but California cooking is also in fact a fusion of tastes from all over the world. The favorite main courses for 2006 of San Francisco's top chefs make the point. They include "seared yellow fin tuna, marinated summer cucumbers, daikon sprouts, yuzu-wasabi crème fraîche," "lobster roe crusted Japanese hamachi with a warm Maui onion shellfish vinaigrette," and "shellfish tom yum noodles with Thai basil pesto."[29]

The fusion of international cuisines is also going on in casual dining and fast food. In 1988, the three Wahoo brothers Wing, Ed, and Mingo founded Wahoo's in Southern California. Their objective was to introduce the Mexican fish taco to the California market but also to give their food a Brazilian flare (they grew up in Brazil) with some oriental highlights (their parents ran a Chinese restaurant in Brazil). Now with 30 locations in California and Colorado, Wahoo's offers fish, chicken, steak, and vegetarian tacos, enchiladas, and burritos. The combo plate comes with ahi rice and black beans or spicy Cajun white beans.[30] Yet even in California, the cheap and portable hamburger is still a hamburger, great for eating while sitting on a freeway. In-N-Out Burger, with around 150 locations in California, allowed customers to order their hamburgers on a two-way speaker in 1948. Jack in the Box, the first drive-through franchise, started selling hamburgers in San Diego in 1951. Fatburger, a California hamburger franchise that claims to be "a culture" and "a phenomenon," started in 1952. McDonald's did not open its first location until 1955, and it was in Des Plaines, Illinois.[31]

It would be far from the mark to say that Chinese food began in California, of course, but Chinese-American food did indeed begin there. Chinese, most from the Canton area, first came to California in the 1840s to work on railroads and in gold mines, often in menial positions. Some Chinese entrepreneurs in the restaurant business discovered that they could sell Americanized versions of Chinese foods successfully. Chop suey houses spread across the nation. Many of them featured traditional Cantonese fare for their Chinese patrons and an English menu with such Chinese-American dishes as egg rolls, wonton soup, chop suey, sweet and sour pork, and even meats with lobster sauce. While Chinese fast food in America is for the most part Chinese-American food, excellent regional Chinese cooking has become available in the United States as Americans' tastes have matured. Cantonese dim sum is very popular. Mandarin dishes like mu-shu pork and pot stickers have become mainstays of Chinese restaurants. Even the hot cuisines of Szechwan and Hunan find their place now in America.[32]

The Pacific Northwest is known for salmon, oysters, apples, berries, and Oregon and Washington wines to drink with them. In fact, however, this area of the country also produces tremendous amounts of wheat, potatoes, lamb, beef, and dairy products. A great variety of vegetables are also successfully grown there. Rainbow trout are abundant in the freshwater streams all over the West, and in addition to salmon, the ocean provides Pacific cod, halibut, pollock, and other varieties of fish. The bays that produce the oysters also produce crab. Dairy production has given rise to local cheese making. Washington produces more apples than any other state. Wild mushrooms abound in the forests. Native berries include raspberries, strawberries, blueberries, blackberries, boysenberries, gooseberries, and the very special huckleberries, to name just a few. Grapes for wine have been grown in Washington since 1825. The developing cuisine of the Pacific Northwest makes use of these local foods much in the spirit of California cuisine. Fresh local food, perhaps with an accent of Asian influence, characterizes the taste of the Northwest.[33]

Fresh fish caught in the Pacific Ocean are often sold in street markets such as this one in Washington. Getty Images/MedioImages.

The luau is Hawaii's version of the New England clambake. Chicken and taro plant leaves cooked in coconut milk is called *luau,* thus the name of this traditional and symbolic feast. Today, of course, a luau may include roasted pig and other meats, fish in great variety, pineapples and coconuts, fruits, macadamia nuts, and so on. Whatever dishes a modern luau may include, it is never without poi, the Hawaiian specialty made by beating tarot root into a paste. Poi, like Scandinavian lutefisk, is an acquired taste. Luaus, without the poi, are popular for parties on the mainland, but in Hawaii, they are held mostly for the benefit of tourists. Indeed, the large Japanese population of the islands has made Hawaii the best state in the nation for Japanese food.

AMERICAN FASHION

That's hot!

—Paris Hilton

Paris, Milan, London, Tokyo, and New York are the recognized fashion capitals of the world. Americans had long looked to Paris for high fashion. It could be argued that only the demise of Paris because of Nazi Germany's occupation of France from 1940 until 1944 brought New York, and thus America, to the party. In fact, however, America had been developing and inventing a distinctive fashion look from its beginning that was purposely democratic, not aristocratic, and decidedly pragmatic, not flashy, and certainly not up to the quality and exacting standards of haute couture. When New York took over the international fashion lead, the effect was to rent the fabric of haute couture, so tightly woven for centuries in France. American fashion designers broke all the old rules, designed for the masses, and clothed them in ready to wear (RTW).

American fashion design was in fact democratized in the face of a mass market. The quintessential old rule that fashion was dictated from on high by a few fashion houses stood in sharp contrast with American thinking and tradition. American designers were quick to give the people what they wanted and placed their imprimaturs on the fashion that came up from the streets, such as grunge and urban hip-hop, that complemented the American casual lifestyle and that put modern twists on American classic styles, including western wear. The great American couture houses make their money from RTW lines of clothing and accessories, not from custom fitting individual clothing items to wealthy patrons. American clothing is mass-produced, most of it outside the country, in what has become a global industry.

Oddly enough, men's clothing was the first to be mass-produced in the United States in meaningful quantities. The problem with mass-producing clothing is that some standard is needed for sizing. The Civil War created the need for mass-produced uniforms, and as a pattern emerged from sizing soldiers, that military standard became the standard for sizing civilian mass-produced men's clothing. While women's clothing began to be mass-produced in the later 1920s, the movement for standardized women's clothing was pushed by population growth and the development of mass merchandisers like Sears, Roebuck and Co. It was not until 1941, however, that the basis for a standard for women's sizes emerged after a national study of women's sizes was published by the U.S. Department of Agriculture in 1941. Yet it was still later, in 1958, that the government published a commercial standard, CS215-58, for women's sizes. The standard was updated and made voluntary in 1971 and then completely withdrawn in 1983.[34] Clothing marketers were quick to understand that a dress marked size 6 but cut to a standard size 10 sold better than the same dress marked size 10 and cut to a size 10.

Americans spent $326.5 billion on clothing and shoes in 2004. At the wholesale level, consumption totaled more than 18.4 billion garments and 2.15 billion pairs of shoes. Imports accounted for 91 percent of apparel and 98 percent of footwear. Most Americans are wearing clothes made in Central America and the Dominion Republic, owing to a trade agreement, and

China and Mexico. Most Americans are wearing shoes made in China, which alone accounted for 82 percent of footwear imports. One indication of the total commoditization of clothing and shoes is that even as retail prices have increased overall by 15.9 percent from 1993 to 2004, the retail prices of clothing and shoes have slipped 9.5 percent and 6.8 percent, while wholesale prices have remained about the same.[35] The fashion industry can make good money in this gigantic market only when it successfully brands its products to support higher noncommodity prices in the marketplace. Of course, a personal fashion statement cannot be made with clothing and shoes alone. The whole package also includes jewelry, accessories like handbags and rucksacks, and a scent. Marketing and advertising are therefore every bit as important as design and fabric in selling the American look.

There was a time even within the frames of baby boomers' lives when Americans traveling abroad were advised not to dress like Americans to avoid being conspicuous in a crowd. Today, however, much of the world dresses like Americans. From Moscow to Capetown, Buenos Aires to Tokyo, and Madrid to Beijing, the casual style invented by America has taken hold in a sea of humanity dressed in jeans and T-shirts. American fashion has long been sent around the world in Hollywood movies and, more recently, as a tie-in to American pop music.

American fashion reflects the diversity and complexity of American society as the personal expression of urban and country, rich and poor, young and old, ethnic, regional, religious, and even musical cultures. In very general terms, northeasterners are said to dress rather formally; southerners dress conservatively and maintain the old-fashioned nostrums—straw hats and seersucker suits may be worn only between Easter Sunday and Labor Day—that are pretty much dead elsewhere; midwesterners are considered to be quite cost-conscious, with a preference for practical and plain clothing; and westerners seem to prefer casual clothing. Cowboy boots and Stetson hats with a business suit would look normal in Dallas and Houston but quite out of place in Boston and Philadelphia. For most of the older immigrant populations, traditional dress comes out only for festivals and special events. Although most American Roman Catholic orders of religious women have abandoned habits for plain dress, religiously inspired dress may be seen occasionally on America's streets. The Hassidic Jews, mostly in New York City, have maintained their traditional garb, as have the Amish who settled first in Pennsylvania and have moved westward over time. Some American Muslim women choose to be in *hijab,* that is, wear head scarves, but it is not unusual to see them maintain the requirement for head-to-toe covering with a sweater or shirt and blue jeans rather than an overgarment. Indeed, it would be the exception, rather than the rule, that any American would stand out in a crowd of fellow Americans by virtue of dress. The mass culture has assured a certain sameness in dress.

While there is no real distinctive eastern, midwestern, or southern style, the same cannot be said of the western style of dress. In fact, if there is indeed an indigenous American style, the western style would be it. The cowboy is, of course, the mythical iconic American. Tough, Golden Rule fair, a true individual in command of all around him, he roams the golden plains freely and uses his gun only when he has to. His dress is simple: cowboy hat; pointed leather cowboy boots; jeans (chaps optional), held on by a sturdy belt with a big buckle; and a denim shirt. On special occasions, he might don a shirt with fancy stitching and pearl buttons and slip on a bola tie. Celebrated in Wild West shows late in the nineteenth century and into the twentieth century, the cowboy mythology grew larger through films and television, even as real cowboys virtually disappeared. Country music appropriated western wear, created singing rhinestone cowboys, and seemingly moved the center of the west to Nashville, Tennessee. Western fashion is very much alive on the rodeo circuits and even in fashion designers' collections. The Wild West continues its hold on the American imagination.[36]

American fashion is in a constant state of rebirth, borrowing from the past, appropriating from the present, and mixing up the signals by crossing traditional lines. It can be value laden; it can be dangerous. It can be practical; it can be outrageous. Fashion can also be confusing. Americans are never quite sure what to wear on occasions that demand formal, black tie optional, semiformal, casual, business casual, or informal attire. A "come as you are" party is an even more daring concept.

A number of famous American fashion designers have contributed in achieving an American look. New York City's Fashion Walk of Fame, which stretches along the east side of Seventh Avenue from 41st Street to 35th Street, is to American fashion designers as the forecourt to Hollywood, California's, Grauman's Chinese Theatre is to American movie stars. The plaques on the Manhattan sidewalks (no designers' footprints, but rather design sketches) honor American fashion designers for their contributions to American fashion. They were elected from 1999 to 2002 by ballots passed around to 150 industry leaders. Nominees were limited to those with "a significant New York presence" who owned their own businesses a minimum of 10 years and who made a "powerful impact on fashion" through their creative designs or use of materials or who "significantly influenced the way America dresses."[37]

Most of the fashion designers memorialized on the Fashion Walk of Fame are household names. Lilly Daché (1898–1989) came to New York City from France when she was only 16 years old. By the time she closed her shop in

1968, she had become the city's most reputed milliner, having added accessories and dresses to her salon. She also designed headgear for movie stars like Marlene Dietrich and Betty Grable. Her sculpted hats helped to define an American look for decades before hats became costume, rather than everyday wear. Maryland-born Claire McCardell (1905–1958), however, is often credited with originating the American look. She believed that fundamental American democratic values could and should be expressed in the clothing she designed. McCardell, working out of Townley Frocks, designed for working-women, not the idle class, and she believed that mass-produced clothing could also be fashionable, comfortable, and affordable. In the 1930s, she came out with the monastic dress, which women could shape to their bodies with a sash or belt. In 1940, McCardell's designs used a natural shoulder and pleats or bias cuts for comfortable wear. Her 1942 pop-over dress was a kind of wraparound. She designed for a casual and free lifestyle—this was American—at the beach, at play, at home, or at work. Even the fabrics she used, from denim and corduroy to seersucker and calico, expressed a basic casual feel.

Designers, of course, continued to cater to the wealthy. Charles James (1906–1978), though born in England, spent much the 1940s and 1950s in New York City designing opulent sculpted ball gowns that each in its own right was considered a work of art. Norman Norell (1900–1972) left Indiana to design clothes for Paramount Pictures in New York City in 1922. He also designed for Broadway productions. In 1944, he and his partner, Anthony, founded Traina-Norell and defined the American look during the war—empire line dresses, fur coats, and sequined evening sheaths. In 1960, with his own label, called simply Norell, he designed classic, impeccably tailored clothes meant to last and, in establishing the New York style, successfully translated couture to RTW. James Galanos (1924–) had his first show in Los Angeles but opened a shop in New York in 1952. His expensive off-the-rack ornamented gowns, favorites of Nancy Reagan, were superbly constructed. Main Rousseau Bocher (1891–1976), branding himself as Mainbocher, was born in Chicago but made his name in Paris. One of his famous clients was Wallis Simpson, the Duchess of Windsor. As war in Europe loomed, he returned to the United States, where he contributed jeweled sweaters and short evening dresses to the American look and designed uniforms for the new women's military units as well as the Girl Scouts. Pauline Trigère (1909–2002) left her Paris birthplace in 1937 and started her own fashion house in New York in 1942. When she began making RTW in the late 1940s, she was already a respected New York label. Her contributions to American fashion, in addition to her costume jewelry, included removable scarves and collars from dresses and coats, classic suits, sleeveless coats, opera capes, and reversible coats.

Anne Klein (1921–1974) was, in her day, the most popular sportswear designer in the United States. Her plaque on the Fashion Walk of Fame notes that the coordinated day and evening separates she developed, including her "body suits and zippered skirts, have become classic staples of the modern wardrobe." In 1948, she founded Junior Sophisticates, and in 1968, Anne Klein and Company, where she nurtured future designers who would impact American fashion. Bonnie Cashin (1915–2000), after designing handbags for Coach, working for 20th Century Fox and, designing women's military uniforms, formed her own business in 1953. Her loose-fitting, layered, interlocking women's clothing and the poncho as fashion as well as canvas and poplin raincoats were designed to express independence, adaptability, and the taste of the wearer.

American fashion could be playful. Geoffrey Beene (1924–2004) set up his own firm in 1962. A dress from his first collection made it to the cover of *Vogue,* and he suddenly had made it in the fashion world. Beene was one of the first to show short skirts, and his football jersey evening gown with jewels gained him some notoriety. Rudi Gernreich (1922–1985) came to California from Vienna in 1938. He formed Rudi Gernreich Inc. in 1964. Gernreich introduced to America and the world such innovations as knitted tube dresses, shirt-waist dresses, the women's topless bathing suit (the fashion sensation of 1964), the no-bra bra, and women's boxer shorts, a statement of the 1980s. Italian by birth and bred in Argentina, Giorgio di Sant'Angelo (1933–1989) came to the United States in 1962 and started a RTW business in 1966. He experimented with stretch fabrics, with the goal of freeing body movement. His body suits, devoid of zippers and buttons, could double as swimming wear.

Iowan Roy Halston Frowick (1932–1990) began his career as a milliner, having designed pillbox hats for Jackie Kennedy. He opened his own design business in 1966 and got into the RTW market. Halston was America's first minimalist designer—clean and simple lines with classic fabrics. Many considered him to be the best evening wear designer in the nation. His foray into mass merchandising a cheaper line with J.C. Penney put his jet set business in a tailspin, but this experience would not hold out for later designers. Ralph Lauren (1939–) is, in many ways, the quintessential American designer. Born in Bronx, New York, he has cleverly reinterpreted great American fashion of the past for the contemporary age and, in the process, has produced classically elegant men's wear and women's wear. His Polo brand is ubiquitous, but he designs beyond clothing for a total lifestyle. Lauren virtually invented the casual preppy style that has defined the look of the well-to-do. Another Bronx native, Calvin Klein (1942–), is perhaps the icon of late-twentieth-century and early-twenty-first century American fashion. From the 1970s onward (Calvin Klein Inc. was founded in 1994 and sold in 2003), Klein defined American fashion, including jeans and underwear, with a minimalist approach and a zest for controversial advertising campaigns. Dominican-born Oscar de la Renta (1932–), on the other hand, is known for his blending of "Latin elegance and American ease." In the late 1960s, he notably featured bejeweled hot pants in his Gypsy collection, but his day wear for working-women, as in his less expensive OSCAR line, is quite restrained. His tasteful use of color maintains his Latin roots.

Bill Blass (1922–2002) bought the company he was working for in 1970, and Bill Blass Ltd. was born. His plaque on the Fashion Walk of Fame notes that he can "rightly be credited as one of the creators of a true 'American style.'" Best known for his women's day wear, it is Blass who can either be blamed or credited for Americans' confusion about what is sportswear and what is formal wear because he "brought the comfort and simplicity of sportswear into the realm of formal dressing." Sometimes referred to as the Dean of American Designers, Blass employed classic fabrics in garments that curved to the body. His designs, favored by notables such as Nancy Reagan and Barbra Streisand, could exude Hollywood glamour or be suitable for a country club setting. Perry Ellis (1940–1986) founded Perry Ellis International in 1978 and shared the designer spotlight with Blass in the 1980s. Ellis made his name in sportswear. He believed it should not be pretentious, and he sought to bring traditional fashion a modern American look. He helped to revive hand-knit sweaters.

Norma Kamali (1945–) opened her first shop in 1968 designing rhine-stoned and appliquéd T-shirts. In 1974, she introduced parachute jumpsuits made of real parachute silk. Her sleeping bag coat came in 1975, and in 1977, she introduced swimwear that would make her famous. In 1978, Kamali opened OMO (On My Own), and in 1980, she introduced another fashion innovation, her Fashion at a Price collection, that featured her sweatshirt collection. She went on to develop fragrances, cosmetics, and gym and athletic wear as well as a no-wrinkle poly-jersey collection for travelers. Philadelphia native Willi Smith (1948–1987) wanted to design fashions that would fit somewhere between formal evening wear and very informal jeans. He founded WilliWear in 1976 and introduced moderately priced, brightly colored clothing oriented to young people that, with baggy pants and oversized shirts and sweaters, precursed the rap and hip-hop styles that would come later. Born in Connecticut in 1942, Betsey Johnson had a background in dance and was a Warhol groupie in the 1960s. She opened a boutique in 1969 and designed rock 'n' roll clothing in the 1970s. In 1978, she and a partner formed the Betsey Johnson label, now with stores worldwide that include accessories as well as clothing. Johnson designs youthful, sexy—microminis—and colorful, even exuberant clothes, often in stretch fabrics that allow ease of movement. Marc Jacobs (1963–) is famous for his wit—the Freudian slip dress—and making grunge high fashion in 1982. His label Marc for the mass market is designed to be edgy and affordable. New Yorker Donna Karan (1948–) worked for Anne Klein and, after her death, designed sportswear for the company. She went out on her own in 1985 with the Donna Karan collection. Karan's designs for women, whether for sports, work, or evening wear, are simple, elegant, and comfortable. She liberated successful, independent women from "the masculine corporate uniform." Her figure suit is casual chic. In 1988, she started DKNY, a less expensive brand more accessible to the masses.

Perhaps in recognition of the global success and preeminence of American fashion design and designers, but certainly not in any recognition of the fact that some Americans designers had reached the highest level of couture as practiced only heretofore in France, five American designers were invited to show their designs at Versailles in 1973 with five French designers. The occasion was actually a fundraising event for the Versailles Restoration Fund, but that Americans were showing their fashions in France was a revolutionary event. The American designers invited included Bill Blass, Anne Klein (Donna Karan filled in for her), Oscar de la Renta, Halston, and Stephen Burrows. Burrows had come to notice after he opened a New York boutique in 1970 and become famous for his chiffons, jersey dresses with lettuce hems, usually in red, and his bright colors. He dressed Cher and became the preferred designer of the disco scene. Thanks in part to the Versailles show, Burroughs became the first African American fashion designer to attain an international reputation. He now sells his lesser designs on television through the Home Shopping Network. With everyone assembled at the palace on November 28, the American designers showed their RTW, while the French designers—Yves Saint Laurent, Hubert Givenchy, Emanuel Ungaro, Pierre Cardin, and Christian Dior—showed their haute couture.[38]

While these noted fashion designers have been instrumental in developing an American look, in truth, there are many American looks, and designers are providing Americans with quite eclectic clothing choices. Carmen Webber and Carmia Marshall of Sistahs Harlem New York attempt to express in their fashions the experience and heritage of New York City's Harlem, from the people of the streets to the upper class. While their style is decidedly American, it is American in the sense that America is a fusion of cultures. One of their collections, for example, is called Rastafarian Street Punk. Tommy Hilfiger, on the other hand, wants his clothes to be fun and to be used to express individuality, a treasured American value. David Rodriguez, a Mexican American, opened his own label in 1998 and quickly became known for his sleek and sexy cocktail dresses as well as his red carpet ensembles. He came out with a fur collection and accessories in 2005. Zac Posen made his name by designing nostalgic gowns worn by movie starlets to suggest their rightful places in Hollywood history. Mark Badgley and James Mischka are also bringing back classic Hollywood glamour in their designs. Michael Kors has been designing chic, upscale, luxurious classics for the jet set since 1981. Kors and Posen have used their success in women's wear to expand into men's wear. While Kors's designs have modern lines, Mary Ping, who launched her own label in 2001, based her designs on the lines of postmodern architecture and the shapes found in nature. Her silk and velvet gowns define chic in rich colors that are not necessarily beholden to symmetry. Luca Orlandi of Luca Luca designs flirtatious, very feminine dresses in bold colors that are inspired by abstract art. Ralph Rucci of Chado Ralph Rucci creates sculpted and sophisticated clothing with prints from his own artwork. His perfection got him invited to show his haute couture in Paris. Kenneth Cole began in the shoe business and continues to design shoes in addition to men's and women's wear that claim a contemporary urban inspiration with black jeans and crew neck sweaters. Born in Colombia and raised in Miami, Esteban Cortazar entered the fashion design business in 2002 at the age of 18. The bright colors of his fabulous gowns give away his consciously Spanish influences. Designer Maz Azria at BCBG combines the sophistication of Europe with the spirit of America in his fashions, which stretch to denim, footwear, and fragrances.[39]

Fashions, like hairstyles, are safe, nonpermanent ways for Americans to express themselves. Take the curious American invention of blue jeans. Levi Strauss began supplying jeans to miners shortly after the California Gold Rush began in 1848. In the 1870s, he and his partner had perfected the jeans known today by reinforcing stress points with rivets. Jeans, both pants and overalls, became and remain the uniform of Americans who work with their hands—farmers, steel workers, assembly line workers, construction workers, miners, cowboys. In the 1950s, they were appropriated by some youths as a symbol of their personal disaffection. Movies passed on the message. In the 1960s and 1970s, however, in one of those strange turns in American political history, jeans became the symbol of the youth culture and its imagined solidarity with working people, a solidarity not sought by most working people. War protesters in blue jeans filled television news stories, but jeans now had taken on a different look. Bell-bottoms and flower and bead designs were in, and the scruffier the pants, the more they were in. By the 1980s, fashion designers had figured out that blue jeans could be cool, even if stonewashed and with holes in the knees. A pair of fashion designer branded jeans could fetch thousands of dollars, even while most Americans were satisfied with a $12 pair of Levis.

Levi's jeans are still one of America's most popular brands. © AP Photo/Eric Risberg.

The 1990s saw the reappropriation of blue jeans into urban fashion. Leading the charge were the hip-hop artists, the rappers. These blue jeans were not sleek designer jeans fit to accentuate the buttocks, but to hide them in loose-fitted, baggy pants worn low on the hips to expose underwear pants and gathered over the ankles. With sneakers, T-shirt, a hoodie, flashy large jewelry, and a baseball cap worn sideways or backward, or a do-rag, jeans helped to make a new fashion statement. This fashion, associated with the pimps and hos of dangerous, young, urban African American and Latino gangsterism, quickly found its way into teenage fashion of all races in all places.

Fashion is changeable as the wind. Teenage fashion is especially fickle. The fortunes of clothing retailers like Abercrombie & Fitch, the Gap, and American Eagle Outfitters that cater to teens rise and fall on the ability of its buyers to catch the wave of what is hot in that season. Large discount retailers have sought to associate themselves with celebrities and fashion design houses to ratchet up their marketing campaigns and increase their profits and cachet. Actress Jaclyn Smith, who rose to fame in the original *Charlie's Angels* television show, has been selling her line of clothing at K-Mart for over 20 years. It has sales of about $300 million a year.[40] Mary-Kate and Ashley Olsen, the Olsen twins, used their celebrity for many auxiliary enterprises, including a line of preteen and young teen clothing sold in Wal-Mart stores. In 2003,

Isaac Mizrahi began designing clothing for Target. Like many fashion designers, Mizrahi continues to work in high fashion, but these cheaper designs produce a big bottom line. Noted designer Vera Wang followed Mizrahi into the mass retail trade in the fall of 2007 with a less expensive line of sportswear, intimate apparel, handbags, and leather accessories along with jewelry, furniture, towels, and lines for the moderately priced Kohl's chain. J. C. Penney has filled its clothing racks with private store labels, and in 2005, Wal-Mart even introduced "Metro 7," its own brand of urban fashion.

The tremendous influx of Hispanics into the United States created a large new market of Latinas, who have proved to be quite fashion conscious. Studies have shown, for example, that 57 percent of Hispanic women preferred clothing that looked better on them for an evening out eating and dancing than clothing that was more comfortable. White and African American women much preferred the more comfortable clothing, at the rates of 45 percent and 46 percent. Hispanic women also spent on average 135.1 minutes in stores shopping for clothing, beating out white women at 89.4 minutes and African American women at 109.27 minutes. In addition, more Hispanic women than the other ethnic groups were likely to use the Internet to shop for apparel.[41] Put all together, this means that Latinas are likely to spend more on clothing. Given $500, a 2004 study indicated, Latinas would spend $305.33 on clothes, whereas African American women would spend $297.51 and white women only $219.58.[42]

Armed with this information, retailers have gone after the Latina market. Celebrity and model Daisy Fuentes teamed up with Regatta to design low-priced clothing with a little salsa for Kohl's. Mexican-born pop music star Thalia Sodi sells her collection of spicy and flirtatious clothing through K-Mart. Color, lace, beads, hoop earrings, and tight-fitting jeans are in. Sears teamed up with Latina Media Ventures, publisher of *Latina Magazine,* to introduce a full line of Latina fashion, shoes, jewelry, and accessories into its stores. Latina fashions are proving to have a large appeal beyond their originally targeted market.

Movie stars are famous for plugging fashion designers on the red carpet runways of such events as the televised Emmy and Academy Award shows. Media representatives dutifully ask them, "Who are you wearing?" and the stars dutifully tell them. While they are selling high fashion at high prices in the Hollywood glamour tradition, it is the rock bands and rappers who establish for teenagers what is cool, and it is the teens who push new looks for their generation. These days, a band or group is not only a musical ensemble, but also a marketing concept. With a market in the United States alone of hundreds of billions of dollars (and American music goes around the world quickly), a fractional percentage of total market sales could establish a successful brand.

Entrepreneur Russell Simmons, a pioneer of hip-hop and cofounder of Def Jam Recordings, among other things, started Phat (for "pretty hot and tempting") Farm Fashions LLC in 1992. With a combination of preppy and hip-hop clothing lines, Russell reached annual sales of $250 million when he sold his clothing line in 2004 for $140 million. Rapper Shawn "Jay-Z" Carter, now CEO of Def Jam Recordings, started Rocawear in 1999. It epitomizes urban fashion, the look of the street, the look of the rappers with their baggy jeans hanging on their hips, exposed underwear, hoodies, and loose-hanging shirts. The women's wear sparkles with sequins and rhinestones. With more than $350 million in sales, Rocawear has signed deals with Tiffany & Co. for luxury accessories and has a licensing deal with Pro-Keds sneakers. There are lines even for toddlers and infants. Things are changing, however, for Rocawear. Noting that once he hit the 30-year mark, he could not show his underwear anymore, Carter has come out with a Custom Fit label meant to appeal to a more mature (older) population. The closer-fitting jeans, shirts, and track jackets look more traditional and only suggest the urban fashion look of an earlier era.[43] Designer Marc Ecko, with his M.E. and Cut and Sew lines, is also trying to bridge the gap between urban and preppy with tailored but comfortable clothing.

Russell Simmons and his former wife Kimora Lee Simmons pose with their children after the debut of one of their fashion collections. © AP Photo/Richard Drew.

If any proof were needed that urban culture and clothing had become mainstream America, certainly Sean "P. Diddy" Combs's receipt of the 2004 Council of Fashion Designers of America Men's Wear Designer of the Year award would be enough. Combs started Sean John in 1998. With this success, he designed a women's line that is both sophisticated and grounded in street culture. Sean John's retail sales exceed $450 million.

Rappers have taken to fashion. Eminem has his brand Shady Ltd. that sells beanies, his famous knit scullcap, T-shirts with logos, sweatshirts, and baggy jeans. St. Louis rapper Cornell "Nelly" Haynes Jr. actually started his men's line, Vokal, before he hit the music scene big in 2000. His football jerseys, sweatpants, jeans, and tracksuits are meant to be clothes that speak for themselves. His later women's line, Apple Bottoms, features sexy slim jeans, V-necked hoodies, flounce skirts, tanks, and tube dresses. Gwen Stefani's L.A.M.B. collection has sales of around $20 million and includes fleece and leopard hoodies as well as plaid jumpsuits and a line of rock 'n' roll clothes. Jennifer Lopez, with partner Andy Hilfiger, have turned their Sweetface Fashion business, started in 2001, into a $500 million business with about a dozen different lines that cover head to toe. Even Justin Timberlake, former Mouseketeer, has a clothing line of T-shirts, jeans, and knits called William Rast, a label he hopes to make a major brand.[44]

American fashion, no matter the price point, represents the liberation of self-expression from old norms and mores. Americans can dress like modern-day cowboys and cowgirls or Hollywood stars, or gangstas, if they like. Young men can show off their underwear and young women their midriffs, or teenagers can demonstrate their inevitable alienation from everything of their parents' generation in grunge or goth or punk—about anything goes fashionwise in America. What most Americans really want in their dress, however, is comfort and flexibility, which is what American designers have given them. Everyday dress in the workplace remains rather traditional—men in business suits, women in business suits and conservative suits and dresses—but even there, old standards have been put into question with the growth of the casual Fridays movement. At home and at leisure, however, the sweatpants and sweatshirts, the jeans, the shorts and the T-shirts come out. That is the American look.

NOTES

1. Phillip Stephen Schulz, *As American as Apple Pie* (New York: Simon and Schuster, 1990).

2. U.S. Bureau of the Census, *Statistical Abstract of the United States: 2004/5*, http://www.census.gov.

3. "2006 Restaurant Industry Fact Sheet," http://www.restaurant.org.

4. Susan Spielberg, "Positive Sales, Growth Trends to Continue, Analysts Say: High Costs Legislative Issues Still Concern Regional Operators," *Nation's Restaurant News*, January 3, 2005, http://www.nrn.com; "More Than Six Out of 10 Americans Will Have Their Mother's Day Meals at Restaurants," *Pizza Marketing Quarterly*, May 4, 2006, http://www.pmq.com.

5. Exxon Mobil Corporation, "Mobil Travel Guide Announces the 2006 Mobil Four- and Five-Star Award Winners," news release, October 26, 2005, http://www.companyboardroom.com.

6. Bruce Horowitz, "NPD Group Survey of 3,500 Respondents to the Question 'What Did I Order at a Restaurant Today?' as Part of a Year-long Survey of Eating Habits in 2004," *USA Today*, May 12, 2005, http://www.usatoday.com.

7. "Pizza Power 2005; PMQ's Annual Pizza Industry Analysis," *Pizza Marketing Quarterly*, September/October 2005, http://www.pmq.com.

8. "Pizza Industry Facts," http://pizzaware.com.

9. U.S. Census Bureau, "Census Product Update: Chow Mein, Cacciatore, or Fajitas?," http://www.census.gov.

10. el Restaurante Mexicano, "Hispanic Market Profile," http://www.restmex.com; "About CRN," http://english.c-r-n.com.

11. "Frozen Food Trends," http://www.affi.com.

12. "Industry at a Glance," http://www.affi.com.

13. "News: 2005 California Wine Sales Continue Growth as Wine Enters Mainstream U.S. Life," *California Wine and Food Magazine*, April 6, 2006, http://www.californiawineandfood.com.

14. "Craft Brewing Industry Statistics: Highlights of 2005," http://www.beertown.org.

15. "Spirits: North American Whiskey," http://www.tastings.com.

16. "Product Variety: Soft Drink Facts," http://www.ameribev.org; "Product Variety: What America's Drinking," http://www.ameribev.org.

17. "Fun Facts about Peanuts," http://www.nationalpeanutboard.org.

18. Helen Mendes, *The African Heritage Cookbook* (New York: Macmillan, 1971).

19. Chef John Folse and Company, "Experience Great Cajun & Creole Food and Recipes with Chef John Folse & Company: History," http://www.jfolse.com.

20. E. A. Oelke, T. M. Teynor, P. R. Carter, J. A. Percich, D. M. Noetzel, P. R. Bloom, R. A. Porter, C. E. Schertz, J. J. Boedicker, and E. I. Fuller, "Wild Rice," in *Alternative Field Crops Manual*, http://www.hort.purdue.edu.

21. U.S. Department of Agriculture, National Agriculture Statistics Service, "Dairy Products 2005 Summary," April 2006, http://usda.mannlib.cornell.edu.

22. "Barbeque Kansas City Style," http://www.experiencekc.com.

23. See Cliff Lowe, "The Life and Times of Chili: Cincinnati Chili—Part Two," http://www.inmamaskitchen.com.

24. "Upper Great Lakes Fish Boil: A Tasty Tradition," http://www.seagrant.umn.edu.

25. White Castle Inc., "Timeline," http://www.whitecastle.com; "About Us," http://www.whitecastle.com.

26. Maid-Rite Corporation, "Unique Loose Meat Sandwich," http://www.maid-rite.com; "Menu," http://www.maid-rite.com.

27. See John Sedlar, with Norman Kolpas, *Modern Southwest Cuisine* (New York: Simon and Schuster, 1986).

28. "Mexican and TexMex Food History," http://www.foodtimeline.org.

29. "Menus & Recipes from the Bay Area's Finest Restaurants & Top Chefs," http://www.sanfranciscocuisine.com.

30. Wahoo's Fish Taco, "Wahoo's Story," http://www.wahoos.com; "Menu," http://www.wahoos.com.

31. Fatburger, "History," http://www.fatburger.com; In-N-Out Burger, "History," http://www.in-n-out.com.

32. Michael Luo, "As All-American as Egg Foo Young," *New York Times,* September 22, 2004, http://www.nytimes.com.

33. "All You Want to Know about Washington Cuisine," http://www.theworldwidegourmet.com; Brendan Eliason, "A 6 Region Exploration: Pacific Northwest," http://www.winebrats.org.

34. U.S. National Institute of Standards and Technology, "Short History of Ready-Made Clothing: Standardization of Women's Clothing," http://museum.nist.gov.

35. "Trends: Annual 2004," http://www.apparelandfootwear.org.

36. "How the West Was Worn," http://www.autry-museum.org.

37. "Fashion Walk of Fame," http://www.fashioncenter.com.

38. Ibid. For biographies of designers, see "History of Fashion & Costume: Fashion Designers," http://www.designerhistory.com.

39. "Fashion Shows," http://www.nymag.com.

40. "Celebrity Style: Coming to a Department Store Near You," http://abcnews.go.com.

41. Cotton Incorporated, "Latina Fashion: From Vogue to K-Mart," news release, October 5, 2005, http://www.cottoninc.com.

42. Cotton Incorporated, "Latina Flavor: Today's Hispanic Woman Feasts on Fashion," http://www.cottoninc.com.

43. Teri Agins, "Jay-Z's Fine Line," *Wall Street Journal,* August 17, 2006, B1–B2.

44. See *Fashion Rocks: A Supplement to the New Yorker,* September 2005 and September 2006 editions.

BIBLIOGRAPHY

Bradley, Susan. *Pacific Northwest Palate.* Reading, MA: Addison-Wesley, 1989.

Cunningham, Patricia A., and Susan Voso Lab, eds. *Dress in American Culture.* Bowling Green, OH: Bowling Green State University Popular Press, 1993.

Glenn, Camille. *The Heritage of Southern Cooking.* New York: Workman, 1986.

Hays, Wilma P., and R. Vernon. *Foods the Indians Gave Us.* New York: Ives Washburn, 1973.

Johnson, Ronald. *The American Table.* New York: William Morrow, 1984.

Jones, Evan. *American Food: The Gastronomic Story.* 2nd ed. New York: Random House, 1981.

Kidwell, Claudia Brush, and Margaret C. Christman. *Suiting Everyone: The Democratization of Clothing in America.* Washington, DC: Smithsonian Institution Press, 1974.

Langlois, Stephen. *Prairie: Cuisine from the Heartland.* Chicago: Contemporary Books, 1990.

Mendes, Valerie, and Amy de la Haye. *20th Century Fashion.* London: Thames and Hudson, 1999.

Milbank, Caroline Rennolds. *New York Fashion: The Evolution of American Style.* New York: Harry N. Abrams, 1989.

Root, Waverley, and Richard De Rochemont. *Eating in America: A History.* New York: Ecco Press, 1976.

Smallzried, Kathleen Ann. *The Everlasting Pleasure.* New York: Appleton-Century-Crofts, 1956.

Stern, Jane, and Michael Stern. *Real American Food.* New York: Alfred A. Knopf, 1986.

Stern, Jane, and Michael Stern. *A Taste of America.* Kansas City: Andrews and McMeel, 1988.

Welters, Linda, and Patricia A. Cunningham, eds. *Twentieth-century American Fashion.* New York: Berg, 2005.

6

Literature

William P. Toth

IN THE YEAR 2006, one of the top best sellers in bookstores across the United States (with over a half million sales) was the *Far Side Boxed Calendar*. The vast majority of the sales in bookstores, however, were actually for books. The Book Industry Study Group has projected 2.5 billion books to be sold in 2006, this despite a trend toward less time spent reading (101 hours per person in 1995 compared to 84 hours per person projected for 2006).[1]

Prognosticators have also looked into their crystal balls and seen trends in the publishing world: more fragmentation, rather than the current consolidation of publishing houses. Publishing in the United States is still dominated by six publishing houses: Random House, Pearson, von Holtzbrinck, Time-Warner, HarperCollins, and Simon & Schuster. There are small press, professional, academic, and numerous other kinds of publishers as well, but even they have been thinned out. This is a trend that has been ongoing for about the past 30 years, but this may be coming to an end as high-tech alternatives to book publishing, such as print-on-demand (POD), portable document format (PDF), and other means of self-publishing, become more popular. Furthermore, thanks to newer means of distribution, especially the Internet, smaller publishing companies can now afford to compete in the market.

Another populist trend is the Oprah Winfrey Book Club. Beginning in September 1996, Oprah Winfrey began to recommend a book a month to her audience of 20 million viewers. She then featured a discussion of the book and author interviews. It has proven to be a powerful book-selling phenomenon. For instance, one of the first books she featured, Jacquelyn Mitchard's

The Deep End of the Ocean, went from a pre-Oprah run of 68,000 books to a post-Oprah run of 4 million and a spot on the *New York Times* bestseller list. The success of her book club has made book clubs in general popular.

Whether the publishing is traditional or part of the new media, it still includes traditional poetry and drama as well as many types of traditional prose, both fiction and nonfiction. One of the modern, nontraditional trends is to blur the distinction between fiction and nonfiction as exemplified by the movement known as creative nonfiction. American literature and even journalism are subject to the same creative impulse that has driven painters, sculptors, musicians, film directors and other artists to break down the old structures and barriers, throw out the old rules, and create new ones. This blurring usually leads to interesting, lively, and exceptional literature, but it also can lead to controversy when fiction creeps too strongly into something that is categorized as nonfiction. For example, several newspaper journalists—using creative nonfiction techniques—in the last few years have been fired or resigned when their editors found out that articles they had written were partially fiction, not just in technique but also in content.

Literature is not always contained in books—there is also performance literature, some traditional, like the theater, and some nontraditional, like slam poetry. Both can exist in book form, but most people experience them through live performances. That is their natural state, and they, too, are important parts of the contemporary American literary scene.

POETRY

The Oral Tradition Goes Hip-Hop

Chicago can be a rowdy town. The words *poetry* and *rowdy* do not traditionally mix, but in November 1984, poets gathering on Monday nights at the Get Me High Jazz Club on the west side of Chicago changed that perception and started a national trend. Breaking from the tradition of polite, serious, and sedate poetry readings, they decided to declaim poetry while walking on bar counters and bar stools, performing and interacting with their audience. Remarkably, this craziness caught on. It became so popular that the poetry gatherings moved to larger digs, the Green Mill Cocktail Lounge, and turned the readings into a competition. The Chicago Poetry Ensemble, led by poet Marc Kelly Smith, called it the Uptown Poetry Slam. Thus began one of the popular contemporary trends in poetry: public, competitive poetry readings, also known as poetry slams.

To be accurate, the oral tradition is as old as poetry itself. The likes of Homer and Sappho performed for audiences, telling tales of valor, fate, and

Suheir Hammad, Beau Sia, and Georgia Me perform in the Def Poetry Jam in New York. © AP Photo/Robert Spencer.

love. The poets of ancient Greece did not, of course, compete for Twinkies, boxes of macaroni and cheese, lottery tickets, or—the biggy—a $10 bill. Nevertheless, these were the much coveted prizes at the early poetry slams.

Smith and the Ensemble (formed in 1985) turned their Monday night readings into a cultural phenomenon and gave slam a mission. The mission was, in part, to turn as large a part of the population of the country as possible into not only lovers of poetry, but also creators of poetry. No longer was poetry limited to the academy and to the insular world of literary magazines and small presses. Now, anyone with the guts to get on stage could be part of the poetry scene. True, they might get booed off the stage, but then again, they might end up eating a Twinkie as well.

So how popular and far-reaching is the poetry slam today? Eighty-four-year-old Doris Gayzagian (her first book was published in 2006) is a regular at the Chelmsford Public Library's poetry slam. The National English Association promotes slam poetry in high schools. It found a niche on television in HBO's *Def Poetry Jam,* which then became a Broadway Tony Award–winning production, *Russell Simmons' Def Poetry Jam on Broadway.* There is even a *Complete Idiot's Guide to Slam Poetry* (written by Marc Kelly Smith and Joe Kraynak).

The poetry itself is often socially oriented, often political, often angry. Some of it arrogantly mocks W. H. Auden's line that "poetry makes nothing happen." The worst of it, like the worst of any art form, is ephemeral: there is nothing there that will be of any human importance beyond the immediate moment. Yet some of it captures—without dissecting—truly human moments that promise universality and timelessness. While the poetics might sometimes be thin, there is another dimension to be considered: the performance itself.

This is poetry that is performed on Broadway stages, television, auditorium stages, and small stages in bars and bookstores. This fact creates an added dimension to the poetry—it is more than just the words; it is also the delivery. On one extreme, the delivery can be graceful and poignant; on the other extreme, it can be like a tuning fork hit with a sledge hammer. The best performance artists use the tools of the actor or the comedian—and all are voice musicians. The star poets are most often the champions of either the National Poetry Slam or the Individual World Poetry Slam.

The National Poetry Slam began in 1990 as part of a poetry festival held in San Francisco. The next year, it took on a life of its own. It has been held every year since at various cities across the country, in Asheville, Ann Arbor, Seattle, and Chicago, among others. It is now a 16-year tradition as well as a happening. The competition is held over four nights and includes team competition—group poems, sometimes choral, but also punctuated with solos, much like a jazz performance—and an individual competition. The Individual World Poetry Slam is a newer event. It began in 2004 and is an offshoot of the National Poetry Slam.

The spirit of slam poetry is to sidestep exclusivity and celebrate democracy, while passionately scorning the concept of the anointed few. Nevertheless, slam poetry has produced some stars and important figures. One is certainly Marc Kelly Smith, the originator of the poetry slam. Though not a competitor in any of the above poetry competitions, he is still a compelling performance poet. He was born in 1950 in Avalon Park, a neighborhood of Chicago. His roots are blue collar, and his speech—pure Chicago dialect—supports this. He first became interested in writing poetry in 1969, at age 19, because (he says) his wife was a poet. He took some classes in literature and a few in writing, but considers himself self-taught. His first poetry reading was at the Left Bank Bookstore in Oak Park, Illinois, where he claimed to have hidden his poems in a newspaper. From this experience and from attending other poetry readings, he came to the conclusion that street conversations were more interesting than poetry readings. While he was learning his craft, he worked as a construction worker. Then, in 1984, he quit to become a full-time poet, and the rest is slam poetry history.

Smith is humble about his poetic abilities (which he considers to be a little above average) but forthright about his role in the creation of slam poetry and its democratization of poetry. He eschews the connection (often made) between the beatniks and slam poetry—he considers the beatniks to have been social dropouts. For him, slam poetry is more akin to the Socialist movement and folk artists like Pete Seeger. Still, often, when he is performing at the Green Mill, he is accompanied by a jazz group called the Pong Unit, thus, ironically, beating the jazzy, bongo beats at their own game.

The subject of many of Smith's poems is Chicago itself: its people, its sights, its sounds. The scene for his poem "Peanuts," for instance, is outside one of Chicago's baseball stadiums. As the narrator of the poem perches himself on a fire hydrant, and as the barking voice of the peanut vender intermittently calls out, he notes the characters around him: cops, fathers and sons, and even a peroxide blond eating a Polish sausage. Some of his other topics are Chicago's famous El train, street musicians, bicycle messengers, and jazz music. The poem he considers his best is titled "My Father's Coat." This is a moving, deceptively complex poem that revolves around the central metaphor of his father's coat and deals with relationships and generations. Equally good is his poem "Small Boy," which deals with three generations, intermingled in memories of childhood captured in a photo.

Like Smith, Bob Holman does not compete directly in any of the national competitions, but he is also a slam impresario of the first magnitude. Holman is the Don King of poetry, promoting himself as well as slam. Born in 1948 in LaFollette, Tennessee, he grew up in New Richmond, Ohio, just east of Cincinnati and across the river from Kentucky. He went to college at Columbia and was highly influenced by Alan Ginsberg and, in turn, by Walt Whitman. He claims to have moved to New York City with a copy of Ginsberg's *Howl* in his back pocket.

Holman coproduced the PBS series *United States of Poetry* and has been extremely active in the promotion of slam and of poetry in general (he did the program *Poetry Spots* for WNYC-TV, was the founding editor of NYC Poetry Calendar, was curator for the People's Poetry Gathering, was founder of the St. Mark's Poetry Project, and much more). For slam poetry, he helped to reopen the Nuyorican Poets Café and is the proprietor of the Bowery Poetry Club. Both establishments host poetry slams and are poetry hot spots in New York City. Most of Holman's poetic style is heavily derived from Ginsberg and Whitman, and at times, he overuses the repetition of words. He is famous for his poem "DiscClaimer," which he reads before every slam that he hosts. In it, he describes slam poetry as "space shots into consciousness" and declares that the best poet always loses.

"Mighty" Mike McGee is the 2003 winner of the individual title at the National Poetry Slam, the 2006 winner of the Individual World Poetry Slam, and a frequent guest on HBO's *Def Jam Poetry*. Born in 1976 at Fort Campbell, Kentucky, he dropped out of college in 1998 and became part of the slam poetry scene in San Jose, California. McGee has an engaging style, laced with a strong dose of humor, and a definite stage presence. With his trademark chin beard and black framed glasses, he eases up to the microphone, and with a somewhat rotund middle section, tells the audience—with a saxophone-like voice and a comedian's sense of timing and rhythm—about his eating duel with death, as related in his poem "Soul Food."

McGee's poetry is also capable of moving beyond Dante-like food fights and into the area of lyrical love poems, like "Open Letter to Neil Armstrong," in which he plays off the clichés of the moon, love, and the stars. He calls himself a traveling poet; he claims that since 2003, he has toured over 170,000 miles throughout the United States and Canada. This is one of the marks of slam stars: they go on the road with bookings in venues all across the country (and even into other countries). The venues might be public libraries, coffeehouses, universities, slam events, bars (like the Green Mill), or even prisons. Like many of the contemporary slam poets, McGee cuts his own CDs, laces the Internet with MP3 files of his spoken word art, and even has a very charming and winning pod cast.

Born in Shreveport, Louisiana, in 1974, Buddy Wakefield was raised in Baytown, Texas, and graduated from Sam Houston State University in 1997. Until 2001, he worked for a biomedical firm. Then, like Marc Kelly Smith, he gave it all up to become a professional performance poet. He is the 2004 and 2005 Individual World Poetry champion. Like most of the really good slam poets, his on-stage presence is unique. Most often, he stands on the stage, feet together, arms extended (or animated), pulsing with emotion. He has what might be called the Wakefield growl as he roars through individual words and frequently peppers his presentation with Texas y'alls. His poems, like "Convenience Stores," often tell stories of lonely people briefly connecting. "Guitar Repair Woman" is a humorous paean to his mother, where he says that he is striving to get comfortable in the skin his mother gave him. And in "Flockprinter," his championship poem from the 2005 Individual World Poetry Championship, he traces a man's life searching for love through a torrent of images and metaphors.

Anis Mijgani was born and raised in New Orleans and attended the Savannah College of Art and Design in Savannah, Georgia. He graduated with a bachelor of fine arts degree in sequential art, focusing in on comic book design, which he says taught him about engaging the audience and about structure. He then worked on his master's of fine arts in media and performing arts. He is the 2005 and 2006 National Poetry Slam individual champion.

On stage, he sometimes looks like Alan Ginsberg on a bad hair day, hands in pocket, slim and with a direct and sincere passion. His poetry is inspirational and his poems explore how to live and how to have faith, depth, and meaning in your life. Mijgani is distinguished from many of his fellow slam poets in that faith, the search for something beyond human pleasure, does play a significant part in his poetry. He addresses the young, the old, the awkward, the disenfranchised, those who might have doubts or who might have given up hope.

Patricia Smith is perhaps the most traditionally literary of the popular slam poets. Born in Chicago in 1950, Smith is a four-time individual winner of the National Poetry Slam (1990, 1992, 1993, and 1995). She also has four books of poetry published: *Life According to Motown* (1991), *Big Towns, Big Talk* (1992), *Close to Death* (1993), and *Teahouse of the Almighty* (2006). *Teahouse* was chosen for the National Poetry Series.

Her subject matter often deals with the tragedy, the unfulfilled dreams, and the limitations of everyday life, often focusing on the life of African Americans, but there is universality about her poetry and an appeal that goes beyond race. Often, there is an edgy—verging on bitter—humor in her poetry. She is a powerful performer and powerful poet, steeped in tradition. In "Medusa," for instance, she takes the persona of the mythical character Medusa, putting a modern spin on her; in this case, she is a cocky, streetwise Medusa who seduces Poseidon. In "Related to the Buttercup, Blooms in Spring," Smith writes about how she came to poetry as a child, giving the advice that the writer must learn to love language, word by word. Her own language is one of vivid, precise words, rhythmic and melodious. Smith's own voice might best be described as one that speaks an honest, true picture of the world around her.

Poetry in Books Is Alive and Well

The written word in poetry is not dead, despite the popularity of slam (or perhaps because of the popularity of slam). Connoisseurs of written word poetry (as well as academics) claim, with some justification, that the overall quality of written poetry is higher than slam. In any case, people continue to purchase books of poetry, though not at the pace of best-selling prose books. For instance, best-selling poet Billy Collins's combined book sales for four books (tabulated in April 2005) was 400,000, whereas John Grogan's nonfiction best seller *Marley and Me* sold 1,307,000 copies from November 2005 through December 2006.

Bookseller statistics show that the two most widely purchased poets in the United States at this time are Mary Oliver and the previously mentioned Billy Collins. Both have had multiple books in the poetry top 30 list for the entire year (2006). There are other active poets who have dominated the top seller list as well. These include Donald Hall, Ted Kooser, Louise Glück, and Claudia Emerson.

In addition to these active poets, there are a number of deceased poets who readers still consider vital enough to purchase, and thus they, too, have been on the best seller list for a good portion of the year 2006. These include the beatnik poets Jack Kerouac and Alan Ginsberg as well as Sylvia Plath, Elizabeth Bishop, and Charles Bukowski. These four poets seem to suggest that there is a portion of the poetry reading public who are attracted to the message of rebelliousness, whether it be beatnik, bohemian, or feminist.

Some of these poets see despair, some loneliness; some are angry at injustice, some see transcendent beauty in nature, some argue for social change, and all know something about love and personal loss.

Mary Oliver, born in 1935 in Maple Heights, Ohio, began to write poetry at age 13. Immediately after graduating from high school, she left Ohio and drove to the home of Edna St. Vincent Millay in Austerlitz, New York. She ended up working for Millay's sister as her secretary for a short while. She then entered Ohio State University in 1955. She spent two years there and then transferred to Vassar. She remained there for only one year and quit to concentrate on writing. Oliver has won many awards, including the Pulitzer Prize for Poetry in 1984 for her third book, *American Primitives.* In 2006, she had seven books on the poetry best seller list, including a new book, *Thirst.*

Oliver is typically described as a nature poet. In comparing her very early works, like *The River Styx, Ohio* (1972)—which is filled with portraits of ancestors—to her newer works, it seems that people have gradually disappeared from her poetry. Her poetry would not be so popular, however, if it were just the "roses are red, violets are blue" kind of poetry. She is, as Billy Collins has noted about poetry in general, interested in seeing life through the viewpoint of mortality. This is not a negative vision. For her, there is a power and a magic and a beauty in nature. It is her ability to create this sensibility in her poems that no doubt draws readers to them. They are mysterious, philosophical, fairy tale–like observations of the natural world, meditations that contrast nature with the world of ambition, greed, and selfishness. These objects in the natural world, as she has said herself, praise the mystery. In *Thirst,* there is a growing connection between this mystery and God. In the title poem "Thirst," she writes about waking with a thirst for a goodness she does not possess, juxtaposing love for the earth against love of God. In the opening poem of the book ("Messenger"), Oliver claims her work is to love the world and to learn to be astonished by it. Her poetry conveys to the reader this sense of astonishment.

Billy Collins was born in New York City in 1941. He went to College of the Holy Cross and, for graduate school, the University of California, Riverside. He has been the recipient of many awards, including the Poet Laureate from 2001 until 2003. During 2006, he had four books on the poetry best seller list, including his newest, *The Trouble with Poetry and Other Poems,* which was the number one seller.

People like to say that Collins writes humorous poetry. In truth, humor is often a vehicle for serious consideration. Though there are poems, such as "Another Reason Why I Don't Keep a Gun in the House," which is about the neighbor's barking dog, and which can only be seen as humorous, other poems, like "The Death of Allegory," are something more. There is humor there: the Virtues are retired in Florida, but there is the realization (created through a humor that is slightly acerbic) that the world is worse off without them.

Since the title of Collins's new book of poetry is *The Trouble with Poetry,* interviewers like to ask him just exactly what the trouble with poetry is. He will often answer that it is pretentiousness, an attempt to be more difficult than necessary; that it is poetry, as he says in the poem "Introduction to Poetry," that needs to be tied to a chair and tortured until it confesses its truth. He admits that when he first started writing poetry, he wrote like that, but in the title poem of *The Trouble with Poetry,* the trouble described is more pleasant. The trouble is that the writing of poetry encourages the writing of more poetry, poetry that can bring either joy or sorrow. It fills him with the urge to sit down and await the muse so that another poem can be written.

Donald Hall, the 2006 Poet Laureate, was born in New Haven, Connecticut, in 1928. He is the most senior of the best-selling authors. Hall is the recipient of many awards besides Poet Laureate. He had an exceptional education, attending the famous prep school Exeter Phillips, then Harvard, Oxford (England), and Stanford. Hall is a prolific writer, excelling in a number of genres. His newest book, *White Apples and the Taste of Stone: Selected Poems 1946–2006,* was a best seller most of the year in 2006. As the title states, this book presents the greater part of his entire career as a poet. With a prolific, long career such as his, there are bound to be many styles of poetry in a book of his collected poems. His poetry often touches on personal relationships and family relationships in a rural New Hampshire setting, where his grandparents owned a farm and where he came to live after he left his teaching job at Michigan State in Ann Arbor. His topics are varied: baseball, poetry itself, Mount Kearsarge, his late wife, the poet Jane Kenyon, loss, death, and the sweep of time.

Another poet who also sees the sweep of time is Ted Kooser. A native of Ames, Iowa, Kooser was born in 1939. Thoroughly a man of the Great Plains, Kooser attended Iowa State and the University of Nebraska. For 35 years, he worked as an insurance executive, retiring in 1998 after a bout with throat cancer. He was named Poet Laureate in 2004. He won the Pulitzer Prize for *Delights and Shadows* in 2005. Many of Kooser's poems are meditations on relatives (most of whom were farmers) and on everyday objects, objects that one might find in a rural antique shop, at a yard sale, or at a county fair. He has said that he is most interested in writing about the so-called ordinary. He has the ability to take a simple object like a pegboard or a casting reel and telescope a sense of time and human connectedness with it. For example, his poem "At the County Museum" notices the black, horse-drawn hearse that has seen a hundred years of service. The poet's eye sees not just the object, but the generations of people who have driven the hearse and who have been carried by the hearse. And, by extension, the metaphor telescopes to include all of mankind. It has been said that Kooser writes about the point where the local and the eternal meet.

Less upbeat than any of the previous poets, Louise Glück was born in New York City in 1943. She attended Sarah Lawrence and Columbia. In 1993, she won the Pulitzer Prize for Poetry, and in 2003, she was named Poet Laureate. She, like all of these poets, is the winner of many other literary awards. Her new book, *Averno,* is what put her on the contemporary best seller list. Some commentators have said that certain lines from Glück's poetry could be used as the basis of a philosophy class. Nevertheless, some readers would find her less accessible than most of the popular contemporary poets. She is sparse, cerebral, and—some would say—gloomy. The classical story of Persephone is the myth that loosely ties the poems of *Averno* together. Like Persephone, the persona of the poems is isolated and caught, seemingly, between worlds. While the tone of the poems is bleak, the totality of them, the artistic structure on which they are built, is a thing of beauty—and all the more so for being placed in an existential desert.

Claudia Emerson is more accessible than Glück. Born in Chatham, Virginia, in 1957, Emerson obtained her undergraduate degree from the University of Virginia. She then spent a number of years not writing poetry, but instead doing odd jobs like rural letter carrier and manager in a used book store. She returned to school at the University of North Carolina at Greensboro to work on her master's of fine arts and began writing poetry. She has since published three books of poetry. She received the 2006 Pulitzer Prize for her best-selling book of poetry *Late Wife,* admittedly autobiographical in nature. In simplistic terms, it is about her divorce, her psychological healing, and her new marriage. The formal titles of the sections are "Divorce Epistles," "Breaking Up the House," and "Late Wife: Letters to Kent." The setting for the poems is often rural Virginia, where she spent most of her life. The poetry in the book is a study of the triumphs and failures of love and of the meaning of loss. It is a book of poetry exploring many small, often domestic experiences, all the while coalescing painful experiences into poetry.

Another personal poet and an icon of the feminist movement, Sylvia Plath was born in Boston, Massachusetts, in 1932 and died in London in 1963. She attended Smith College and Cambridge University. One of the things about her 2006 best seller that attracts readers is the fact that it is a so-called restored edition of her final book of poems, *Ariel,* and that it has been restored by her daughter, Frieda Hughes. Hughes argues that her mother's poetry should be seen in the widest sense possible—as works of art—and not solely in a narrow way (i.e., as a battle cry for the women's movement). At the same time, she honors her mother's integrity and aesthetic sensibility by presenting *Ariel* exactly as her mother had instructed. For some, this focus on the aesthetic, rather than on the politics, of her poetry is a controversial stance. Hughes had been attacked by some of the British public and much of the press for not allowing a plaque to be placed in the house where Plath committed suicide—which for some people represents a final defiant act, an ultimate political statement. Instead, Hughes wanted it placed in the house where her mother was the most productive and happiest.

Plath's poetry in *Ariel* is strong, even viscous. It is certainly easy to see why some might connect it to a rebellion against male oppression. She describes her relationship with her husband, the British poet Ted Hughes, as equivalent to being filled by the constriction. Most dramatically, there is the famous poem, "Daddy," that compares her German father to the Nazis. Hughes hints in her introduction that the origin of her mother's anger is more complex than male oppression alone and certainly closely related to Plath's lifelong battle with severe depression. In any case, the poetry is still powerful and arresting.

A Pulitzer Prize winner for poetry, Elizabeth Bishop was the consummate artist and perfectionist. Born in 1911 in Worcester, Massachusetts, she died in 1979. Often, she would work on a poem for years (even decades) before she would publish it. The 2006 best-selling book *Edgar Allan Poe and the Juke-Box* is a compilation (often with photographs of various drafts of poems) of her unpublished works.

Bishop lived in many parts of the world and traveled extensively when she was young, visiting Europe, North Africa, and Mexico. Much of her poetry deals with this travel and often creates strong vignettes of place and sensibility. The two places where she lived that provided some of her best subject matter were Key West and Brazil. The title poem of the book is a good example of one of her Key West poems.

In "Edgar Allan Poe and the Juke-Box," Bishop paints a picture of mid-century Key West, sometimes seedy and certainly decadent. The setting is a honky-tonk, and the poem is a downward motion on many levels; Poe-like, it descends into the psyche. Almost all of works in the book are tone poems of place. In the books published while she was alive, she managed to refine out her own personal angst, leaving nothing but pure poetry. In many of these poems, the angst shows through. Despite the fact that she did not feel that the poems were good enough (refined enough) for publication, many of the poems in *Edgar Allan Poe and the Juke-Box* are of high quality.

Jack Kerouac, along with Alan Ginsberg, represents the current culture's fascination with the beatnik and hippie generation. Kerouac was born in Lowell, Massachusetts, in 1922 and died in 1969. He began college at Columbia University on a football scholarship but dropped out after a dispute with his coach. While at Columbia, he made friends with some of the future elite of the beatnik and hippie generation: Alan Ginsberg, William S. Burroughs, and Neal Cassady. His education then truly began as he started his life "on the road." First, he joined the Merchant Marines and traveled to Greenland. Afterward, he traveled the road crisscrossing America, often with Neal Cassady.

Kerouac is famous for his novels, especially *On the Road,* and his poetry, as in *Mexico City Blues.* Though not quite as unfiltered and spontaneous as legend would have it, his writing technique was to write his final draft—even of some of his novels—in a single burst. He was just the opposite of Elizabeth Bishop. The writing was always based on years of notebook entries. This is the case with his recent best seller, *Book of Sketches.* This book is made up of 15 of his notebooks that he wrote between 1952 and 1954. In 1957, he typed up the pages but never published them. Just as the title implies, they are poetic word sketches of people and sights from his cross-country travels. To paraphrase painter George Condo (who wrote the introduction), Kerouac is the Charlie Parker of words, great at spur of the moment improvisations. There is a difference in these poems and his later works. Unlike the other beatniks, Kerouac was politically conservative during the 1960s; in fact, he supported the Vietnam War. In these poems, on the other hand, there is more of the typical beatnik criticism of American culture.

Alan Ginsberg, whom the *New York Times* called the "poet laureate of the Beat Generation," was born in 1926 in Newark, New Jersey. He died in 1997. Ginsberg attended Columbia University and, like Jack Kerouac, spent time in the Merchant Marines traveling to the Atlantic and Gulf coasts and to Africa. He is known for his book *Howl,* which became the object of a major twentieth-century freedom of speech battle. He became an icon for the hippie generation and a major protestor against the Vietnam War. Readers are now drawn to his book *Collected Poems 1947–1997.* It is chronologically arranged by each of his published books and, of course, includes the famous book (and poem) *Howl,* which, in many ways, became the emotional manifesto for the entire beatnik generation.

Of the deceased poets, Charles Bukowski is perhaps the most popular with contemporary readers. The fact that he had four books in the top 50 list for a single year (2006), *Slouching toward Nirvana: New Poems; Come On In;*

Sifting through the Madness for the World, the Line, the Way; and *The Flash of Lightning behind the Mountain,* says something for his staying power and for his fascination for the contemporary reading public. He was born in 1920 in Andernach, Germany, to an American serviceman and a German mother, and he died in 1994.

Some people like to lump Bukowski in with the beatnik poets—mostly because he was writing at about the same time they were—but he is really a thing unto himself. He attended Los Angeles City College for two years, but never graduated. He suffered psychologically from an acute case of acne that disfigured his face and worked a series of often menial jobs: factory worker, warehouse worker, store clerk, and postal worker. Gradually, Bukowski became a prolific poet, short story writer, journalist, novelist, playwright, and screen writer. His poetry is edgy, raw, and often brutally honest. There is sex, drinking, belligerence, fighting, and escapes from landlords who want their money. There is, at the same time, often a sensitivity and sadness.

There are many other poets of note who are widely read and currently popular. These include Brian Turner, Jane Hirshfield, Mary Karr, Wendell Berry, Galway Kinnell, Jim Harrison, Jack Gilbert, Jane Kenyon, Franz Wright, Stanley J. Kunitz, Naomi Shihab Nye, Kay Ryan, David Tucker, W. S. Merwin, Sharon Olds, Richard Wilbur, Richard Siken, Mark Strand, and Charles Simic.

In addition, there are classic poets who continue to be anthologized and to influence contemporary poets. For example, Walt Whitman (1819–1872) is a kind of grandfather for American poetry. His free verse style infused poetry with raw power and natural speech. Emily Dickinson (1830–1886) is also considered one of America's first true poets, but unlike Whitman she was quiet and nonstentatious and used traditional forms instead of free verse. Ezra Pound (who was politically controversial) was not only a great poet but also an innovator and mentor to many of America's finest poets. He was born in 1885 and died in 1972. T. S. Eliot (1885–1965) wrote one of the most famous and difficult modernist poems, "The Waste Land," in 1922. Robert Frost (1874–1963) is still one of the most popular poets in America and is considered by some to be the first poetry "super star." And finally, Langston Hughes (1902–1967) brought the jazz beat to poetry and was part of the Harlem Renaissance.

DRAMA

It was not until the twentieth century that America had any significant playwrights. This past century (as well as the current one) has seen a number of writers who are often read and studied, including Eugene O'Neill,

Tennessee Williams, Arthur Miller, Edward Albee, August Wilson, and Wendy Wasserstein. Their plays are included in many drama anthologies and often appear in print as single plays. The themes reflected in these dramas are in large part a history of the breakdown of traditional, inherited values. Received ideas about religion, the traditional family, sexuality, gender, capitalism, and patriotism, among others, come under sharp, critical attack or analysis in many of these plays.

New York City native Eugene O'Neill (1888–1953) was really the first of the American dramatists who contemporary readers find important. He won four Pulitzer Prizes for Drama and is the only American dramatist to win the Nobel Prize in Drama. While O'Neill often wrote realistic plays, he also realized that the melodrama and farce (those forms used up to this point) were insufficient to create great drama. He frequently turned, instead, to Greek tragedy for structure and sometimes plotline (as in *Mourning Becomes Electra* in 1931). He also introduced experimental techniques like expressionism that helped to articulate psychological truths. As with many writers, he was influenced by the ideas of Sigmund Freud, Carl Jung, and—in his case—Friedrich Nietzsche. *Desire under the Elms* (1924) is another of his plays based on Greek tragedy and tells a story laced with oedipal complex tensions. The implied sexual taboos landed it in trouble with the police in New York City for its so-called immorality. His most famous play is *A Long Day's Journey into Night* (1956). It was not only a study of a dysfunctional family, but at the same time, it was also considered by many to be the best tragedy ever written by an American. It, too, dealt in part with the conflicts between fathers and sons.

Tennessee Williams (1911–1983), born in Columbus, Mississippi, also broke with many of the conventions of nineteenth-century theater, both stylistically and thematically. Some of his more prominent themes included the destructive tensions of family life and sexuality. He also broached many then taboo subjects like homosexuality and venereal disease. *The Glass Menagerie* (1945) was about the destructive nature of living according to false illusions. Only the play's narrator, Tom, can break free of the shackles of his repressive family situation. *A Streetcar Named Desire* (1947) was a much more sexually charged drama. Its three main characters, Stanley, Stella, and Blanche, have become part of American pop culture, and their interaction in the play displays the dynamics of raw sexual power.

Arthur Miller (1915–2005) was another New York City native. He graduated from the University of Michigan. Though he was a liberal socialist, and though his plays generally reflected his ideology, they nevertheless did not suffer from the didacticism of many socialist plays written in Communist countries. They stand as works of art on their own. For example, *Death of a*

Salesman (1949) can be seen as an indictment of capitalism, but it is also a tragedy of the average man disillusioned by the amoral forces of his world.

Another important contemporary American dramatist, August Wilson (1945–2005), was born in Pittsburgh, Pennsylvania. He won the Pulitzer Prize twice, in 1987 for *Fences* and in 1990 for *The Piano Lesson.* Wilson was most famous for a cycle of 10 loosely interrelated plays, one for each decade of the twentieth century. The setting for most of the plays was Pittsburgh's Hill District, where he grew up. The plays dealt with the difficulties of living in a world where racism exists. The lead characters often had their ambitions and talents thwarted by racism. The final play in his series was *Radio Golf* in 2005. In this play, which takes place in 1997, Wilson explored the perils of losing one's ethnic identity.

Born in Brooklyn, New York, Wendy Wasserstein (1950–2006) was possibly America's best known woman playwright in a field often dominated, on the commercial side (meaning Broadway), by men. She attended Mount Holyoke College, City College of New York, and Yale University. She is considered a pioneer in the portrayal of contemporary women—those struggling with independence, ambition, and traditional values of romance and family. This is especially evident in her most famous play, *The Heidi Chronicles.*

This play won the Pulitzer Prize, the Tony Award for Best Play, and the New York Drama Critics' Circle Award for Best Play. In this work, the life of the lead character, Heidi Holland, was traced from the 1960s to the 1980s. She saw her friends go from the radicalism of the 1960s, to the feminist movement of the 1970s, and back to the traditions they claimed to have rejected. Wasserstein's first produced play, *Uncommon Women and Others,* appeared off Broadway at the Phoenix Theatre in 1977. That play had one of the characteristics of all of her plays—a comedic underpinning that featured a peppering of funny, satirical barbs.

The dean of current American playwrights, Edward Albee was born in 1928 in Washington, D.C. He was expelled from two private schools as a youth and then dropped out of Trinity College in Hartford, Connecticut. He is the only dramatist to have won the vote for the Pulitzer Prize, only to have it taken away before the award was given out—on the grounds that the 1962 play *Who's Afraid of Virginia Woolf?,* now a classic of the American theater, gave an unwholesome picture of America. During his long career, Albee has, among other things, helped to introduce absurdist theater to the United States. *Who's Afraid of Virginia Woolf?,* for example, presents the existential dilemma of living a life trapped in enervating illusions that keep the individual from authentic living. The two main characters, George and Martha, have gone to the absurd extreme of even pretending that they have a child. This they do to fill their lives with meaning, until they realize that the imaginary child, now with them for 21 years, must be let go.

PROSE

It is prose that sells the most books in the United States. It is highly diverse, made up of both fiction and nonfiction, and its most popular sellers are not always what most people would call literary.

There are two major ways to look at what is going on in fiction literature in contemporary America. First, there are anthologies and required readings: readings that are assigned in colleges and high schools across America. These are often not readings of choice, but instead readings that are required for a grade. This literature comes under what is known as the canon: the proscribed list of those works of high quality and an enduring value. These books would, in most people's minds, be considered classic or academically important or—as they may be in the most recent canons—politically and morally correct. Related to this, there is also a group of novels that are fairly current and that are considered literary by a number of serious critics. These novels have won prestigious literary awards but are not always popular with the general public.

Then there are the books that are made important by the general public: the works that are read by choice. These are gauged by popularity, that is, by book sales. Many of them may be forgotten in a few years, but they are, nevertheless, a measure of what contemporary America finds important, in kind if not in quality. The fact is, Americans love to read romance novels, science fiction, fantasy, horror, and mystery novels. Often, these subgenres (as with science fiction, fantasy, and mystery novels) are even taught in colleges and universities.

The Canon

So what is appearing in the anthologies? To a large extent, it is not what used to appear prior (roughly) to the 1990s. Beginning in the 1960s, literary scholars (those who make up the canon) began to attack the traditional canon as overly represented by "dead white men." The social forces of feminism and multiculturalism (related to both ethnic background and sexual preference) began to attack the older canon and gradually to substitute and expand the required reading list. Of course, this is not the first time that the canon has been altered, nor will it be the last. Literary reputations come and go as each generation or two searches for what it needs. Even many of the most historically famous of writers have wavered in importance over the years—Herman Melville, for one.

Today, there are two major anthologies that represent the canon and that are often the source for required readings in colleges: the *Norton Anthology* and the *Heath Anthology*. Both have a series of books, each representing a particular time period. For Norton (the more conservative of the two), there are still some writers from the older canon. In the contemporary edition, writers like Eudora Welty, John Updike, and Bernard Malumud are still represented, but there are also more African American writers, Native American writers, women writers, Asian American writers, and Hispanic American writers.

In Heath's contemporary edition, there are perhaps fewer male writers from the older canon than Norton's, but as in Norton's, multiculturalism and women writers are extensively represented. In addition, Heath's has a section on prison literature, a section called "Cold War Culture and Its Discontents," and a section called "A Sheaf of Vietnam Conflict Poetry and Prose."

There are also required books, especially in high schools. These are usually books that have become part the social and cultural identity of the country. These include such writers as Nathaniel Hawthorne, Mark Twain, John Steinbeck, Harper Lee, J. D. Salinger, Alice Walker, and Toni Morrison. All of these writers are part of the contemporary American's literary experience. They can be seen—apart from their art—as reflections of a maturing national character, and possibly, they may have helped to shape that character.

An often assigned novel is Nathaniel Hawthorne's *The Scarlet Letter*. Hawthorne, who was born in 1804 in Salem, Massachusetts, and who died in 1864, is considered one of the first truly American writers, not just a writer imitating the English and European style, though as with any great artist, his works have universal dimensions. *The Scarlet Letter* (first published in 1850) is considered a psychological allegory. Among other things, it contrasts the European influence of a strict, community-centered society—Puritanism—with the developing American ethos of individuality and freedom. Hester Prynne and her daughter Pearl are used by society as moral objects, warnings to the rest of the citizens to stay within the bounds dictated by the Puritan code. Hester's dignity and good works defy the Puritan society's attempts to take her humanity away, and even when the elders decide to allow her to remove the scarlet letter, the symbol of her adultery, she refuses to allow them to dictate her actions and keeps the scarlet letter. The book also has profound things to say about sin and guilt and their psychological effects on a person. Perhaps most significantly, however, *The Scarlet Letter* also functioned, a mere 74 years after the Declaration of Independence, as an aesthetic declaration to the world that America's writers were independent, free, and capable of creating art that reflected the American experience.

Missouri-born Mark Twain (Samuel Clemens; 1835–1910) wrote a number of classics, but his most read book today is *Huckleberry Finn* (published in 1884). It was published after the Civil War and during the corruption of Reconstruction and the Jim Crow laws. As anyone who has read it knows, this book is not about the sophisticated or Puritan culture of the East; it is a rollicking western-set comedy with a serious message.

While the society of *Huckleberry Finn* is not as extreme as the Puritanism of *The Scarlet Letter,* it is still one that tries to control and dehumanize. One of the major aspects of the novel is that Huck defies all "sivilizing" attempts, and in so doing defines an even better moral order, one that rejects racism and romantic, unrealistic, and debilitating ideals (such as Southern aristocracy). Twain's ideal America, seen in the guise of Huck, is one of individualism, fairness, and equality. It is an America where the individual thinks for himself and is suspicious of the boundaries of the so-called social norm. This is not to say that Twain saw America as actually living according to these standards, but his humor chastises and shows the way.

Another writer who is still read by contemporary readers is John Steinbeck, especially his book *Of Mice and Men,* first published in 1937, during the hard economic times of the Great Depression. Steinbeck was born in 1902. He won the Nobel Prize in Literature in 1962 and the Pulitzer Prize in 1940 (for *Grapes of Wrath*). He died in 1968. At the end of *Huckleberry Finn,* Huck sets out for the territories, where possibility and hope lie, but this idea of the American dream is cruelly dashed in *Of Mice and Men.* The Great Depression had made a mockery of it. Capitalism, human nature, and perhaps the universe itself have the power to inevitably crush anyone's dream. For the book's characters, for gentle giant Lenny, for George, Candy, and Crooks, life is not fair. Denied the dignity they deserve as human beings, they are inevitably dragged down a road toward a tragic, ironic fatality, where the best that can be affected is a rough kindness, a brutal, unsentimental kindness. The book's pathos serves as a powerful, emotional argument for human dignity. The reader is left to hope that ordinary people can have a life beyond the tragedy Steinbeck depicts.

Proving that Twain's antiracist message was little heeded, *To Kill a Mockingbird* by Harper Lee was first published in 1960 in the midst of the country's most serious and effective attempt at instituting civil rights. Lee was born in 1926 in Monroeville, Alabama. She studied law (her father was a lawyer, a newspaperman, and a member of the state legislature) at the University of Alabama and then studied for a year at Oxford. After this, she took time to write her only novel. This book, which won the Pulitzer Prize in 1961, is widely read by high school students across the country.

Though certainly more positive than Steinbeck, Lee's story clearly delineates the evil of racial prejudice and the destruction of innocence by evil (thus the central image of killing a mockingbird, an innocent creature of nature that sings with beauty). Yet, like Twain, Lee has sketched a moral way out of hatred and ignorance. It is Atticus Finch (also a song bird) and his young daughter, Scout, who represent this way out. The book is, in large part, about moral education, as Atticus, a lawyer living in a small Alabama town, defends the falsely accused Tom Robinson and teaches his own children (especially Scout) and the town itself the way to justice and human dignity.

Another book often read by America's youth is J. D. Salinger's *Catcher in the Rye* (first published in 1951). Salinger was born in 1919 in New York City. While his book was a best seller when it was first published, it actually gained popularity over time, becoming a cult classic for the 1960s generation and influencing its sensibilities. There is both a psychological, moral attraction to this book as well as an admired social criticism. With humor and poignancy, it portrays the pains of growing up in a modern America. Holden Caulfield, the 17-year-old main character and narrator, longs to be a "catcher in the rye," saving children before they fall to their death. The only question is whether Holden can save himself. Holden is also critical of superficial people, adults in general, the establishment, and phony, sell-out artists. These are all criticisms that the 1960s generation made famous.

And then there is Alice Walker's classic American novel *The Color Purple* (1982), which addresses the twin evils of racism and sexism. Born in 1944 in Eatonton, Georgia, the daughter of sharecroppers, Walker attended Spelman College and Sarah Lawrence College. She worked briefly as a social worker and then began writing, living for a while in Mississippi during the civil rights movement of the 1960s. There she experienced many of the indignities of racism, including having her marriage declared null by Mississippi law (where it was illegal to have a mixed race marriage). The book is more difficult than many read by students; it is in epistolary format (written as a series of letters) and touches on difficult and controversial topics. It obviously argues against racism and sexism, but also against submission of any human being to another, particularly women to men, and especially submission through violence. It also has the important message that love can redeem.

A final writer to be considered in this category is Toni Morrison, who was born in 1931 in Lorain, Ohio. She is the first African American woman to receive the Nobel Prize in Literature. She attended Howard University and Cornell. *Beloved* (1987), for which she won the Pulitzer Prize, is perhaps Morrison's most powerful book. With great emotional force, it reminds the reader of the destructive, dehumanizing effects of slavery on all people and is based on the true story of a runaway slave who murdered her own child (named "Beloved" in the book), rather than allowing her to be returned to slavery.

There are other classic fiction writers, in addition to those mentioned above, who still have an impact upon the contemporary reader. James Fenimore

Cooper (1789–1851) is today famous for his Leatherstocking Tales, especially *The Last of the Mohicans* (1826), which explores the importance of the frontier and new beginnings to Americans. *Moby Dick* (1851), by Herman Melville (1819–1891), is outwardly an adventure tale, but in truth it is a difficult and long philosophical allegory. F. Scott Fitzgerald (1896–1940) explored the Jazz Age and all of its moral implications, especially in *The Great Gatsby* (1925). Richard Wright (1908–1960) provoked controversy with his now classic look at racism, *Native Son* (1940). Joseph Heller (1923–1999) fueled antiwar sentiments and introduced a phrase into the American vocabulary with his classic novel, *Catch 22* (1961).

Literary Fiction

An important question (one that would no doubt make for a good plotline in literary fiction) is what makes a book literary fiction, as opposed to popular fiction. The glib answer (and perhaps one not too far from the truth) is because the critics say so. Certainly these books are often difficult, they often eschew normal plotlines, they often put a premium on verbal fireworks, they are sometimes based on some obscure, difficult philosophy (preferably French), and they are often playful, especially with the concepts of reality. Unfortunately, they do not always give a very comfortable answer to the question, What does it mean to be a human being?

One of the better known writers of literary fiction (and more accessible to the average reader) is Philip Roth. In the public's mind, he is probably best known for *Goodbye Columbus* (1959) and, especially, *Portnoy's Complaint* (1969). Born in Newark, New Jersey, in 1933, Roth's latest book, *Everyman* (2006), presents a "medical biography," tracing the inevitable deterioration of a man's body, his struggles with sexual desire in old age, and his death—all seen from the bleak aspect of an atheist. *Portnoy's Complaint*—considered by many as scandalous in its day—is the confessions from a psychiatric couch of a man who is obsessed with the subject of masturbation. *The Breast* (1972) is a Kafka-like novel about a man who wakes up as a giant breast. Roth has also placed himself into one of his novels, *Operation Shylock* (1993). Many of his books are about topical American subjects and about the modern American Jew. Roth has won many awards for writing, including several National Book Awards and the Pulitzer Prize.

Perhaps the most private of literary authors (more private even than the reclusive J. D. Salinger) is Thomas Pynchon. He does not give interviews, let alone an address, and is rumored (and no one really knows) to be constantly on the move to avoid detection. Pynchon was born in 1937 in Long Island, New York. Extremely bright and precocious, he graduated with top honors from his high school at age 16. Pynchon was (and probably still is) a voracious reader. He has a background in engineering and in technical writing. All of these things play a part in his novels. Most of his novels are long and labyrinthine in plot structure. The only exception to this is the highly comedic, but paranoid, *The Crying of Lot 49* (1966). This book is short and tightly plotted. His most famous book to date is *Gravity's Rainbow* (1973). Often compared to Melville's *Moby Dick* because of its complexity, length, and demonstration of encyclopedic knowledge, *Gravity's Rainbow* tells multiple stories centered on Nazi Germany and the building of the V-2 rocket. It satirizes contemporary culture and explores the relationship between death and sex. The book won a number of prestigious awards, including the National Book Award. The Pulitzer Prize advisory committee, on the other hand, turned it down, describing it with a series of adjectives: turgid, overwritten, obscene, and unreadable.

Also a satirist, Don DeLillo was born New York City in 1936. Many of his novels are critiques of American media and current culture. His tour de force—the one for which he won the National Book Award—is *White Noise* (1985). *White Noise* is based on the philosophy of Jean Baudrillard. DeLillo's reoccurring thesis is that Americans hide from the reality of death by creating simulated realities through the media, consumerism, and other personal evasions of what really is. According to DeLillo, Americans are awash in data for a reason. The novel is highly satiric, yet menacing.

Running a close second with Thomas Pynchon for privacy is novelist Cormac McCarthy. His fiction could hardly be called playful, unlike some of the other writers in this category. McCarthy's works, on the contrary, are often violent and graphic. Born in Providence, Rhode Island, in 1933, he attended the University of Tennessee but left to begin his writing career. While McCarthy has given at least two interviews (unlike Pynchon), and while there are numerous photographs of him, he prefers a spartan life, one that best puts him in contact with the harsh realities lurking beneath civilized lifestyles. He refuses lucrative speaking engagements and has lived in motels and in a dairy barn. He uses Laundromats and has been known to cut his own hair—even after some financial success. Two of McCarthy's best known works are *Blood Meridian* (1985) and *All the Pretty Horses* (1992). Like Greek tragedy, his works take the reader to the very edge of civilization (mostly the American West, in his case) and into an uncomfortable moral zone that suggests the most primitive dimensions of the human psyche. His style, when the narrator is speaking, can have a difficult Faulkner-like complexity, while his characters often speak in sparse, simple language.

Popular Fiction

There is no set canon for most popular fiction. People have their own favorite authors in each subgenre. The following is a representative sampling of some of the best in each of the major fiction categories: romance, mystery, science fiction, fantasy, and horror.

It is estimated that over one-half of all of the paperbacks sold in the United States are romance novels and that they account for 39.3 percent of all fiction sold in the country. Despite the charges by literary critics that romance novels are formulaic or trite, they are immensely popular, generating over $1.5 billion in sales yearly. They are, simply put, what many readers are reading, and in fact, they are part of a long literary tradition. Some people trace romance novels back to the Renaissance, though most scholars would place the beginnings in the nineteenth century with Jane Austin.

Nora Roberts, one of the most popular of the contemporary romance writers, was born in 1950 in Silver Spring, Maryland. She has a high school education and worked briefly as a legal secretary. As she tells it, she began her writing career in 1979 while trapped at home during a blizzard with two small children and running out of chocolate. Since then, she has been immensely successful.

To date, Roberts has published over 140 romance and mystery novels. (She sometimes publishes the mysteries under the name J. D. Robb.) She has over 127 million copies of her books currently in print. Roberts has won the Rita Award, given by the Romance Writers of America, in various categories

Nora Roberts has written close to 200 novels, remaining one of America's favorite authors. © AP Photo/Chris Gardner.

19 times since 1982. A typical novel of hers, such as the 2004 Rita Award winner *Carolina Moon,* is best described as romantic suspense. Her heroine is vulnerable, searching for answers—answers that put her in mortal danger. In this case *(Carolina Moon),* she is trying to solve the mystery of who murdered her childhood friend, and then, as befitting a romance, she is befriended by a male character with which she develops a romantic relationship. Her novels are generally typified by excellent character development and taut plotting.

There are scores of other successful romance writers and almost as many subgenres, from the naked pirate romances to vampire romances. Two other standout authors are Danielle Steel and Catherine Coulter. Steel, born in 1947 in New York City, has been known to write two and three books a year (she has sold over 530 million copies of her books). Often made into television movies, her books feature a female protagonist whose romance may or may not work out, but who always becomes a stronger, more successful, and better woman by overcoming adversity.

Catherine Coulter was born in Cameron County, Texas, in 1949. Her books frequently appear on the *New York Times* best seller list. Generally, she writes two books a year and is known for having popularized romance trilogies. She has a master's degree in nineteenth-century European history, which helps to explain why she has successfully written many historical romances. Like Nora Roberts, she has also branched into contemporary suspense novels.

While romance is still important in these books (as the genre title indicates), these novels have also brought a belief to several generations of women that strong women are to be admired and that women do not need to accept the dictates of a prudish, Victorian sensibility. Women, as reflected in these books, have come a long way since Hester Prynne, though she certainly pointed the way.

Mystery fiction (which includes the spy novel, crime novel, various forms of the detective novel, and the thriller) is also very popular. This genre began with the American writer Edgar Allan Poe, who, in 1841, introduced Inspector Dupin in his short story "The Murders in the Rue Morgue." This short story, along with "The Purloined Letter," also often appears in contemporary college and high school anthologies. The pattern Poe created of the genius detective with the less than genius sidekick continues to influence many writers, with the best and most popular duo being that created by the English writer Conan Doyle: Sherlock Holmes and Watson. During the 1930s, however, another major strain of detective fiction was created: the hard-boiled detective story (often associated with film noir). Since then, the genre has divided into many subgenres (the procedural novel, the serial killer novel, etc.).

A classic American writer of mystery and detective fiction, one who is still read and studied, and one who often wrote in the noir, hard-boiled style, is Dashiell Hammett. Hammett was born in 1894 in St. Mary's County, Maryland. He died in 1961. His own life was as colorful as one of his characters: a dropout from school at age 13, he went to work helping out his family, joined the army—twice (once for the First World War then, at age 48, for the Second World War), worked for the Pinkerton detective agency, drank a lot, and smoked a lot. Hammett's most famous character is probably Sam Spade, and his most famous novel is probably *The Maltese Falcon* (1930). In Hammett's fictive world, society is corrupt, greedy, and capable of brutality and senseless, shallow grasping after monetary gain. His heroes, like Spade, expose evil and bring moral balance into the world. He has been much imitated. Writers with similar hard-boiled styles who are still read include Raymond Chandler, Mickey Spillane, and Ross MacDonald.

Detroit resident Elmore Leonard is one of the most popular and prolific of America's contemporary mystery novelists. Born in 1925 in New Orleans, Louisiana, he attended the University of Detroit and worked for a while in advertising, all the time moonlighting as a novelist. At first, he wrote westerns; the most popular was *Hombre* (1961), which was made into a movie starring Paul Newman. His first mystery was *The Big Bounce* (1969). Leonard's signature protagonist is someone who is not quite straight, someone who often has a streak of larceny in him (or her). For instance, *Get Shorty,* one of his better known mystery novels, features Chili Palmer, an almost comic gangster who decides to invade Hollywood and make a movie. Leonard himself likes to say that the main attribute of his novels is character, rather than plot, and he enjoys exploring moral pathology. Leonard is also the prototypical writer who immerses himself in the milieu of his novels. To get things authentic, he will do such things as spend days in a courtroom watching arraignments and interviewing cops. He is especially good at capturing the dialogue of thieves and cops and at describing the minutia of their dress. At age 82, he has just published his latest novel, *Up in Honey's Room* (2007).

Walter Mosley, born in Los Angeles, California, in 1952, writes primarily in the hard-boiled school of mystery fiction. The settings of his novels are often the tough post–World War II African American neighborhoods of Los Angeles, teeming with big-city prejudices. In his famous Easy Rawlins series of novels, he also has his own twist on the detective sidekick: Raymond Alexander, nicknamed "Mouse," whose job it is to meet violence with violence. As with Hammett, Mosley's mystery fiction also deals with moral balance, but again, it is with a twist. In Mosley's case, it deals with racial prejudice. His protagonists may have to skirt the law at times—they are forced to do so because of the prejudices around them—but justice, both racial and legal, is eventually served, and the protagonists are better off. One of Mosley's stated goals is to create black male heroes. He does this within the Easy Rawlins series, the Socrates Fortlow series, and the Fearless Jones series. The important features of a Mosley hero are that he works hard, while demanding and gaining respect—by force, if necessary.

Consistently on the best seller list since 1982, Sue Grafton has created a popular woman detective in Kinsey Millhone, a character who is a former policewoman turned private detective. Grafton was born in 1944 in Louisville, Kentucky. She is best known for her alphabet mysteries, starting with *A Is for Alibi* (1982). While not exactly in the hard-boiled school of American mystery writers, Grafton does follow Hammett in bringing moral order to the world. Her main character, Kinsey Millhone, is eccentric (and a little on the seedy side), smart, caustic, and independent: a role model that clearly knocks the ruffled, silky edges off the woman on a pedestal archetype.

Science fiction, a third popular subgenre, begins in the nineteenth century in England (H. G. Wells) and France (Jules Verne). There was no significant writer of science fiction in the United States until Edgar Rice Burroughs, who wrote his first science fiction in 1912. Then began the age of pulp fiction, with such magazines as *Amazing Stories,* launched by Hugo Gernsback in 1926. Also known as speculative fiction, it extrapolates into the future (occasionally into the past) some scientific idea: robots, computers, space travel, and so on. Sometimes (though rarely in contemporary writers) this extrapolation will lead to a positive fictional world (utopia), but more often, it leads to a dystopia (a world filled with problems). It reflects the American fascination with, as well as suspicions about, science and technology. There are possibly more personal favorites among science fiction readers than there are among romance readers.

One standout is Ursula K. Le Guin, who is also known for her Earth Sea fantasy series. Born in 1921 in Berkeley, California, her mother was a writer, and her father was a distinguished anthropologist. Le Guin's most famous science fiction book is probably *The Left Hand of Darkness* (1969), in which she extrapolates genetics into the future and explores its consequences. This is a book that begins to look at the feminist idea of androgyny by creating a planet, Gethen, where most of the time, its inhabitants are indeed now androgynous. Le Guin wrote two later essays, the titles of which ask, Is gender necessary? While she herself feels that *The Left Hand of Darkness* did not go far enough, it is still seen as a first of its kind: feminist science fiction.

The extraordinarily prolific Isaac Asimov was born in Petrovichi, Russia. He died in 1992. Asimov attended Columbia University for his undergraduate and graduate schooling and ended with a PhD in biochemistry. Like fantasy writers, he often created fictional worlds that were presented in a series of books. His two most famous are the Foundation series and his Robot series. The Robot series is famous for delving into the moral quandaries associated with artificial intelligence. Asimov created the famous three laws of robotics to deal with the problem.

This is a good place to discuss a writer who was more than just a science fiction writer and whose work is often required reading in high schools and colleges. Kurt Vonnegut Jr. was born in 1922 in Indianapolis, Indiana, and died in 2007. He studied at Cornell and the University of Chicago, gaining a background in chemistry, biology, and anthropology.

One of his best known science fiction works was *Cat's Cradle* (1963), which tells the story of the potential destructiveness of technology in the form of ice-nine, an invention that can freeze all water on the planet. Even more critically acclaimed was his 1969 book *Slaughterhouse-Five; or, The Children's Crusade.* Vonnegut is often compared to Mark Twain, especially the later Twain, who became pessimistic about humankind, and this comes across in this novel. In this book, a World War II prisoner in Dresden (Vonnegut himself was a prisoner there and witnessed the effects of the fire bombing) is abducted by aliens, who place him in a zoo on their planet and mate him with a movie star. As with most of his works, there is humor, but it is a disturbing, critical, dark humor.

Fantasy literature can be seen as the flip side of the coin from science fiction. While science fiction puts a premium on science and rationality, fantasy focuses in on magic and the irrational. It, of course, has connections to fairy tales and began to become somewhat popular for adults during the nineteenth century, but it really was not until the English writer J.R.R. Tolkien introduced the world to *The Lord of the Rings* in the mid-twentieth century that it really became popular with adult readers. One of the attractions of fantasy is that there is usually a clear demarcation between good and evil. It is consoling to see good triumph over evil, and it is equally comforting to enter a world of wonder and magic.

The Sword of Shannara (1971) was Terry Brooks's first book of fantasy, and it was the first American fantasy novel to make it to the *New York Times* best seller list. Brooks was born in Sterling, Illinois, in 1944. His first series, the Shannara series, has sometimes been criticized for being too close to Tolkien, but since then, he has gone on to create numerous original fantasy worlds. He is a good example of the trend in fantasy writing to create a series of books based in a single secondary world.

Robert Jordan (pen name for James Oliver Rigney Jr.) was born in 1948. His hometown is Charleston, South Carolina. A Vietnam War veteran, he attended the Citadel and graduated with a degree in physics. His most famous series is the Wheel of Time series. There are currently 11 books in the series, a series that has been written over a 16-year span. Like most fantasy, it is a quest, a journey of discovery of epic proportions. Like all good fantasy writers, Jordan has created an entire mythology, and even a language (as Tolkien did). The series is scheduled to be finished with the next book, but Jordan was recently diagnosed with a rare cancer.

The horror genre is also popular in the contemporary United States. Again, just as with mystery fiction, the American strain of horror and gothic fiction can be traced to Edgar Allan Poe ("The Fall of the House of Usher," "The Tell Tale Heart"). In most cases, what horror fiction suggests is a metaphysical or spiritual side to reality, even when that metaphysical side is of the evil type—this in the midst of an increasingly secular society—and, according to Stephen King, it also works as a catharsis for the darker side of human nature lurking in all of us.

The superstar of contemporary horror is indeed Stephen King. Born in Portland, Maine, in 1947, his first novel, *Carrie* (1974), began a long line of successes, including two outstanding nonhorror novellas, *The Body* and *Rita Hayworth and the Shawshank Redemption,* both appearing in 1982. King writes with realistic detail, which helps to intensify the horrors. Vampires, ghosts, and other examples of the supernatural are often part of the story fabric, but so is the exploration of the potential horrors in contemporary society as well as the potential for violence and evil in ordinary people. He is also known for his experimentation with serialization and distribution of books on the Internet. King's *The Green Mile* (1996) is a perfect example. The book was originally written and published in six volumes, ala Charles Dickens. The real horror and evil in the book is the murderous capabilities of William Wharton, a vicious child killer, as well as the realities of capital punishment.

Anne Rice, who was born in New Orleans, Louisiana, in 1941, began her writing career blending horror (vampires and witches) with the sensual and erotic. Her first horror novel was *Interview with a Vampire* (1976). Her unusual take on a traditional tale was to see the story from the vampire's point of view, and, as she herself has pointed out, the vampire becomes a metaphor for her. To read one of her vampire books is to partake of an existential exploration of living in a world where God does not exist and where the vampire must commit evil just to be. Her delving into the philosophy, psychology, and angst of this situation is what draws many people to her novels. Since 2005, with the publication of *Christ the Lord: Out of Egypt,* Rice has vowed to approach the metaphysical from a traditional perspective. She plans on writing the biography of Jesus Christ and to never write a vampire book again.

A totally different take from Rice on the Dracula tale is Elizabeth Kostova's *The Historian* (2005). Kostova was born in 1964 in New London, Connecticut. She attended Yale and then received an master's of fine arts from the University of Michigan. Her first and only book, *The Historian* (2005), took 10 years to write. It has remained on the best seller list and has every sign of becoming a horror classic. Much more in the spirit of the traditional story, it is told from the perspective of the victims, and Vlad Tepes (Dracula) has no redeeming values and no philosophical angst. The story is told in an interesting and effective way, simultaneously on three timelines (sometimes more when there is a story within a story) and primarily through narrative letters.

Popular Nonfiction

It is estimated that nearly 80 percent of the 50,000 or so new books published every year are nonfiction. These are often self-help books, cookbooks, political diatribes, and the like. These are not considered literature; they are more related to journalism and its factual, sometimes ephemeral and time-sensitive nature. Yet there are a number of subgenres of nonfiction that have the potential to be called literature and to endure.

All these important subgenres of nonfiction have been affected by creative nonfiction. While there are still many academic, purely factual and thesis-driven nonfiction works, the works that have the greatest potential to be enduring classics as well as popular with the public merge narrative techniques with fact, history, information, and social commentary. Most affected by the trend of creative nonfiction have been history works, biographies and autobiographies, and travel books.

At times, academic historians are at odds with the first category: popular history. The academics argue, accurately, that they have often already written the same observations, facts, and insights as popular historians have. They have been there and done that, but with little public acclaim. And they claim, often again with justification, that popular historians can be sloppy with their documentation. Generally, though, they write in a different style from popular historians: they debunk and theorize, often in excruciatingly ponderous prose and dry, intellectual analysis. Popular historians, on the other hand, make history come alive by imposing on it a narrative structure and an arresting prose style; thus their works are sometimes called *narrative history*. Simply put, popular historians tell a story, and that is what makes them well-liked and their works candidates for enduring literature.

The dean of contemporary popular historians, David McCullough, is from Pittsburgh, Pennsylvania. He was born in 1933 and is a graduate of Yale University. He began his career writing for magazines—*Time, Life,* and *American Heritage*—and switched to writing popular history books in 1968 with *The Johnstown Flood.* He also writes popular biography. The central research technique in all creative nonfiction is immersion. McCullough is a prime example. He is a meticulous researcher. His research focuses not just on the facts, but also on the words, thoughts, and ideas of a time period, including its art and culture. He reads what his characters read; he embraces their philosophies, their art, their literature, and their values. He tracks down personal and official letters, not only of the famous, but also of the minor characters in the narrative. He physically traces the steps of his characters making their settings his settings. He puts himself there and, by doing so, puts his readers there as well. Like most of the popular historians, McCullough focuses in on dramatic, pivotal moments, especially those that illuminate the national character. *1776* (2005), for instance, focuses on the crucial year in the American Revolution when it seemed that the Americans had no chance at all. It illuminates the character of George Washington and of the men who served under him. McCullough has won the Pulitzer Prize for two of his biographies, *John Adams* (2002) and *Truman* (1993), as well as the National Book Award for several of his histories.

One of the topics of fascination for American readers of history is the American Civil War. It, too, is a pivotal moment in American identity, with many human dimensions. One of the most popular writers on this subject is Greenville, Mississippi, born Shelby Foote (1916–2005). Foote dropped out of college at the University of North Carolina, joined the army as a captain of artillery, was court-marshaled and dismissed for going out of bounds to visit his girlfriend (later his wife), and then promptly enlisted in the Marine Corps as an infantryman. Foote began as a novelist (thus gaining a good insight into narrative structure) and then spent 20 years writing a three-volume history of the Civil War titled *The Civil War: A Narrative,* finally completed in 1974. He is often remembered as one of the primary narrators of Ken Burns's documentary *The Civil War.*

Another war historian, though certainly more controversial, is Stephen Ambrose. He was born in 1936 in Decatur, Illinois, and died in 2002. He received a PhD from the University of Wisconsin and began his career as an academic historian; in fact, he was the official biographer of Dwight Eisenhower. In the 1990s, Ambrose began writing popular history, focusing especially on World War II, beginning with *Band of Brothers* in 1993. His books soon became best sellers. This frequently made him unpopular with academic historians for not being rigorous enough, and his 2000 book, *The Wild Blue,* brought charges of plagiarism for not putting quotation marks around borrowed material (though he did footnote it).

The autobiography and biography subgenre is peppered with transitory works about, and by, recording artists, actors, sports figures, and people generally in the public eye. Much of it is ghost written and more titillating than significant. Keeping in mind that some of the earlier discussed historians

(McCullough, especially) are also significant biographers, the following are a few of the others who are contemporary and popular.

Mitch Albom and John Grogan are definitely not in the school of rigorous academics, but their books are classified as biography, and they are both often assigned for high school students to read, probably because they are upbeat and have solid life lessons to teach. Mitch Albom was born in 1958 in Passaic, New Jersey, and is well known for his book *Tuesdays with Morrie* (1997), about teacher and sociologist Morrie Schwartz, his former sociology professor at Brandeis University. Though classified as biography, it is not a rigorous study of Schwartz's entire life. It focuses on the last days of his life—14 Tuesdays, to be exact. It is based on the conversations that Albom had with him and on the wisdom, insights, and lessons that Albom recorded. Often criticized by intellectual reviewers, it nevertheless remained on the best seller list for six years. Albom has since written books that could best be described as fantasy literature, but with the same result: immense popularity and often assigned to high school students to read (these include *The Five People You Meet in Heaven* [2005] and *For One More Day* [2006]).

John Grogan has written one of the most unusual—but very popular—of books, *Marley and Me* (2005). But is it an autobiography? Or is it a biography, perhaps? Grogan was born in Detroit, Michigan, in 1957. He attended Central Michigan University and Ohio State and has worked as a journalist and editor. Curiously, Marley is a dog, so while technically, it is the biography of a Labrador retriever, the book is really the autobiography of a family written with great humor.

Another popular historian, Walter Isaacson, was born in 1952 in New Orleans, Louisiana. He is a graduate of Harvard and a Rhodes Scholar at Oxford and has been a journalist, an editor, and the CEO of the Aspen Institute. His latest biography is of an icon of the twentieth century, Albert Einstein, who has had a profound effect on the way we conceive reality. In *Einstein: His Life and Universe* (2007), Isaacson focuses on both *life* and *universe* as his narrative presents the human side of Einstein as well as an attempt at explaining his theories to mere mortals.

Doris Kearns Goodwin, the last of the biographers to be discussed, is also an example of the strengths and weaknesses of creative nonfiction. She was born in 1943 in Brooklyn, New York. She attended Colby College and received her PhD from Harvard. Her books often make the best seller lists—the Pulitzer Prize–winning *No Ordinary Time: Franklin and Eleanor Roosevelt: The Home Front in World War II* (1995), for example. Like McCullough, she immerses herself in her subject, but like Ambrose, she has been embroiled in a controversy over plagiarism. The general criticism of creative nonfiction is that in a rush to have the next best seller, writers sometimes get sloppy, or they invent. In her case, it seems to have been a case of sloppiness. Her latest book looks at one of the most important of American leaders, Abraham Lincoln, in *Team of Rival: The Political Genius of Abraham Lincoln* (2005).

And finally in the biography/autobiography category is Maya Angelou, born in 1928 in St. Louis, Missouri. Born into poverty and a broken family, Angelou is considered by many to be a modern renaissance woman, successfully dabbling in poetry, acting, singing, writing plays, and directing. In addition, she is a historian and an educator. She has lived in many parts of the world and held many jobs. While she never attended college, she has received a number of honorary degrees. But she is probably best known for her series of autobiographies, especially the first one, *I Know Why the Caged Bird Sings* (1969). The latest in the series is *A Song Flung Up to Heaven* (2002), which relates her life up to 1968 and the turbulent years of the Civil Rights Movement.

Travel literature in the United States goes back to Mark Twain and his *Innocents Abroad* (1869), but worldwide, it can be traced back much further. In any case, it is and always has been a natural for creative nonfiction. Good travel literature (unlike guidebooks, which are a kind of journalism and easily dated) has the universality and agelessness of any good literature. The technique of immersion used in travel literature, as in autobiography, is based on personal experience, but it inevitably also includes traditional research. It invites commentary from the writer in many areas: politics, history, economics, sociology, psychology, art, conservation, and so on. Travel literature is also, obviously, about place. At its best, it is a journey through physical, psychological, intellectual, and moral space.

Bill Bryson is one of America's premier travel writers. Born in 1951 in Des Moines, Iowa, Bryson dropped out of college (he would later finish school) to begin a life as a traveler. He began by hiking through Europe, first on his own, then with his friend Stephen Katz (a pseudonym for a reoccurring character in several of Bryson's books). Since then, Bryson's travels have been source material for books on the United States, England, Australia, and Africa. His perennial best seller *A Walk in the Woods* (1998) is a good example of his style. This book takes the reader onto the great Appalachian Trail, which runs from Georgia to Maine. It blends an ironic, often deadpan humor with encyclopedic information and a critical eye for American foibles. Though he is obviously a conservationist, he still takes a realistic view of nature: it is big, sometimes scary, and sometimes just boring.

Tony Horwitz, a Pulitzer Prize–winning reporter, has immersed himself in both travel and history, whether it is in the Civil War South, the Pacific of Captain Cook, or the Middle East. Born in Washington, D.C., in 1958, he studied history at Brown University and journalism at Columbia. His travel books often blend his own journeys with those of historical figures, as in *Blue Latitudes* (2002). The book has a dual structure: the telling of the journey of Captain James Cook and the telling of Horwitz's own journey as he retraces Cook's explorations, even subjecting himself to sailing on a replica of Cook's ship, the *Endeavor*. The reader not only learns the history and biography, but also gains an understanding of the sociological impact of eighteenth-century exploration.

Paul Theroux is a prime example of the difference between a traveler and a tourist. Both a novelist and travel writer, he was born in 1941 in Medford, Massachusetts. He graduated from the University of Massachusetts and joined the Peace Corps and thus began a life of travel that has led to 12 highly respected travel books. Theroux does not seek out the planned and the well organized. In his opinion, one cannot really know a country or a place by visiting it in the cocoon of the travel agent's agenda; striking out on one's own, perilously if necessary, is a requirement. A traveler must see the place as it really is, not as others want him or her to see it. For example, in his first travel book, *The Great Railway Bazaar* (1975), Theroux travels alone, without outside help, going mostly by train from London to Vietnam and back. Less encyclopedic than some other travel writers, he is instead more novelistic, and he has an eye for the absurd and eccentric. Characters are finely developed, and his descriptions of place have the astute economy of a poet.

Finally, John Berendt takes the technique of immersion to an even more extreme degree than any of the previously mentioned travel writers, with the exception perhaps of Paul Theroux. He has lived for years in the two places he has written about: Savannah, Georgia, and Venice, Italy. Berendt was born in 1939 in Syracuse, New York. He graduated from Harvard and has written for *New York* magazine and *Esquire*. His focus is often on character—especially the upper classes—on artisans, and on the eccentric. He also has a way of making the cities he writes about become characters in themselves. In both of his travel books, *Midnight in the Garden of Good and Evil* (1994) and *City of Falling Angels* (2005), Berendt finds a dramatic moment to wrap his narrative around. In *Midnight in the Garden of Good and Evil,* it is a murder trial, and in *City of Fallen Angels,* it is the tragic and mysterious burning of the historic La Fenice opera house. In this regard, he is like the popular historian who finds a dramatic, pivotal moment on which to reveal the essence of the city.

CONCLUSION

Paraphrasing Billy Collins again, to look at the world of contemporary American literature is to look at the history of the nation's heart—and conscience and mind. Literary works are sometimes critical of the culture (especially when ideals are not met). Americans are even willing to be chastised, especially if it is done with humor, as by Mark Twain, or with powerful emotional resonance, as by Toni Morrison or Harper Lee. American drama and literary fiction are purveyors of the currents of world intellectual thought, though even horror novels can sometimes be philosophical, and romances can sometimes teach about feminist ideals. Americans find solace and beauty in their poets as well as wisdom. Americans celebrate virtues and successes (and sometimes mourn failures) in biographies and histories. Americans dream and learn with the fantasy writers, the travel writers, and the romance writers.

Critics sometimes accuse American popular prose of having a Pollyanna mind-set, but that is only true if being positive is unrealistic. In truth, Americans both embrace and worry about the effects of science, big business, and industrialization, especially in science fiction, and Americans love to bring moral order in mystery fiction because the world can be evil and greedy. The sum total equals a love for the richness of language and the emotional power of a story, even the scary stories of good horror novels.

NOTE

1. The industry statistics for this chapter come from several sources. The Book Study Industry Group provided many of the raw numbers, especially as they are distilled in Albert N. Greco, "The Economics of Books and Magazines," in *Media Economics: Theory and Practice,* ed. Alison Alexander et al. (Mahwah, NJ: Lawrence Erlbaum Associates, 2004), 127–48. Some of the information also comes from the U.S. Census Bureau (http://www.census.gov). The statistics for poetry sales were provided by the Poetry Foundation (http://www.poetryfoundation.org). General prose book sales were calculated by the Nielsen BookScan service. Romance book sales were provided by the Romance Writers of America (https://www.rwanational.org). Statistics on nonfiction book sales were provided by Lee Gutkind, *Creative Nonfiction* (Chicago: Chicago Review Press, 1996), 7.

While some of the texts for the slam poets can be found on their Web sites and in books, many of their works have to be experienced through Google's video search engine, either under the poet's name or simply under "slam poetry."

Biographical information comes from author and publisher Web sites and from online interviews.

BIBLIOGRAPHY

Algarin, Miguel, and Bob Holman, eds. *Aloud: Voices from the Nuyorican Poets Cafe.* New York: Holt, 1994.

Bloom, Harold. *Novelists and Novels.* Philadelphia: Chelsea House, 2005.

Elliot, Emory, ed. *Columbia Literary History of the United States.* New York: Columbia University Press, 1988.

Fussell, Paul, ed. *The Norton Book of Travel.* New York: W. W. Norton, 1987.

Goia, Dana. *Disappearing Ink: Poetry at the End of Print Culture.* Saint Paul, MN: Graywolf Press, 2004.

Gunn, James, ed. *The Road to Science Fiction.* Vol. 3, *From Heinlein to Here.* Lanham, MD: Scarecrow Press, 2002.

Gutkind, Lee. *Creative Nonfiction.* Chicago: Chicago Review Press, 1996.

Hart, James David. *The Oxford Companion to American Literature.* New York: Oxford University Press, 1995.

Klinkowitz, Jerome. *Literary Subversions: New American Fiction and the Practice of Criticism.* Carbondale: Southern Illinois University Press, 1985.

Mass, Wendy, and Stuart P. Levine, eds. *Fantasy.* San Diego, CA: Greenhaven Press, 2002.

Newbery, Victor E. *The Popular Press Companion to Popular Literature.* Bowling Green, OH: Bowling Green State University Popular Press, 1983.

Regis, Pamela. *A Natural History of the Romance Novel.* Philadelphia: University of Pennsylvania Press, 2003.

Smith, Marc Kelly. *The Complete Idiot's Guide to Slam Poetry.* Indianapolis, IN: Alpha Books, 2004.

Sternlicht, Sanford. *A Reader's Guide to Modern American Drama.* Syracuse, NY: Syracuse University Press, 2002.

Tanner, Tony. *City of Words: American Fiction, 1950–1970.* London: Cape, 1971.

Tanner, Tony. *The American Mystery: American Literature from Emerson to De Lillo.* New York: Cambridge University Press, 2000.

7

Media and Cinema

Agnes Hooper Gottlieb

Today we are beginning to notice that the new media are not just mechanical gimmicks for creating worlds of illusion, but new languages with new and unique powers of expression.

—Marshall McLuhan

AMERICA AND ITS MEDIA

ASSESSING THE STATUS of the media in the United States in the early twenty-first century is a little like predicting the outcome of a bird flu pandemic: anything could happen. Media convergence has become a popular topic at academic conferences, but just how the media will converge and what will capture the interest of the American people is an educated guess. For years, pundits predicted the likes of video telephones and electronic supermarkets, but no one could have imagined the proliferation of the Internet and its corresponding transformation of the ways Americans live, work, and relax.

Personal computers started off in the 1980s as little more than fancy typewriters; the evolution was slow. By the time the century ended, however, the Internet and the World Wide Web had reshaped daily activities, created a new branch of media and consumerism, and profoundly changed American culture. It provided new avenues of entertainment, while at the same time forcing newspapers, magazines, television, radio, and cinema to rethink their markets and audiences. How well the individual media adapt to the new kid on the block will determine just who survives during this second communication revolution (the first being in the fifteenth century, with the invention of moveable type).

Apple's new iPhone hit U.S. shelves in late June 2007. This gadget does it all: With the touch of a button users can access their music, text messages, phone calls, photos, e-mail, and Internet. © AP Photo/Jason DeCrow, file.

ABC News, for example, has created an interactive Web site that encourages viewers to "engage with the news" and to "be seen and be heard" by providing news stories, photos, and videos. Cell phone cameras that can capture news as it occurs allows the *everyperson* to be involved in news gathering and reporting. Video footage of brush fires, floods, and other natural disasters find their way onto the Web site. In 2005, YouTube, a video-sharing technology, premiered and gave aspiring filmmakers an instant massive audience.

While media changes like these occur rapidly and constantly in today's society, the media evolved slowly up until 1900. From that moment on, however, the media have been evolving, morphing, and recreating into new and ever-changing formats. Where newspapers once stood alone, radio, cinema, television, and the Internet have crowded in to demand consumers' time and attention. While the twentieth century was transformational for media, the evolution did not end with the dawn of the year 2000.

Perhaps the hardest thing to get one's arms around with a broad topic like the American media is just what constitutes the media in this new millennium. While it is easy to categorize newspapers, magazines, and old-fashioned television, media convergence means that mainstream media outlets morph into new and different media. The *New York Times* newspaper still wields incredible authority as a preeminent and elite newspaper, but no one waits to read about breaking news stories like the 9/11 terrorist attacks in a newspaper. A newspaper like the *Times* might help readers put cataclysmic events in context, but it no longer bears the burden of informing readers that an event has taken place. The American people turn on their televisions and, to a lesser extent, go online to learn about breaking news events. In the space of 100 years, the roles and responsibilities of newspapers—initially the only game in town—were transformed by competition that came from many venues.

NEWSPAPERS

The last century in the story of newspapers in the United States could be billed as the media version of the Hundred Years' War. Newspapers hunkered down with the advent of radio and fought off competitive threats (both perceived and real), outliving the predictions of doomsayers who regularly forecast the demise of daily newspapers when their dominance was challenged, first by radio, then by television, and finally by the Internet. Newspaper publishers grew fond of quoting Mark Twain's clever quip, "Reports of my death have been greatly exaggerated." By the end of the century, most newspapers were still thriving, though profit margins and readership had shrunk and changed.

Newspapers, slow to take hold in the Americas, had long been the dominant medium in America once they established their presence. There were two printing presses on the Mayflower when it docked at Plymouth Rock in December 1620, but 70 years went by before the first newspaper was attempted. That product, *Publick Occurrences Both Foreign and Domestick,* appeared only once, on September 25, 1690. Publisher Benjamin Harris stated his intention to publish once a month, or more frequently if news events occurred, but the newspaper was banned four days after it appeared by the Massachusetts governor, riled because it had been published without permission.

Publick Occurrences proves an interesting artifact, however, because it demonstrates that what we would define as news today can trace its roots back all the way to the beginning of the American press. The four-page newspaper contained 20 paragraphs of news, mostly domestic, although there were two foreign items. The publication had three pages of news, with the back page left blank so that readers could add their own items as the newspaper was circulated. The stories included information about the kidnapping of two children by Indians, a suicide, a fire in Boston, an epidemic of small pox, and skirmishes between the English and the French and Indians. While little is written in U.S. newspapers today about small pox epidemics, the scourge that is AIDS continues to take headline space, and while the wars have changed with the decades, the U.S. involvement in Iraq was the leading story in American newspapers in 2007.

After *Publick Occurrences'* short-lived appearance, 14 years passed before another newspaper was undertaken. On April 24, 1704, John Campbell, the postmaster of Boston, edited and published (with permission) the *Boston News-Letter*. Campbell had been sending handwritten letters to the governors of all the New England colonies for at least a year before he had his missives typeset. The journal had no advertisements at first, and Campbell charged two pence a copy (or 12 shillings a year). Campbell gathered together foreign news from four-month-old London newspapers that passed through his post office and added local news. Campbell, a postmaster, not a printer, worked with printer Bartholomew Green, establishing early in American printing history the dual roles of editor and printer. The *Boston News-Letter* continued under various editors for 72 years before folding during the American Revolution.

Founding father Benjamin Franklin looms large in the story of American newspapers. Franklin began as a printer's apprentice to his older brother James, who was printing the *Boston Gazette*. In August 1721, James Franklin began publishing the *New-England Courant* with the backing of a group of investors opposed to the Massachusetts governor. Franklin flaunted his position that he was publishing without permission. The *New-England Courant,* the third newspaper in Boston and the fourth in all the colonies, provided the platform for the Silence Dogood essays that young Ben Franklin penned when he was 16. The *Courant*'s contribution to journalism history is twofold: its publication of essays, letters, and verse expanded the purview of newspapers in the eighteenth century and provided readers with what they liked, not just what they needed to know; and its publication without permission sounded the death knell for that form of prior restraint in the colonies.

Ben Franklin ran away from his domineering brother's influence to Philadelphia, where he became editor and publisher of the *Pennsylvania Gazette*. Franklin's competition in Philadelphia was Andrew Bradford, whose father, William, was one of the pioneer printers in the colonies.

Most memorable from the pre–Revolutionary War period of American history was the ongoing struggle between press and government, the outcome of which established the parameters that helped create a tradition of press freedom that was formalized in the First Amendment to the U.S. Constitution. In 1733, John Peter Zenger, a semiliterate German immigrant who printed the *New York Weekly Journal* for a group of backers, clashed with officials in power in New York colony. Zenger, who barely spoke English, was merely the conduit for their antiadministration views, but it was he who bore the brunt of Governor William Cosby's wrath. Cosby hand-picked a justice and ordered him to obtain an indictment. When the grand jury declined to indict, a group of the governor's council came forward with an action against Zenger, who was arrested in November 1734 and charged with sedition. Zenger was jailed for nine months before his trial (his weekly newspaper continued to be printed by Zenger's wife, Anna). Lawyer James Alexander, one of the newspaper's writers and backers, was disbarred when he challenged the validity of the charges. Zenger's cause was championed by revered Philadelphia attorney Andrew Hamilton, 80 years old at the time. An admission that the printer had actually been responsible for printing such material was in essence an admission of guilt, but Hamilton argued that although Zenger was indeed the printer, he had done nothing wrong because what he had printed was true. Hamilton argued that for a statement to be libelous, it had to be false, malicious, and seditious. Hamilton's eloquent argument carried the day, and Zenger was found not guilty. Although the verdict had no effect on libel law of the day, it was the first case to establish the concept that truth was the best defense of libel, a principle that was finally recognized in the 1790 state constitution of Pennsylvania.

Newspapers played a major role in the American Revolution, first as a propaganda tool that fueled colonists' fervor for war. Foolishly, the British government alienated the press as early as 1765, when it passed the Stamp Act, which required all legal documents, official papers, books, and newspapers to be printed on stamped (or taxed) paper. For newspapers, this would have amounted to about a penny for a standard four-page tome. The act passed in March but was not to be effective until November, which gave angry colonists time to work up opposition to the law. The opposition included the very people who had the wherewithal to fight it: the printers. Newspapers rallied around the charge of taxation without representation leveled against the British Parliament, which was making laws governing the colonies, although the colonies had no voice there.

The summer of 1765 was a hot one in the colonies. Newspapers printed the names of tax collectors, while colonists burned them in effigy during organized protests. Some newspapers flaunted the law by printing without their mastheads so that they were technically no longer newspapers. Some briefly suspended publication. None of the approximately 35 newspapers in the colonies published with the stamp. Reacting to the furor, the Parliament rescinded the Stamp Act in March 1766, but communication was such that the colonies did not learn of the repeal until mid-May.

Patriot Samuel Adams, considered one of the driving forces behind the colonial independence, wrote for the pre-Revolutionary newspapers using about 25 different pen names. And although newspapers had no formal editorial pages, they were important in fueling public opinion against the British.

The success of the Stamp Act protest taught colonists the effectiveness of organized protest. Adams realized that to lure the masses to his cause, he needed to present the colonists with reasoned arguments against the British. And since the men who would be the foot soldiers for the cause were not highly literate, the campaign had to be waged in simple terms. Thus began what some historians have called America's first organized public relations campaign, masterminded by Adams and his compatriots. When British troops fired into a mob of protestors in Boston in 1770, Adams labeled it a massacre in print. When the British government taxed tea, Adams led a group of colonists in a staged media event to dump tea in Boston Harbor.

If Adams can be considered the public relations man of the Revolution, Thomas Paine is its poet. Paine's 1776 essay *Common Sense* is credited with speaking plain language that could be understood by the common (and often uneducated) patriot. It laid out a clear argument for a break with Britain and argued in favor of independence.

After the Revolution, newspapers served as the sounding boards for the two major political platforms, the Federalists and the Republicans. The press of the period was a partisan one, with major newspapers arguing about the ratification of the U.S. Constitution and the legality of the Alien and Sedition Act and reporting the sordid and sensational rivalry between two of America's Founding Fathers. *The Federalist Papers,* a series of essays published in newspapers and pamphlet form, set out a methodical argument in favor of passage of the U.S. Constitution. Written in part by James Madison, Alexander Hamilton, and others, the essays argued point by point in favor of the Constitution. They also set out an argument for press freedom, a principle that was solidified in a few words as part of the First Amendment in the Bill of Rights.

Hamilton, first publisher of the *New York Post* (1801), was considered the leader of the Federalists, while Thomas Jefferson, champion of the common man, was his counterpart among the Republicans. Hamilton, who served as George Washington's secretary of the treasury, met his fate in a now legendary duel with Aaron Burr in 1804.

By 1800, journalism was thriving in the young United States. Philadelphia had six daily newspapers, New York had five, and Boston, which had been the birthplace of American journalism and the hotbed of the American Revolution, had none. Journalism continued to grow in the early decades of the 1800s and expanded into new regions as the United States outgrew its borders. The cost of a daily newspaper, however, was out of reach for most of America, filled as it was with rural farmers and modest merchants. Newspapers cost about six cents (about the same price as a pint of whisky).

Slow and tedious handpresses that physically limited the circulation of newspapers gave way in 1830 to the first steam press, which overnight tripled the speed of printing. Production capabilities grew at the same time as the reading public swelled. Thus began one of the golden ages of American journalism, the penny press, beginning in 1833 with the four-page *New York Sun.* The *Sun,* founded by Benjamin Day, introduced a breezy reporting style that appealed to a new class of readers. With little emphasis on politics, the penny press moved away from partisan reporting and focused instead on local news, entertaining information. Sensationalism, still with us today, reared its ugly head.

The shift to cheap newspapers made them accessible to America's uneducated or poorly educated workers, but a newspaper that appealed to workers was fundamentally different from one that appealed to America's upper crust. Human interest news and local stories became more important; news shifted away from partisan politics and changed the definition of what news was. At the same time, penny papers were accused of overemphasizing crime and sex and pandering to bad taste, a recurring theme in American culture.

While the papers actually sold for a penny for only a short time, the drastic reduction in price and the shift in readership signaled a societal change that never turned back. With the help of the fruits of the Industrial Revolution, which enabled and enhanced the printing of many newspapers, journalism became mass communication for the first time.

Leaders in the penny press era of journalism included James Gordon Bennett Sr., who founded the *New York Herald,* and Horace Greeley, publisher of the rival *New York Tribune.* New York became the center of publishing in the United States, and its newspapers flourished throughout the nineteenth century.

Technology and technique were two majors themes for newspapers during the nineteenth century. Technology furthered the way newspapers were printed, opening the possibility of mass circulation. The telegraph, invented by Samuel Morse in 1840, transformed how information was gathered, allowing timeliness to creep into the equation of what made a newspaper stand out. Modern modes of transportation extended circulation areas and fueled the desire to get the news to the public first.

While news of the battle of Lexington and Concord that started the Revolutionary War took six weeks to make its way from Boston to a Savannah newspaper in 1775, the telegraph allowed daily reports of the Civil War to appear in modern New York newspapers. The telegraph is also credited with triggering the use of reporters' bylines, which began to appear in the 1860s under the tagline "by telegraph."

The telegraph also has been credited with changing how journalists reported their stories. American journalism initially adhered more closely to the rules of fiction, featuring a beginning, a middle, and an end. When Aaron

Burr and Alexander Hamilton faced off in a duel, for example, the *New York Morning Chronicle* described how the two men arrived at the scene, how they counted out 10 paces and loaded their pistols. In the story's last paragraph, the author wrote, "The fire of Colonel Burr took effect, and General Hamilton almost instantly fell."[1] The development of the telegraph, however, coupled with the unreliability and high cost of the new technology spurred the development of what is known today as the inverted pyramid style of writing. The reporter's first paragraph, called a lead, focuses, instead of setting the scene, on explaining the most important thing that happened. The reporter is charged with answering the five *W*s and *H*: who, what, when, where, why, and how.

Correspondents during the Civil War were uncertain that their transmission would go through in its entirety, so it became imperative to put the most important information first. In addition, these correspondents in the field had to find a telegraph office and pay for the transmission themselves. A poorly paid group in the first place, that financial burden in itself was enough reason to keep the transmissions terse.

Photography also came of age during the Civil War, although the newspaper technology lagged. While it was still too difficult to reproduce photographs in a daily newspaper, the Civil War was notably the first American war to be recorded in photographs. Mathew Brady and about 20 of his photographers trekked the war's battlefields and created a record of about 3,500 pictures that survive in the National Archives. Since photography was unavailable to newspapers and periodicals, war artists proliferated. In theory, the artists' renderings of battles could provide insight into the military techniques of the day, but in practice, not all artists thought it necessary to witness the battles. Some of the drawings that were published were based on what the artist, safely ensconced in a newsroom far from the action, thought the battle might have looked like.

Other common journalistic techniques emerged at mid-century. Horace Greeley's interview of Brigham Young, published in the *New York Tribune* in 1859, was highly criticized at the time because, the critics claimed, it was contrived to make news. It signaled the beginning of journalistic interviews designed to illuminate the private details of a celebrity's life. Greeley, a moralistic and opinionated publisher, interviewed Young, leader of the Mormon church and husband to 15 wives, in Utah and printed the verbatim interview in his *Tribune*. The description of polygamy prompted a national debate that ended in its prohibition by Congress three years later.

The explosion in technology also transformed the speed in which readers received information. James Gordon Bennett, of the *New York Herald,* then the largest paper in the United States, kept a fleet of small boats cruising off the coast of New Jersey to intercept incoming steamers from Europe to get the news from that continent to its readers first. Carrier pigeons also were used by enterprising editors to send stories back to the newsroom swiftly. The expansion of the railroad westward, the ever-increasing miles of rails and telegraph wires, played their part in the explosion of mass communication in the United States.

Later in the century, the glow of gas lamps and, later, electric light increased the usefulness of the newspaper by expanding the reading day. This innovation, coupled with technology that allowed for swift gathering and printing of news, ushered in the heyday of the afternoon newspaper. Selling itself as the most up-to-date information available, the afternoon newspaper appealed to commuters returning from their jobs in the city and to women who were able to find the time to read after they had completed their daily chores. The evening papers included closing stock prices, the day's sports scores, news of the day, and the department store advertising aimed at women readers. By the 1870s, journalism in America's cities featured morning papers and, in many cases, independent afternoon newspapers, owned by the same company, but with different staffs and content. There were 16 daily English-language newspapers published in New York in 1892; 7 of those appeared in the evening. Sunday newspapers also rose in popularity at this time, fueled by the reading public's desire for the news seven days a week and by a U.S. population that was increasingly educated and literate.

The 1890s in New York journalism was punctuated by the legendary rivalry between two of the major personalities of American newspaper history: Joseph Pulitzer and William Randolph Hearst. Pulitzer, generally cast in the role of hero of this story, was an unlikely leading man—a Hungarian immigrant whose eyesight was so bad that he was rejected by the Austrian Army and the French Foreign Legion before he was deemed fit enough for the Union Army during the Civil War. He began his journalistic career after the Civil War as a reporter for a German-language daily in St. Louis. Pulitzer bought the *St. Louis Dispatch* for a song at a sheriff's sale in 1878, merged it with the *St. Louis Post*, and established his *St. Louis Post-Dispatch* as a profitable and most important evening paper in that city. Pulitzer stormed into New York four years later with his purchase of the *New York World* and used that newspaper as the flagship for his new journalism style. Readers flocked to his newspaper, and later to his *New York Evening World*. His new style affected newspapers around the country. Pulitzer was an incorrigible self-promoter. He backed crusades against crooked politicians, championed the little guy, and exposed companies and contractors who stole and lied to the poor. His so-called stunt journalism triggered a national phenomenon. The most notorious of the stunt girls, journalism's Nellie Bly, was his employee when she made the news as well as reported it by going around the world in fewer than 80 days.

While Pulitzer had a natural nose for news and loved the kind of stories that caught readers' attention, he also loved responsible journalism. He tempered his sensationalistic approach to news with an editorial page that was thoughtful and insightful. He saw the editorial page as the heart of his newspaper and the main reason for the paper to publish.[2]

If Pulitzer is the hero of this epoch, Hearst is the villain. Generally considered to be the founder of so-called yellow journalism, Hearst went head-to-head with Pulitzer in a circulation war that pitted the *New York Journal* against Pulitzer's newspapers. Hearst, who was tossed out of Harvard for playing a practical joke, learned the newspaper business in San Francisco after his father bought the *San Francisco Examiner* and handed over its management to his young son. Hearst arrived in New York and bought the *Morning Journal* in 1895 and almost immediately declared war on Pulitzer's papers, which were topping New York's circulation. He stole away Pulitzer's best and seasoned writers and editors and built a following on sex and crime stories that appealed to readers' prurient interests. He also played fast and loose with the facts. He relied on screaming headlines set in extra-large type. The term *yellow journalism* came to describe this popular style of writing after Hearst stole away Pulitzer's artist, who drew the "Yellow Kid" for his comic section. The comic featured a street urchin dressed in a long, flowing, yellow coat. When the artist, Richard Outcault, moved to the *Journal* and began penning the comic for that newspaper, Pulitzer hired another artist and continued the comic. Pundits began referring to the "Yellow Press," and the moniker stuck. Today, the term *yellow journalism* is still used to represent the most base of newspaper and television reporting.

Muckraking, mostly a phenomenon in U.S. magazines, rose to prominence in the new century, perhaps in direct response to the growing perception of an irresponsible press that flourished because of yellow journalism. The term *muckraking* was meant as an insult to news reporters when it was coined by President Theodore Roosevelt, who compared the investigative reporters of the day to the man who rakes the muck in the then popular allegory *Pilgrim's Progress*. Journalists, however, embraced the term and continued their campaigns against political, social, and business corruption in earnest.

THE TWENTIETH CENTURY: MULTIMEDIA EMERGE

Newspapers in the twentieth century fended off challenges to their supremacy from radio and newsreels before succumbing, at least in part, to the power of television in the 1960s. After the Great War, American life shifted radically.

People were anxious to forget the troubles of war. It was the day of the flappers, women who were embracing their newfound right to vote, while at the same time shedding the bondage of their clothing for knee-length dresses and pushing the boundaries of societal restrictions. Today, we call the era the Roaring Twenties, while the newspapers of the time represent jazz journalism. Newspapers responded to the looser times by a preoccupation with sex, crime, and entertainment and the rise of tabloid newspapers. Tabloids initially referred to the small size of the newspaper, making it cheaper to publish and easier to read for commuters on trains and subways, but tabloid journalism came to mean the kind of sensational journalism that includes screaming headlines, lots of photos, and appeals to the working class. Sports reporting increased; Hollywood stars became celebrities in the press. In New York, the birthplace of American tabloid journalism, the *New York Daily News* and the *New York Post* typified the tabloid brand of journalism even into the twenty-first century.

Newspapers were frightened by the power of the nascent radio industry. Although radio did not initially compete with newspapers to report the news, it was clear from the beginning that it could threaten newspapers' monopoly on information. In January 1922, there were 30 radio stations broadcasting in the United States; 14 months later, there were 556. Newspapers were reporting on the phenomenon of radio in their columns. The listening audience grew quickly—there were about 50,000 radio sets in 1921 and more than 600,000 in 1922. By 1930, that number had risen to 14 million.[3]

Newspapers were not challenged by radio broadcasts per se. In fact, many newspaper publishers dabbled in radio by purchasing stations or sponsoring programs. Yet the newspaper industry was, indeed, frightened by the possibility that it would lose advertising dollars to the new industry and by the fear that radio stations would begin reporting news. Even though the American Newspaper Publishers Association's radio committee sagely took the official position that news on the radio stimulated newspaper sales, owners were not convinced.

One way to curtail the growth of radio as a vehicle for news was to attempt to ban it. The Associated Press (AP), founded in 1848 as an organization that shared news and the expenses incurred covering world events, initially tried to prevent radio stations from using their news copy to broadcast radio newscasts. It fined the *Portland Oregonian* $100 for broadcasting the results of the 1924 presidential voting. Four years later, the AP, United Press International (UPI), and the International News Service had caved in and supplied the results to the radio stations. The candidates themselves had purchased radio air time to get their messages across.

At first, radio broadcasts complemented newspaper coverage: the 1924 political conventions, the 1925 Scopes Monkey trial in Tennessee, the arrival of Charles Lindbergh in Washington after his flight to Paris in 1927. Sports events found a natural venue in radio. The 1927 Jack Dempsey–Gene Tunney prizefight was carried on 69 stations. One of the major concerns for newspaper publishers, however, was that the press associations were actually giving information to the radio stations before the newspapers had actually published the information. They were fighting a losing battle. Bowing to pressure from their newspaper clients, the wire services agreed to stop selling their news items to radio stations. Radio responded by gathering the information itself. Finally, the newspaper-radio war of the 1930s ended with UPI creating a news report specifically for radio broadcast. The AP fell into line shortly thereafter.

While news moguls were debating what role radio would play in the gathering and dissemination of news, there was no dispute over the new medium as a vehicle for entertainment. America's love of popular music became apparent. Dance music and band leaders found a home on the radio. Just as sports figures like Babe Ruth and Jack Dempsey became celebrities in part because of their national exposure through radio, singing stars like Bing Crosby and Al Jolsen made a name for themselves over the airwaves. Radio also appeared to be a natural venue for dramas, situational comedies, and variety shows. The most enduring drama genre, the soap opera, traced its beginning to radio. The genre was so named because the syrupy romantic dramas with ongoing plotlines that brought fans back to listen day after day were sponsored by soap companies, most notably Proctor & Gamble. The first soap opera was *Guiding Light,* which came on the air in 1937, made the transition to television in 1952, and was still broadcasting 70 years later.

It is hard to separate the history of radio from the stories of the other media with which it competed. It has basically weathered four distinct periods: 1890 to the 1920s, in which radio was developing into a distinct medium; the 1930s to the 1940s, the golden age of radio programming; the 1950s to the 1960s, the television age, in which radio needed to adapt its programming to accommodate the new medium; and the posttelevision age, which continues today.[4] Radio includes a wide range of programming choices, including call-in shows, sports radio, shock radio, advice, interview, all-news, and commentary, in addition to the traditional music stations.

Radio, however, enjoyed a short-lived period as the entertainment medium of choice. While it has continued into the twenty-first century as a medium of news, entertainment, sports, and talk, its influence is minimal. Americans gathered around their radio sets in the 1940s to listen to broadcasts from World War II, calming words from President Roosevelt, and the music, comedy, and dramas that had come into fashion. That cozy tableau with a radio in the center did not last.

While the destruction of newspapers by the new medium of radio never materialized, the second battle focused on how people chose to spend their time. The movie industry, which began in earnest in the 1920s, captured people's attention, and their expendable incomes. When television arrived on the scene in the late 1940s, radio was pushed aside quickly. People moved their chairs from in front of the radio and settled down to watch an evening of television. Radio has continued as a secondary medium. People tend to listen to radio while they are doing something else—most notably, driving.

Television had the potential to snuff out radio and newspapers on all fronts: it could consume Americans' time in the evening, time previously spent reading newspapers or listening to radio; it could take a serious chunk out of limited advertising revenues; and it could be the medium of choice for viewers hungry for the day's news. The shift did not happen overnight. It soon became abundantly clear that newspapers could not compete on timeliness or immediacy with television news. Americans—indeed, the world's citizens—turned to their televisions on November 22, 1963, when President John F. Kennedy was gunned down in a motorcade in Dallas, Texas. While some afternoon newspapers published special editions to update their readers on the nation's tragedy, the published information was outdated before the ink was dry. Three days later, the man suspected of being the trigger man, Lee Harvey Oswald, was shot on live national television.

For newspapers, television's ascendancy should have raised a red flag and forced publishers and journalists to rethink what they did and how they did it, but newspapers continued to carry on business as usual, despite other warning signals. Newspapers had spent too many centuries as the only game in town and were slow to react to change. They still are.

As the decade of the 1960s unfolded, television demonstrated its power as a news medium during the Vietnam War, when America's confidence in its government was shaken. Anger at U.S. policies in Vietnam was fueled by press coverage, especially the television video from Southeast Asia. It was the first time Americans' witnessed the horror of war on film. They did not like what they saw. Americans began questioning their government and their leaders in earnest. When U.S. president Richard Nixon ordered the invasion of Cambodia in 1970, college campuses erupted in violence. One-third of the universities in the United Sates were shut down that spring in the wake of student walkouts, protests, and sit-ins. Four students at Kent State were killed when the National Guard in Ohio fired their rifles into the protesting crowd.

America was in crisis. Then, during the presidential campaign of 1972, the Democratic National Committee headquarters at the Watergate Hotel were burglarized. Two local reporters for the *Washington Post,* Carl Bernstein and Bob Woodward, began investigating and reporting about the burglary and its aftermath. Ultimately, their reporting revealed a conspiracy to cover up the involvement of highly placed Republicans and a campaign of "dirty tricks" designed to make the Democrats look bad. The trail of responsibility led directly to the White House, and on August 8, 1974, Nixon resigned the presidency. As a result of its coverage of the Watergate affair, as it came to be known, the *Washington Post* newspaper won journalism's top award, the Pulitzer Prize.

Societal developments also had an effect on newspapers and their readership. The last half of the twentieth century saw a shift in the types of writing by journalists. A second wave of new journalism was evidenced beginning in the 1960s with writers who took a fiction approach to nonfiction, book-length topics. Truman Capote's *In Cold Blood,* serialized in *The New Yorker* in 1965 and published in book form later that year, told the story of the senseless murder of a family in Kansas. Writers like Norman Mailer, Tom Wolfe, Jimmy Breslin, David Halberstam, and Gay Talese were known for this novel approach to news. A genre of book publishing, true crime, emerged from this new journalism. These edgy books complemented well the tastes of the American public, who were becoming enamored with being entertained by television.

Another book genre, the kiss-and-tell phenomenon, also emerged. Most notably, the 1977 publication of *Mommy, Dearest,* by Christina Crawford, laid out in gruesome detail the maternal mess that was her mother, the famous and glamorous movie star Joan Crawford. It opened the floodgates. Tell-all books became popular. Magazines that made public the private lives of movie stars and celebrities proliferated. *People Weekly,* one of the profitable national magazines owned by Time Inc., and its imitators gave rise to television programs like *Entertainment Tonight, Extra!,* and *The Insider.* The lines between news and entertainment blurred. Is extensive reporting of stories like the death of celebrity Anna Nicole Smith and the ensuing paternity battle over her baby daughter journalism? When Fox News interviews the contestants as they are voted off the ultrapopular *American Idol* song contest, is it news or blatant self-promotion?

During the twentieth century, the United States also saw the professionalization of the news reporter. Early in the century, uneducated news hacks often rose from positions as copy boys into full-fledged reporters. Ultimately, however, the route into journalism came from college, with hundreds of journalism programs springing up at universities around the country. Journalists also became specialists in their beats, beginning about 1960. Urban reporters, consumer writers, and science writers joined the ranks of other established beats: war correspondents, political writers, foreign correspondents, and feature writers. During the 1970s, the environment also became an established area for journalists.

Not only did the type of journalism change, but the profession was profoundly affected by technological advances throughout the century. While reporters initially pounded out their stories on manual typewriters, they ultimately ended the century by carrying portable laptop computers with them on assignments. Conversations could be recorded, first on large, unwieldy machines, but in the 1980s, portable minirecorders made that job simpler. In the 1990s, cell phones provided added flexibility, while e-mail became a tool for interviewing. The subjects of interviews found comfort in their ability to write down the words that could be used as quotes, while reporters were able to cast a wider net in researching a story. The Internet also made journalistic research quick and efficient. What could have taken hours just 10 years earlier could be had in an instant. Tracking down a court opinion, for example, could have required a journalist to travel miles to a courthouse and cost hundreds of dollars in photocopying. With the Internet, it could be located and printed in minutes.

The wire services also changed. The incessant noise of newsrooms at mid-century was caused by the *clang-clang* of the wire service teletypes, which became obsolete with the shift to computer technology. That was not the only difference. The fierce rivalry exhibited between the nonprofit cooperative, the AP, and its for-profit counterpart, UPI, slowly faded. Once considered vital for a large newspaper to subscribe to both of the big wire services, that expense became a luxury as costs accelerated with the years. The AP more often became the wire service of choice, while newspapers supplemented their output with one of the specialized wires, like the Dow Jones, the Gannett wire, or the New York Times News Service. UPI changed hands repeatedly but clung to life by trimming its employees and limiting its offerings. As UPI faded, the British wire service, Reuters, rose in prominence in the United States, with its focus on business and international news.

The decline of the cities and the rise of suburbia took their toll on newspapers. In 1940, there were 181 cities that had competing daily newspapers. That number shrank to 30 by 1981. New York City, once a mecca for newspapers, whittled down to three regular dailies: the *New York Times,* the *New York Post,* and the *New York Daily News.* The *Wall Street Journal* also published five days a week. Those four papers numbered among the top 11 papers in the country in 2006.

Meanwhile, suburban newspapers grew in number and influence. *Newsday,* which covers the mostly suburban Long Island, New York, was founded in 1940 and tapped into the growing number of bedroom communities that sprang up in commuting distance to New York City. *Newsday* is the 19th largest newspaper in the United States, with a circulation in 2006 of 488,825, according to the Audit Bureau of Circulation.[5]

USA Today, founded by the Gannett newspaper chain in 1982, provided the nation with its first truly national newspaper. With 2.5 million circulation, *USA Today* publishes five days a week and looks the same no matter where it is purchased (by contrast, the national edition of the *New York Times* is a truncated version of the edition that circulates in the New York metropolitan area). Although the U.S. journalism community initially reacted to *USA Today* as if it were a bad joke, the newspaper ultimately made an indelible mark on all U.S. newspapers. Its use of color, its reliance on graphics, its streamlined layout, and its abridged approach to news led journalists to dub *USA Today* "McPaper," flippantly calling it the fast food of newspapers. Yet all American newspapers, even the "Gray Old Lady" (the nickname for the *New York Times*), have been affected by its innovations.

JOURNALISM OUTSIDE THE MAINSTREAM

Journalism has long been a tool in the United States for people who lack a voice. While the costs of a mainstream newspaper initially stood in the hundreds of thousands, daily newspapers today trade hands for hundreds of millions of dollars. That prohibitive cost has always stood in the way of making newspapers the voice of the little guy, but grassroots movements have long recognized the power of modest methods in mass communication.

In the nineteenth century, the abolitionist cause and the suffrage battle were waged in the press. Although mainstream newspapers ignored—or worse still, mocked—these social justice crusades, the proponents found an outlet for their arguments by creating their own newspapers. Abolitionist newspapers appeared early in the century. The *Philanthropist* was published in Ohio beginning in 1817; the *Manumission Intelligencer* had its home in 1819 in Jonesboro, Tennessee. The *Genius of Universal Emancipation,* the most influential of these early journals, was published by Benjamin Lundy beginning in 1821. Lundy hired William Lloyd Garrison to work on the *Genius.* Lundy traveled the country drumming up readers and supporters to the cause, while Garrison published the paper. Garrison and Lundy had philosophical differences that ultimately led to a split and the publication of a new journal, Garrison's the *Liberator.* Garrison spewed fire. His strong language against slavery and the people who traded in it had tremendous shock value. He published for 30 years. His last issue, on January 1, 1866, celebrated the ratification of the constitutional amendment to abolish slavery.

The black press was also born during the nineteenth century. It marked its founding with the publication of *Freedom's Journal* in 1827. By the time the Civil War began, about 40 black newspapers had been founded. Black newspapers, however, were poorly funded and slow to take hold, most certainly because of the lack of education available to the nation's black Americans and the high illiteracy rates among slaves and free blacks. While abolition clearly was an important topic in the black newspapers, they also were concerned with the lives of black Americans and provided news and information about this completely marginalized and disenfranchised group. Black editors and publishers numbered in the dozens, but most famous of all was former slave Frederick Douglass. Douglass escaped from slavery in 1838 and traveled widely throughout Europe, speaking on the horrors of the practice. When he returned to the United States, Douglass began his own publication, *The North Star,* in 1847.

Many of America's suffragists began their activism in the abolitionist movement, where they often were treated like second-class citizens. Publications like Amelia Bloomers's the *Lily* and Paulina Wright Davis's the *Una* gave women's rights the soft sell. Elizabeth Cady Stanton and Susan B. Anthony would have none of that when they published the *Revolution* beginning in 1868. A few years later, the *Woman's Journal* began a 47-year tenure as the voice of the woman's movement in America. It was merged with several other like publications in 1917, just three years before the 19th Amendment to the Constitution gave women the right to vote in 1920.

One major characteristic of the abolition and suffrage publications was that they suffered from a perpetual lack of funds. They were not alone. Any grassroots publication that relied mostly on the beneficence of its readers, rather than the income of advertisers, could anticipate difficulty in meeting a payroll and financing the costs of printing.

In the 1930s, for example, Dorothy Day founded the *Catholic Worker* to spread the word of the Roman Catholic social justice movement. Day began her journalism career on the *New York Call,* a socialist newspaper, and the *Masses.* She began publishing the *Catholic Worker* in 1933 with Peter Maurin. Published in the kitchen of a New York tenement, the *Catholic Worker* appealed to many of the Great Depression's unemployed with its message of a benevolent, caring Church. Day had to sell her typewriter to get a second edition of the monthly paper published. While the circulation of Day's newspaper has always been modest, its success has always been in publicizing the goals of the movement.

Day was not alone. I. F. Stone, one of the earliest of the twentieth century's alternative journalists, was a staunch opponent of Senator Joseph McCarthy's Communism witch hunt in the 1950s, when he began his newsletter dedicated to liberal ideals, *I. F. Stone's Weekly,* in 1953. Stone's newsletter lasted until 1971.

Stone and Day are among a handful of writers who are credited with paving the way for the underground press that began in the 1960s. These cheaply printed newspapers were the forerunners to the now-popular newsletters that were made possible by personal computers in the 1990s. Underground newspapers were not confined by the dictates of fair play and objectivity that often constrained mainstream newspapers. The publishers of these radical newspapers did not worry about polite language and did not care if they made enemies of the rich and powerful. At a time when the nation was in turmoil, when college campuses were hotbeds of unrest, when the civil rights movement was simmering and the Vietnam War was triggering ugly protests, the underground press fueled the fires. The *Village Voice* seems a mainstream paper to many today, but it was considered the most powerful voice of the underground when it began publishing in 1955. *Rolling Stone,* which first appeared in 1967, became a hugely successful commentator on popular music and society. Other papers came and went. Some published on college campuses, others at high schools.

Today, the Internet has supplanted traditional newspapers or cheap newsletters in giving a voice to the silent. The zine, a Web magazine, was popular for a period before blogs, short for *weblogs,* took over. Literally millions of blogs are published on the Internet, giving voice to people who want to share their thoughts, their actions, their private lives, and their public opinions with an anonymous world. Like the underground newspapers of the 1960s, which abandoned the rules and customs of newspapers, the veracity and reliability of a blog is not guaranteed. Often the ravings of the passionate and irate, blogs have evolved from online diaries into a no-rules free-for-all.

TELEVISION

Television was introduced to the American public in 1939 at the New York World's Fair. There were a few hundred television sets in the United States by then, and about 40 million radio sets, when Franklin D. Roosevelt was televised at the opening ceremonies for the fair. World War II slowed down the steamroller that television ultimately became, and FDR confined his cozy fireside chats to radio, but the entertainment value of television slowly emerged during the 1940s. By October 1950, there were 8 million sets in America's homes. There was no turning back.

While Johannes Gutenberg gets credit for the sixteenth-century invention of the printing press, and radio points to Guglielmo Marconi as its inventor, television can single out no one person. The technology necessary to translate both sound and picture through the air waves and into people's homes took many minds. A few of the innovators, however, stand out. In 1929, Russian Vladimir Zworykin was working for Westinghouse in Pittsburgh when he invented the cathode-ray tube, which made the television picture possible.

Meanwhile, American engineer Philo Farnsworth lays claim to producing the first rudimentary television broadcast in 1927. While the engineers spent decades perfecting the science behind the technology, a true visionary in creating television as the ultimate mass medium in the twentieth century was David Sarnoff.

Sarnoff honed his communication skills in radio. He understood that if radio was to be a mass medium, it had to be simple to use. His streamlined vision of a little box appealed to American consumers. It worked. Then, Sarnoff diversified his company, RCA, into television. Determined to do for television what he did for radio, Sarnoff had the first television studio built in the Empire State Building in 1932. The 1930s proved to be a decade of mere preparation for the medium that was to come. Broadcasts occurred but were limited, of poor quality, and unavailable to all except the select few who had TV sets.

It was not until 1941 that the Federal Communications Commission (FCC), which had been established to sort out the radio air waves, approved commercial broadcasting for 18 television stations. They were approved to offer 15 hours of programming each week. The federal government froze development of more stations during World War II, and at war's end in 1945, only six stations were still on the air.

Television as a powerful mass medium truly was born in the 1950s. It was then that the three networks, the National Broadcasting Company (NBC), the Columbia Broadcasting System (CBS), and the American Broadcasting Company (CBS), solidified their positions. The networks traced their roots to radio—NBC was first in 1928, when it established a coast-to-coast network of 58 stations. CBS appeared on the scene in 1929. ABC was the latecomer; it was formed in 1945, when NBC was forced to sell part of its network by the FCC. The big three ruled television programming for decades and were joined in 1987 by Fox Broadcasting. Later, UPN and the WB (Warner Brothers) debuted in 1995 by focusing on programming to lure young audiences and African American viewers to their offerings. UPN and the WB, which often competed for the same audience, transformed into one unit, the CW network, in September 2006.

Cable television, which actually had been operating since 1948, made it possible for remote areas to receive television programming. However, the biggest boon to cable came with the advent of pay television, for which viewers pay a premium for extra television stations. Home Box Office (HBO) debuted in 1972 and featured newly released movies that had never been seen on television. It ultimately expanded its programming to include exclusive concerts, performances, sporting events, and its own comedies and dramas, most especially the long-running Mafia drama *The Sopranos.* The

1980s was a golden age for cable. The Entertainment and Sports Programming Network (ESPN) debuted in September 1979, while the Cable News Network (CNN) was founded in 1980. Despite skeptics who predicted that an all-news or all-sports channel could never survive, those two channels thrived. As programming on cable accelerated, more and more households made the conversion. The Cabletelevision Advertising Bureau asserted that nearly 93 million households (85%) in the United States used cable television in 2005.

The rules for cable television were different. While standard television programming adhered to specific rules and limits that were monitored by the FCC, cable television flourished without them. Comedians on network television had to watch their language and punch lines, but cable television provided a venue for adult situations, nudity, and risqué topics. Parents who objected to racy content had two choices: not buying cable at all or programming their televisions to black out objectionable shows.

Cable also served as the great media equalizer. Television was an expensive technology far beyond the means of the common person. Its initial capability was limited to a small number of channels. Cable's wide breadth of channels provided the possibility of access to a wider spectrum. Local access channels opened broadcasting to groups and communities without extensive resources and allowed television to provide news coverage that normally was reserved for small weekly newspapers.

In addition to cable viewing, how Americans watched television was profoundly affected by the mass marketing of the video cassette recorder (VCR) beginning in the late 1970s. Two different systems, the VHS and the Betamax, competed in the United States initially, but VHS ultimately dominated. The advent of the VCR affected television viewing in three major ways: first, it opened up a rental market that allowed viewers to borrow movies and watch them at home; second, it allowed viewers to record their favorite shows and watch them at their leisure—gone were the days when viewers had to stay home and watch their favorite shows at an appointed time; third, it allowed viewers to fast-forward past unwanted commercial advertisements. The VCR technology was slowly replaced by digital video disks (DVDs), which resemble music CDs and computer disks but allow television programs and movies to be replayed on televisions. DVDs were first marketed in the mid-1990s but slowly replaced VCRs as the state-of-the-art recording method.

The latest television technologies to capture the pocketbooks of the American people were flat screen TVs and high-definition TVs (HDTVs). Flat screen televisions allowed consumers to hang their sets like a picture on the wall, while HDTV provided an incredibly sharp, seemingly three-dimensional picture. Often, the two technologies were marketed together.

Television programming in the United States initially borrowed from radio. Comedies and dramas that had captured America's attention on radio segued into live television. The popular radio personalities like George Burns and Gracie Allen broadcast initially in both television and radio, but television clearly was more suitable to the situation comedies and soap operas that had been popularized on radio in the 1930s and 1940s. Ultimately, radio abandoned its pursuit of these broadcasts and concentrated instead on the news, talk, music, and sports to which it was more suited.

Television made big celebrities quickly. Comedian Milton Berle became known as Mr. Television because of his understanding of and ability to play comedy to a television audience. He began his shtick on television in 1948 on the *Texaco Star Theater* variety show. People stayed home on Tuesday nights to watch the program, which was credited with contributing to the sale of millions of TV sets.

Most programming in the 1950s was broadcast live. Several genres emerged during that time and have remained closely identified with the medium. News broadcasts, both local and national, became a staple at dinnertime. Newscasters like Edward R. Murrow, Walter Cronkite, and Howard K. Smith made the transition to television news. Murrow, whose voice calmed an anxious nation during World War II, brought his popular *Hear It Now* radio program to television on CBS. *See It Now* began on television in 1951 and was supplemented in 1953 with his *Person to Person.* Murrow tackled difficult subjects in both of his shows, most notably his refusal to report objectively on the histrionics of Senator Joseph McCarthy and his campaign to root out hidden Communists in America. By the time Murrow died in 1965, Walter Cronkite was seen as the face of news. On NBC, the news came to the American people via the *Huntley-Brinkley Report,* featuring Chet Huntley and David Brinkley as anchors, from 1956 to 1970. NBC's *Meet the Press,* which premiered on television in 1947 (making the transition from radio), is the longest-running program in U.S. television history. NBC also popularized morning television when *The Today Show* began in 1952. It made celebrities of a series of news interviewers, including Barbara Walters, Katie Couric, Jane Pauley, Tom Brokaw, and Bryant Gumbel. The other networks imitated, but even into the new millennium, *The Today Show* was king.

The immediacy of television was its strength. Americans watched John F. Kennedy take the oath of office as president in January 1961; they were glued to the television when John Glenn made the first manned orbit of the moon; they were transfixed when the much-loved Kennedy was felled by sniper fire the following year. When Neil Armstrong walked on the moon in July 1969, it was an event witnessed by an estimated 600 million people back on earth, thanks to television.

NBC's *Today Show* draws large crowds to Rockefeller Center every weekday morning. © AP Photo/Jason DeCrow.

The love affair with television news continued and accelerated, much to the chagrin of the presidents and their administrations. The journalistic coverage of the Vietnam War in the 1960s and 1970s often is credited with affecting its outcome. America had never seen a war up front and personal before because technology had stood in the way. But by the time the U.S. involvement in Vietnam accelerated in the 1960s, television was ready. For the first time, Americans watched the war unfold in their living rooms. The carnage was live and in color. Reported in newspapers and reinforced on television, the news from Asia was not pretty. America revolted. The protests that erupted on college campuses and in Washington, D.C., were also played out on the evening news. In March 1968, several hundred unarmed Vietnamese civilians were slaughtered by American troops in the village of My Lai. The devastation was covered up by the army but made public by a news reporter in November 1969. Two years later, the trial of Lieutenant William Calley for mass murder led the national newscasts night after night.

As the number of television stations increased, broadcasters took advantage of the ability to target both a local and a national audience. Local news shows usually focused on providing viewers with information they needed to know: weather and traffic, crime and punishment, and government. National news programs basically synthesized the national headlines of the day.

Situation comedies, dubbed *sitcoms,* roared to popularity in the 1950s with early shows like *Our Miss Brooks* (which had been a radio favorite) and Lucille Ball's *I Love Lucy.* That comedy, which lasted in various forms into the 1970s, garnered the largest television audience of the 1950s, when 21 million families turned on their sets to watch the episode when a pregnant Lucille Ball gave birth to her television son, Little Ricky, in January 1953. *I Love Lucy* also pioneered the now-standard practice of taping episodes, thus creating the concept of a rerun, which allows the show to be shown over and over. In fact, TV programs sometimes earn more money after they officially go off the air by being sold in syndication to television stations that can re-air them in a new time slot. *Seinfeld,* a popular 1990s comedy "about nothing," is the highest-earning sitcom ever in syndication.

As early as 1950, sitcom producers introduced a laugh track into their shows. This canned laughter provided viewers with cues on when to laugh and what was supposed to be funny. Sitcoms are the most enduring genre in television entertainment. *The Simpsons,* an animated show that actually parodies the genre, is the longest-running sitcom in U.S. history. It premiered in 1989 and was still running in 2007. Other popular sitcoms over the years included *All in the Family,* which pioneered the concept of biting

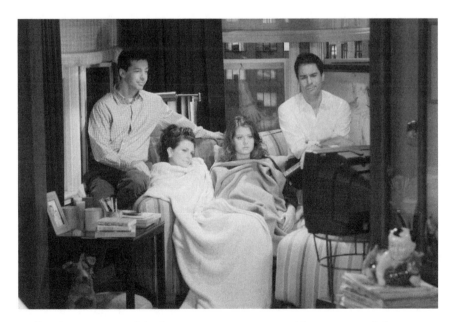

Will and Grace is one of the first American sitcoms to address issues with homosexuality. Courtesy of Photofest.

social commentary in the 1970s with its bigoted leading character, Archie Bunker; *Friends,* which chronicled the lives of six single New York friends; *Cheers,* which centered on the lives of people who worked and hung out in a bar in Boston; and *The Cosby Show,* about the family life of a lovable obstetrician, played by Bill Cosby.

Game shows also were popular in early television, before they were rocked by a cheating scandal that made producers shy away from the genre for a time. *The $64,000 Question* was the CBS television network program that brought the hammer down on game shows. Airing from 1955 to 1958, it was wildly popular and spawned imitations at other networks, including the show *Twenty-one.* The bubble burst when a contestant who lost on *Twenty-one* began talking publicly about how the show was rigged. Congress got involved and ultimately passed a federal law barring game tampering. Game shows slowly regained popularity in the 1960s and continue to appeal to viewers today. *Jeopardy!,* which first aired in 1964, had several lives under several television hosts, before it was broadcast in the early evening beginning in 1984 with Alex Trebek as its host. That game, which provides the answers and requires contestants to ask the questions, was still on the air in 2007. Produced by Merv Griffin, it usually aired just before or after *Wheel of Fortune,* a game that required players to guess common word phrases by filling in the blanks with letters. The game show genre produced several other notable programs, including the more recent *Who Wants to be a Millionaire?,* which had different versions in more than 60 countries around the word, and the granddaddy of them all, *The Price is Right,* which began in 1956.

Television dramas take two forms: soap operas, a carryover from radio and still a strong daytime staple on networks, and nighttime dramas, which feature recurring characters and often feature lawyers, police officers, detectives, cowboys, and doctors as the protagonists. Shows like *Perry Mason, Medical Center, Law & Order, Gunsmoke, Kojak, Matlock,* and *Marcus Welby, M.D.,* typically last one hour and are self-contained dramas. Soap operas feature ongoing story lines, and they need to be watched daily to understand the story line. *Guiding Light,* which premiered on television in 1952, is the longest running of this genre. Nighttime soap operas also have their niche. *Dallas,* which ran in the 1980s, was the most popular of this type. The show created an international buzz when the leading character was felled on the last episode of the 1980 season and viewers had to wait until the fall to learn the answer.

Sporting events were a natural draw for television. Live action sports generate great excitement. In fact, it was the promise of one of the longest-running sports variety programs in television history. "Spanning the globe to bring you the constant variety of sport...the thrill of victory...and the agony of defeat...the human drama of athletic competition...this is *ABC's Wide World of Sports!*" was the voice-over introduction that opened the show, which debuted in 1961, beginning in the 1970s. The Super Bowl has become a national television event since 1967, generating a day of Super Bowl parties and prompting advertisers to create custom-made commercials for the broadcast. In fact, the commercials, the half-time show, the singing of the National Anthem, and the pregame events are often as much a part of the day as the game itself. Ninety-three million people in the United States watched Super Bowl XLI in 2007, according to the Nielsen Media Research.

In the early days of television, the anticipated broadcast of a sporting event could generate sales of television sets. The technology today has come a long way from the single, black-and-white camera positioned along the third base line for the Princeton-Columbia baseball game in 1939.[6] Some of the earliest broadcasts included the baseball World Series and boxing bouts. Television was, in some instances, able to deliver a better game than would be had at the ball park. The instant replay, which was put to limited use in 1955, allows viewers to decide whether officials got the call right. Powerful and sensitive cameras positioned in the outfield allowed fans to call balls and strikes. The 1st and 10 line provides television viewers with a virtual yellow line that marks the next first down.

Finally, no discussion of television genres would be complete without reporting on the most recent development, the reality show. *Candid Camera* featured people caught looking foolish on hidden camera, and the *Ted Mack Amateur Hour,* a talent show, both debuted on television in 1948, but the genre never gained the kind of wild devotion it experienced in the new millennium. In the United States, the most recent forerunner of the genre was probably *The Real World* on MTV. A group of young people who lived together were filmed in their daily lives. Then, competition was added to the genre in 2000 with the show *Survivor,* which brought a group of contestants to a remote island, challenged them with physical hurdles, and then had them voted off the show one by one. *American Idol,* a singing competition that allowed viewers to vote for their favorite contestants, began in 2002 and enjoyed the distinction as the most popular show on television in 2007. Reality television was king in the first decade of the new millennium and included off-beat and sometimes bizarre shows like *Wife Swap,* where two mothers changed places for a week; *Nanny 911,* in which a British nanny taught parents how to control their wild children; *The Bachelor,* in which a man got to woo a cadre of beautiful women and get rid of someone each week; and *Extreme Makeover,* in which a person was completely redone using plastic surgery.

Survivor started a new trend in American television. A combination of reality TV and game show, contestants are placed on teams and are given physical and mental challenges. At the end of each episode, one person is voted off of the show. Courtesy of Photofest.

CINEMA

The story of American movies traces its beginnings to the nineteenth century, but the industry really was a child of the twentieth century. In the United States, inventor extraordinaire Thomas A. Edison's preoccupation with capturing moving objects on film fueled a $44 billion industry in 2006. From the five-second black-and-white film *Fred Ott's Sneeze,* which featured Edison's assistant in 1894, the movie industry burst on the entertainment scene.

While the newspaper industry fought off competition from other media, the film industry's story is one of adaptation. Television, VCRs, DVDs, pay-per-view, and other innovations could have decimated the film industry, but instead, it has thrived. The movie industry is a vital and vibrant industry that in the United States generates about 600 films each year.[7] It is the United States' biggest export.

Filmmaking in the United States began modestly enough. Edison's Black Maria studio in West Orange, New Jersey, began producing film shorts, including a 20-second popular item, *The Kiss,* which created a furor and was notable for starting the discussion of censorship in regard to film as early as 1896.[8] Early short films found an audience in cities at Kinetescope Parlors, which allowed viewers to see snippets of film by paying 25 cents, an exorbitant price at the time.

The Great Train Robbery, produced in 1903 by one of Edison's employees, Edwin S. Porter, was notable for its creation of the modern film technique of using several camera positions for the same scene and then editing the film to enhance suspense, create tension, and improve the narrative. That 12-minute silent film also gave rise to the western film genre.

Films found a home at the nickelodeon, movie houses where viewers could see a series of short films beginning about 1905. They spread quickly around the United States, creating a huge demand for new films. Thus an industry was born. By 1909, there were 9,000 movie theaters in the United States. America was not alone in its interest in the budding film industry. Foreign films like *The Cabinet of Dr. Caligari* in 1919 (from Germany) and others found audiences in the United States and contributed to the developing artistic techniques that included both direction and camera work.

While the narrative story emerged quickly as the vehicle for popular films, the films themselves were short, lasting only about 12 minutes (one reel), until David Wark Griffith developed an interest in directing. Griffith had been hired as an actor in Edison's studio but liked being behind the camera instead. He convinced financiers to back his idea for a longer, melodramatic approach to the cinema. Griffith not only influenced the development of the film industry with his innovative ideas, but he also was at least partly responsible for the concentration of the business in the Los Angeles neighborhood we know as Hollywood.

Griffith was working for Biograph as a filmmaker, when he was sent to California with a troupe of actors in 1910 to film *In Old California.* The residents of the Hollywood neighborhood welcomed the actors. The rest is history. Hollywood, the location, has become synonymous with Hollywood, the film industry, and while not all movies are filmed in Hollywood today, it is without a doubt the capital of the moviemaking industry, not just in the United States, but in the world.

Griffith's cinematic contributions included the development of a full-length feature film. He also began the long-held tradition of translating a novel into a film. Griffith purchased the right to the Thomas Dixon novel *The Clansman,* and began filming. When *The Birth of a Nation* was released in 1915, it ran a whopping 3 hours and 10 minutes and changed the direction of film production. *The Birth of a Nation,* which presents the story of the Civil War and Reconstruction from a Southern perspective, has been dismissed as a racist interpretation of history, but in terms of cinematic development, its importance cannot be overstated. It firmly established the concept of story-telling and proved that viewers were willing to sit still and watch raptly if the movie was presented in a gripping fashion. It also established Griffith as a powerful force in the industry. Griffith continued his filmmaking career, and other directors imitated his methods.

Another early innovator was Mack Sennett, who worked with Griffith but left in 1912 and started his own studio, Keystone. Sennett had a knack for comedy and was adept at preserving the humor while filming. He was responsible for the development of the biggest star of the silent film era, Charlie Chaplin. Most famous for his persona of *The Little Tramp,* Chaplin donned a bowler hat, sported a tiny mustache, and twirled a cane in films, while he became embroiled in ridiculous, and funny, predicaments. Chaplin reigned supreme throughout the silent film era of the 1920s but faded as a leading man after sound was introduced with the movie *The Jazz Singer* in 1927.

The silent film era included the development of serial stories that were updated periodically, a precursor to the soap operas of radio and television. Notable in this group was *The Perils of Pauline,* which began in 1914 and featured a damsel in distress who was regularly saved from burning buildings, railroad tracks, and the side of a cliff. The series played on the concept of a cliff-hanger ending that brought the viewers back to see the next episode.

The impact of sound in film history is enormous. Audiences flocked to *The Jazz Singer* and clamored for more. Actors whose voices did not lend them to film were swept aside in favor of those who were photogenic and whose voices were pleasant.

Moviemaking grew into an industry that was centered around a few powerful studios. The studio system, as it came to be known, revolved around five companies: RKO, Paramount, 20th Century Fox, MGM, and Warner Brothers. Most of the financially successful films of the 1930s and 1940s were produced and distributed through these studios.

Despite the desperate financial situation of many Americans during the Great Depression of the 1930s, people went to the movies. Whether it was to escape their dreary existence, or live vicariously through the exotic lives of film stars, or merely to pass the time for a few hours, Americans loved the movies. As movie production and techniques became more sophisticated, the film industry became the leviathan of the entertainment industry—about 80 million people (more than half the U.S. population) went to the movies every week. Films like *Gone with the Wind* and *The Wizard of Oz* in 1939 showcased the industry's storytelling and techniques in living color.

The 1930s also saw the introduction of feature-length animation, most notably the work of master animator Walt Disney. Disney Studio's foray into filmmaking began with *Snow White and the Seven Dwarfs* in 1937 and continued with such instant classics as *Pinocchio* (1940) and *Sleeping Beauty* (1959), to name a few. Even after Disney's death in 1966, and into the new millennium, Disney Studios continued its preeminent position among animators with films like *The Lion King* (1994), *Beauty and the Beast* (1991), and *Tarzan* (1999).

World War II saw the film industry become an arm of U.S. propaganda. Some leading directors, including Frank Capra and John Ford, actually made films for the government. Stars like Clark Gable, who actually joined the army, and his wife, Carol Lombard, who died in a plane crash during a campaign to sell war bonds, typified Hollywood patriotism during the war.

Newspapers were not the only medium threatened by the invention of and consumer love affair with television. The 1950s and 1960s saw the rise of television as a prominent and popular medium. Hollywood quaked. The studio system faded, while American films tried to demonstrate that watching a film in a theater was a bigger and better experience.

As the influence of Hollywood spread around the world, filmmaking branched into many genres. Musicals were made possible when sound was introduced in 1927; films like *Singin' in the Rain* in 1952 and *The Sound of Music* in 1965 are still considered classics. Musicals are still a viable genre. *Chicago* won the Academy Award in 2002, while *Dreamgirls* was critically acclaimed in 2006.

The romantic comedy genre made stars of Cary Grant, Doris Day, Rock Hudson, and Jimmy Stewart beginning in the 1930s. Moviegoers came to expect nail-biting suspense films whenever Alfred Hitchcock directed, and his films, including *Rear Window, The Thirty-nine Steps, Vertigo,* and *North by Northwest,* delivered spine-tingling fear in viewers. Director John Ford and star John Wayne typified the western genre, while Frank Capra focused on uplifting, happy endings typified by the still popular Christmas classic *It's a Wonderful Life* or the patriotic and inspirational *Mr. Smith Goes to Washington.*

It would be remiss not to note the contributions of current-day directors and actors. Director George Lucas's six-part Star Wars epic revived the science fiction genre with the release of the first film, *Star Wars,* in 1977. Steven Spielberg is one of the foremost contemporary directors and producers, whose oeuvre includes 1975s *Jaws;* 1981s *Raiders of the Lost Ark,* which launched Harrison Ford to superstardom; and 1993s best picture, *Schindler's List,* which also won him his first Academy Award for Best Director.

Other leading directors of contemporary Hollywood included Woody Allen, Martin Scorsese, Oliver Stone, Spike Lee, Penny Marshall, and Quentin Tarantino. Among movie actors in 2007, Keanu Reeves raked in about $206 million for his work in the *Matrix* sequels; Tom Cruise, Tom Hanks, and

Jack Nicholson were also good dealmakers by insisting on a percent of the box office.

While other media compete for Americans' time and can lure them away from theaters, the movies are still king. In 2006, the Motion Picture Association reported that the total U.S. box office take came to $9.49 billion, with *Pirates of the Caribbean: Dead Man's Chest* pulling in $423 million. Yet while going to the movies is still a viable activity, Americans are increasingly staying home to watch their flicks. In the United States, 37 percent preferred to watch movies in the comfort of their own home, according to the Motion Picture Association.[9] That trend began in the 1980s, when the VCR first was made available in the United States. Video stores allowed consumers to rent relatively newly released movies to watch at home. The technology shifted in the late 1990s to DVDs, but the home market remained strong. Cable television also entered the fray with pay-per-view technology that allowed consumers to watch feature films and on demand offerings.

The story of film censorship in the United States is almost as old as the industry itself. As early as 1907, nickelodeons were shut down for allowing children to view inappropriate short films. The film industry wasted no time policing itself. By 1916, the National Association of the Motion Picture

The movies in the *Pirates of the Caribbean* series have been some of the world's highest-grossing films. Courtesy of Photofest.

Industry was formed to oversee film content, and when that failed, to satisfy critics, filmmakers created the Motion Picture Producers and Distributors of America, led by former postmaster William H. Hays. The association accepted a Production Code, which came to be known as the Hays Code, in 1930. This self-censorship initiative was responsible for shaping the treatment of sex and violence in Hollywood in the 1930s. Some did not think it went far enough. The Catholic Legion of Decency was formed in 1934 to combat what it believed was a corruption of morals by the film industry. The list created by the Legion condemned certain movies it deemed inappropriate for anyone. Others it listed as appropriate for children or for adults. The list lasted until 1978 and condemned such movies as *From Russia with Love, Rosemary's Baby,* and *Grease.*

In 1968, the Motion Picture Association of America created its own voluntary film rating system, which is still in use today. The initial system included the ratings G for general audiences, M for mature audiences, R for restricted (under 16 not admitted without a parent or guardian), and X for no one under 17 admitted. The system has been fine-tuned over the years to include the PG (parental guidance suggested) and PG-13 (parental guidance suggested for age 13).

While the earliest film actors were anonymous, the star system emerged during the 1920s. The Marx Brothers epitomized comedy; Jean Harlow was a vamp; Edward G. Robinson was a gangster; Bela Legosi was typecast in horror films; Cary Grant and Clark Gable were two of the earliest leading men. As Hollywood actors and actresses became celebrities, they were able to command large sums of money for their work. Hollywood became known as Tinseltown.

The success of the 1939 film *Gone with the Wind* ushered in a golden age for Hollywood. The movie, based on the runaway best seller by Margaret Mitchell, won 10 Academy Awards in 1939 and held the record for making money for many years, before contemporary ticket prices knocked it out. It still holds the record for the most tickets sold.

The Academy Awards to recognize achievement in film were begun in 1929 in Los Angeles. The winners were given a distinctive gold statuette of a man to honor their achievements. Legend has it that film star Bette Davis, who won two and was nominated 10 times, dubbed the statue "Oscar" because it reminded her of her first husband. Held annually in the spring, the Oscars attract an international audience and generate hoopla for celebrities, who prance along a red carpet into the auditorium.

While other countries have established notable film industries, most especially Japan, India, and Italy, American films are the undisputed world leader. In fact, as moviegoing habits shifted with television viewing and then the VCR technology that brought the theaters into homes, American filmmakers turned increasingly to the export market to make up the financial difference. By 2007, more than half of American film revenues came from the foreign market, forcing filmmakers to pay attention to how a movie will play with foreign audiences. It was by no means a one-way street. Increasingly, Americans were open to viewing foreign films. The Chinese film *Crouching Tiger, Hidden Dragon* grossed $128 million in the United States in 2000.

MAGAZINES

Everyone reads magazines in the United States. Americans can be found thumbing through pages in doctors' and dentists' waiting rooms, at the barbershop, and even in line in the supermarket. Magazines, which are often highly specialized, are big business. In 2005, the average circulation for all magazines was a whopping 369,620,102—that is more than one magazine for every man, woman, and child. The Magazine Publishers of America estimates that 84 percent of the population over age 18 reads magazines, while it counts 18,267 separate titles, with 6,325 consumer titles.[10] In fact, in 2005, 350 new titles were introduced, most focusing on the niche marketing that has been so successful for magazine publishers. While broad-based magazines like *Newsweek* and *Time* continue to attract readers, publishers are more likely to find success introducing publications that fill small markets, such as *Arthur Frommer's Budget Travel, Acoustic Guitar,* and *Bow & Arrow Hunting,* to name a few.

Magazines began in the United States in 1741 in the American colonies. Ben Franklin's *General Magazine* debuted three days after his rival, Andrew Bradford, circulated his *American Magazine* in January 1741. The colonies might have been ready for one magazine, but two was just too much. Neither succeeded. Within six months, they had both folded. Over the next three decades, magazines tried to gain a foothold in the colonies, but none thrived. While newspapers became important propaganda tools during the Revolution, they were unable to garner a stable circulation base.

From the onset, magazines were a potpourri of many topics. Poetry, essays, politics, and the arts came together under one cover. The paper was cheap newsprint, and the covers were plain. Artwork and illustration were uncommon, although Paul Revere provided a series of cartoon engravings on copper for the *Royal American Magazine* that was published just before the war began. In all, 98 magazines were published during the eighteenth century, but one by one, they succumbed to economic realities. Magazines during that century were anything but vehicles for mass circulation and hovered at a circulation of about 500.[11]

It was not until the nineteenth century that magazines grew to be a staple of news and information. The *Saturday Evening Post* began publishing in

Philadelphia in 1821. Around this time, there also was a growth in literary magazines and religious publications. Initially, magazines appealed to the upper classes, with their literary content and the high subscription costs. Yet that characteristic faded as the century, with its swelling literacy and education rates, progressed. *Harper's Monthly* and *Atlantic Monthly* appeared at mid-century and catered to literary minds, but publications like *Frank Leslie's Illustrated Newspaper* and *Harper's Weekly* drew a more popular audience. The illustrations in these magazines, especially during the Civil War, appealed to the masses and paved the way for the picture magazines like *Look* and *Life* that captured American imaginations beginning in the 1930s.

The age of muckraking was most visible in magazines beginning about 1900. *McClure's* magazine had been founded in 1893 by Samuel McClure, who charged only 15 cents for each edition. By 1900, it had a solid circulation of 350,000, when it began poking its nose in the public's business. With solid staff writers like Ida Tarbell and Lincoln Steffens, *McClure's* was poised to make some noise. It became known as the most rigorous of the muckrakers after the publication of Tarbell's exposé of the abuses of Standard Oil and Steffens's series of articles on public and political corruption. The fervor of muckraking magazines faded with the onset of World War I. A new type of magazine emerged in the decade following the war. The weekly news magazines that we still know today trace their roots to this period. *Time* magazine was founded by Henry Luce and Briton Hadden. Hadden's involvement was short-lived, and the magazine in many respects reflected the tastes and politics of Luce. The first issue appeared on March 3, 1923. The news was mostly information rewritten from the week's *New York Times*. Editorial analysis was a part of the news coverage. The success of *Time* gave way to other ventures, including *Fortune, Life,* and *Sports Illustrated,* all of which survive to date. *Time* remained the most robust of the newsweeklies, ranking 11th in circulation, with a weekly circulation of 4 million. *Newsweek,* founded in 1933, ranked 16th, while the third popular news magazine, *U.S. News and World Report,* ranked 32nd.

The importance of women's magazines and their growth throughout the nineteenth century cannot be overstated. Women's place was the home and its domestic responsibilities, and women's magazines celebrated this sphere of influence. *Godey's Lady's Book,* which set the standard for women's publications for about 70 years, was begun in 1830 as the *Lady's Book* by Louis Godey. He then purchased the *Ladies' Magazine* and merged the two publications into *Godey's Lady's Book* and hired as its editor Sarah Josepha Hale. *Godey's* published original material at a time when many magazines were merely repositories for previously published articles. Hale sought out the nation's popular authors and poets for her monthly magazine and was rewarded with the likes of Harriet Beecher Stowe, Edgar Allan Poe, Nathaniel Hawthorne, and others. The magazine also provided women hungry for the fashions of Europe with illustrations of the latest dress styles. The magazine declined in popularity after the Civil War and eventually ceased publication in 1898, but its influence on generations of women's magazines is indisputable. Its mix of fashion, literature, and domestic, health, and child-rearing advice is evidenced in magazines even today. As *Godey's* circulation waned, *Ladies' Home Journal* gained ground. It topped the 1 million circulation mark in 1889, providing short stories, serialized novels, good artwork, and the promise, in an age of disreputable advertising, that it monitored the claims of its advertisers. In an era when newspaper and magazine editors were celebrities in the way that movie stars are today, *Ladies' Home Journal*'s editor Edward W. Bok, who took the reins in 1890, was the visible head of this women's publication for 39 years.

The *Seven Sisters,* a term that referred to the most powerful women's magazines of the twentieth century, included *Good Housekeeping, Ladies' Home Journal, McCall's, Redbook, Better Homes & Gardens, Family Circle,* and *Woman's Day.* These were the biggest guns in the women's magazine category, with astounding circulations throughout most of the twentieth century. *McCall's,* initially a vehicle to sell McCall's dress patterns to consumers, had a circulation of 6 million at its peak in the 1960s. In response to the growing popularity of *O, the Oprah Magazine,* the Hearst Corporation monthly that debuted in 2000, *McCall's* changed its name to *Rosie* in 2001 in an attempt to serve as a platform for talk show celebrity Rosie O'Donnell. That relationship flopped, and the magazine folded in 2002. All of the other Seven Sisters still publish. *Better Homes & Gardens,* with a circulation of 7.6 million, was the fifth largest magazine in the country at the end of 2005. *Good Housekeeping* was seventh, with 4.6 million; *Family Circle, Ladies' Home Journal,* and *Woman's Day* rounded out the top 10, according to the Audit Bureau of Circulations. *O* enjoys a 2.5 million circulation and a national ranking at number 23.[12]

While traditional women's magazines enjoy healthy circulations, niche magazines are the prevailing trend today. Magazines like *Southern Living, Brides, Parents, Endless Vacation,* and *Cooking Light* relied on smaller circulation populations but featured readers hungry for information about their topics. By playing to small pockets of readers, magazines have managed to thrive during a time that newspapers saw their influence waning.

The largest-circulation magazine in the United States in 2005 was the *AARP* magazine, with a 22.6 million paid circulation (membership in AARP was considered a subscription to the magazine); the *AARP Bulletin* ranked second, followed by *Reader's Digest.* That monthly magazine, which began in 1922, was the brainchild of DeWitt Wallace and featured articles condensed from other publications. That formula is still successful today. A staple for years in doctors' and dentists' offices, the *Digest* also relied on monthly regular features, including humor columns that featured pithy anecdotes sent in from readers. The oldest continually published magazine, the *New England Journal of Medicine,* began in 1812.

MEDIA IN THE TWENTY-FIRST CENTURY

In 2005, the Kaiser Foundation asked 8- to 18-year-olds to describe what media they had used the day before. The results are enough to send fear into the hearts of some of the media. Eighty-one percent of the group had watched television for an average daily time of a numbing three hours and four minutes. Twenty-one percent of the group had watched for more than five hours. Fifty-four percent had used the computer for recreational purposes totaling an hour. Thirty-four percent had read a newspaper (that figure contrasted with the 42% who had glanced at a newspaper five years before). The term *glanced* is correct, indeed, because the average time the group had looked at the newspaper was six minutes. Magazines fared slightly better: 47 percent had read a magazine in 2004 (compared to 55% in 1999). The average interaction lasted 14 minutes.[13] If this, then, is the future of the media, traditional newspapers and magazines have reason to be concerned. Newspaper readers are a loyal group, but it is a learned habit, and clearly the younger generation is not taking to it. By contrast, 67 percent of adults over age 65 read a newspaper in 2006. The bad thing about that group is that they have a tendency to die; just two years earlier, that figure had been at 74 percent.

Another national survey in 2005 showed that 59 percent of people get their news from local television, while 38 percent read a local paper, and only 12 percent read a national newspaper.[14] The demands for leisure time are great. Electronic explosions continue with new and better gadgets introduced each year before the holiday buying time: television, Tivo, iPods, Play Station, satellite radio, cell phones, Blackberries, Sidekicks, and always new and better computers.

Newspapers have been forced to change. Internet sites like Craig's List, eBay, Monster.com, and Autotrader have taken a bite out of the once lucrative classified advertising. Combined classified ads peaked in 2000 with earnings of more than $19.6 billion. Those dollars are slipping—by 2003, the total had slipped to $15.8 billion, according to the Newspaper Association of America. Classified ads had provided a cash cow for years; they were cheap to produce, with little overhead but a typist. Now, newspapers are fighting to regain their position as the purveyor of classified ads by making alliances with online providers.

Overall, the future is grim for newspapers. Profit margins have slid from 26 percent in 2000 to about 17 percent in 2007.[15] Circulation was also slipping, even though 51 million people still buy newspapers.

The smartest news organizations have accommodated the change and embraced Internet avenues. Newspapers, for example, have banded together to create a national employment service, CareerBuilder, to challenge the domination of Monster. In other advertising areas, the well-being of the newspaper revenues reflects the health of business and industry in general. Fewer large department stores translate into fewer Sunday ad sections. A downtrend in home sales means a dip in real estate advertising.

Not all the news for newspapers is dismal. Some newspaper companies have taken a lesson from magazine publishing and turned to niche publications. *The Miami Herald,* for example, has a separate daily edition in Spanish for its large Hispanic population. Gannett, the country's largest media conglomerate, has 90 newspaper markets but more than 1,000 niche publications in those areas, focusing on travel, health, and other topics of interest to its readers. Some newspaper companies have diversified onto the Internet, buying online companies or establishing joint ventures with some of the online giants. The message to newspapers is clear: change or die.

Newspapers are the oldest form of mass communication, but in the twenty-first century, they constitute just one aspect of an increasingly complex media system that is constantly evolving. The United States—indeed, the world—is in the midst of a communication revolution whose ultimate outcome cannot easily be predicted. How Americans will interact with their media in the future is fodder for science fiction writers.

Much is at stake. The future of journalism as a profession is unclear. News organizations have turned to their viewers and readers to provide information. Audiences respond to instant polling because it gives them a chance to have their voices heard. Popular television programs like *American Idol* can generate millions of viewers' votes: 74 million votes were cast in the *American Idol* finale in 2007. News outlets get hundreds of thousands of votes when they ask viewers their opinions on topical survey questions, and when a news outlet like CNN asks its viewers to submit news tips and stories, they respond. The news outlet then shares video clips of dramatic fires, eyewitness accounts of natural disasters, and first-person stories of human interest. The Internet, with its unlimited capacity for news, has opened the news hole. When news radio WINS tells listeners, "You give us 22 minutes, we'll give you the world," it underscores the fact that the radio station only has 22 minutes' worth of news and information. Network news shows last 30 minutes, including commercials. A typical newspaper is 60 percent advertising, 40 percent news stories. Thus the role of editor includes the burden of gatekeeping: deciding what news is and what is not. The Internet, with its limitless capacity, negates that role. News media can post any number of stories on their sites and let the reader or viewer decide what he is interested in.

The communication revolution continues. Like Winston Churchill's quip during World War II, this revolution is nowhere near its end. It is not even the beginning of the end, but it is, perhaps, the end of the beginning. Where it is headed is unclear. The only thing that is certain is that it will continue to be one heck of a ride.

NOTES

1. "Joint Statement by William P. Van Ness and Nathaniel Pendleton on the Duel between Alexander Hamilton and Aaron Burr," *New York Morning Chronicle,* July 17, 1804, reprinted in Louis L. Snyder and Richard B. Morris, eds., *A Treasury of Great Reporting* (New York: Simon and Schuster, 1962), 38–39.

2. Frank Luther Mott, *American Journalism* (New York: Macmillan, 1962), 438.

3. Mott, *American Journalism,* 679.

4. M. Thomas Inge and Dennis Hall, eds., *The Greenwood Guide to American Popular Culture* (Westport, CT: Greenwood Press, 2002), 4:1466.

5. Audit Bureau of Circulations, "Top 100 Newspapers in the United States," March 31, 2006, Information Please Database, http://www/infoplease.com/ipea/A0004420.html.

6. See "Sports and Television" from the Museum of Broadcast Communications, http://www.museum.tv/archives/etv/S/htmlS/sportsandte/sportsandte.html.

7. See the Motion Picture Association of America statistics, http://www.mpaa.org.

8. A time line of film industry development can be seen at http://www.filmsite.org.

9. For current film industry statistics, see the Motion Picture Association statistics at http://www.mpaa.org.

10. See *The Magazine Handbook,* Magazine Publishers of America, http://www.magazine.org.

11. Sammye Johnson and Patricia Prijatel, *Magazine Publishing* (Lincolnwood, IL: NTC/Contemporary, 2000), 49.

12. Audit Bureau of Circulations, "Top 100."

13. "Use of Individual Media by All 8 to 18 Year Olds," in *Generation M: Media in the Lives of 8–18 Year-Olds* (Menlo Park, CA: Henry J. Kaiser Family Foundation, March 2005), 23–33.

14. "News Source: Where People Get News," Pew Internet Project December 2005 Survey, http://www.infoplease.com.

15. Anya Kamenetz, "Public Interest," *Fast Company* 114 (2007): 38.

BIBLIOGRAPHY

Cousins, Mark. *The Story of Film.* New York: Thunder's Mouth Press, 2004.

Davies, David R. *The Postwar Decline of American Newspapers, 1945–1965.* Westport, CT: Praeger, 2006.

Emery, Michael, Edwin Emery, and Nancy L. Roberts. *The Press and America: An Interpretive History of the Mass Media.* 9th ed. Boston: Allyn and Bacon, 2000.

Endres, Kathleen L., et al., eds. *Women's Periodicals in the United States: Consumer Magazines.* Westport, CT: Greenwood Press, 1995.

Endres, Kathleen L., et al., eds. *Women's Periodicals in the United States: Social and Political Issues.* Westport, CT: Greenwood Press, 1996.

Inge, M. Thomas, et al., eds. *The Greenwood Guide to American Popular Culture.* Vols. 1–4. Westport, CT: Greenwood Press, 2002.

Johnson, Sammye, et al. *Magazine Publishing.* Lincolnwood, IL: NTC/Contemporary, 2000.

Martin, Shannon E., et al., eds. *The Function of Newspapers in Society: A Global Perspective.* Westport, CT: Praeger, 2003.

Miraldi, Robert, ed. *The Muckrakers: Evangelical Crusaders.* Westport, CT: Praeger, 2000.

Mott, Frank Luther. *American Journalism: A History, 1690–1960.* 3rd ed. New York: Macmillan, 1962.

Project for Excellence in Journalism, et al. *The State of the News Media, 2007: An Annual Report on American Journalism.* http://www.stateofthenewsmedia.com.

Sloan, William David. *The Media in America: A History.* 6th ed. Northport, AL: Vision Press, 2005.

Snyder, Louis L., et al. *A Treasury of Great Reporting.* New York: Simon and Schuster, 1962.

Washburn, Patrick S. *The African American Newspaper: Voice of Freedom.* Evanston, IL: Northwestern University Press, 2006.

8

Performing Arts

Pamela Lee Gray

The thing about performance, even if it's only an illusion, is that it is a celebration of
the fact that we do contain within ourselves infinite possibilities.
—Sidney Smith (1771–1845)

AMERICANS LOVE TO be entertained. *American Idol, Ted Mack's Amateur
Hour,* and a host of other similar television and radio programs broadcast
over the decades illustrate the American fascination with live performance,
professional or amateur. A century ago, social commentators argued whether
the country should consciously develop a shared performance culture. Instead, the geography of the American continent influenced development of
a regional character, and instead of sculpting a shared identifiable tradition,
these regional styles, along with some borrowed elements from the country's
immigrants, created a unique culture in theater, music, and dance.

THEATER

Early American theater mimicked European performances and acting techniques. Although records are incomplete for this period, most theater scholars name Anthony Aston as the first professional actor in America in 1703.
(Aston was, however, preceded by Native American spiritualists who regularly played roles in rituals.) Williamsburg, Virginia, boasted a dance school
and theater as early as 1716. Philadelphia constructed a playhouse where
Pickleherring pieces, a genre of acting that followed European clowning
techniques, were performed. The City of Brotherly Love was the center of

colonial theater activity until 1825. Walter Murray and Thomas Kean took simple shows on tour through many of the colonies. Charleston surged ahead of the other colonial cities with a new theater constructed in 1736; at that time, the New York City theater scene paled in comparison.[1]

The London Company of Comedians (later changed to the American Company), led by Lewis Hallan Sr., and then by David Douglas, held a monopoly on professional theater productions from 1752 until 1755, when Hallan's son took over his father's part of the team. The pair constructed and revitalized theaters throughout the colonies, much to the disapproval of religious groups, who held that plays advocated immoral behavior (despite the subtitle *A Moral Dialogue* attached to most plays' titles). Douglas built two of the most important theaters in the colonies in New York in the 1760s and put on the first play written by a native playwright. The Continental Congress banned all stage performances in October 1774, but American playwrights continued working even as British troops captured cities and put on their own military performances in the colonial theaters. The period after the Revolutionary War was a time of rapid theater construction, as acting companies returned and new troupes were formed. French-speaking theaters were constructed in New Orleans and Charleston. New York challenged Philadelphia for the title of theater capital of the colonies but was not recognized as a serious contender until 1800.[2]

There is a perception in America of a clear division between art and the business of art. Vaudeville and musicals were considered a separate venue from Chautauqua and operatic performances. Eighteenth- and nineteenth-century promoters of stage musical and dance performances found that production funds were easy to obtain if the act was perceived as having a reasonable morality, but more importantly, a chance for widespread popularity. Stephen Price, the first professional manager in America, began promoting European actors in the United States in 1809. American actors, however, were not cast in important plays in Europe until much later. Edwin Forrest was the first American actor to make a name abroad. Playwriting contests, beginning in 1828, encouraged homegrown American writing.

As the United States acquired land with each act passed by Congress beginning in 1815, theaters and acting companies moved into the new territories. Floating theaters were located on showboats that traveled the Mississippi River. The Boston Museum began its stock touring company in 1841, and the troupe prospered for nearly 50 years. San Francisco received professional acting troupes from the east in 1850; actors were well compensated for their long journey and for facing dangers in the western territories.

The 1850s established a clear American tradition on the stage, with the high period for theater profits running from the Civil War era until 1915.

Matilda Heron, an actress with an overtly dramatic technique, rose to fame in 1857 in historical costume dramas that were all the rage. Most of the plays, if viewed today, would be considered campy with their stilted, unnatural dialogue, but the theater moved toward a more realistic approach in the following decades. The melodrama, a style that rose to popularity in the 1860s, always had a dramatic turning point such as the rescue of someone (usually a damsel tied to railroad tracks). One of the most famous of the moral plays was *Uncle Tom's Cabin,* which opened in 1852 with a mostly white cast in blackface. Blacks played other roles, but not the major parts in the production. Translations of French plays were also popular during this decade.

By the 1870s, plays about social issues were in vogue; comedies and dramas covered timely issues. Territorial expansion and the rise of the American West was a popular topic that aligned with the phenomenal sales of the dime novels, purportedly chronicling the lives and times of gunslingers, outlaws, and mysterious natives of the new territories. A star system developed beginning in the 1880s, with Edwin Booth, Edwin Forrest, and Charlotte Cushman commanding top salaries. John Drew and Georgina Drew Barrymore (an ancestor of the contemporary Drew Barrymore) followed. Popular actors, prior to the turn of the century, regularly built their own theaters to showcase their talents.[3]

Circuses attracted crowds in Europe, and this performance tradition was brought to the colonies. The first tented show was used in 1825 for the (Joshua Purdy) Brown and (Lewis) Bailey Circus. This allowed flexibility in folding up the tent and transferring the performers, animals, and temporary structures to a new city along the route. Prior to that time, circuses required large structures or construction of a semipermanent building for even the smallest shows. With names such as the Great Overland, Dog and Pony, and the Wild West Show, troupes of acrobats—performers skilled in shooting, knife throwing, and horseback riding—brought to eastern cities a stylized version of the West.[4]

Buffalo Bill and Pawnee Bill had traveling shows that recreated fictionalized battles between Native Americans and cavalry troops. Buffaloes were transported from town to town in an attempt to recreate the West for eastern audiences. The largest modern circuses were the Ringling Brothers, founded in 1886, and C. F. Bailey & Company's Famous Menagerie, collected originally in 1870 by P. T. Barnum to tour under the name Grand Traveling Museum, Menagerie, Caravan and Circus. When the two combined, they came close to living up to the billing Barnum used for the company, "The Greatest Show on Earth." The circuses of Bailey and Barnum, when combined with the huge touring company of the Ringling Brothers—Gus, Alf, Al, Charles, John, and Otto of Baraboo, Wisconsin—were without competition in 1907 for the title of greatest on earth. Ringling Bros. and Barnum & Bailey shows continue to perform today, with two touring troupes throughout the United States and Canada. Each year, a performer is selected to be the featured headliner for marketing the tour.[5]

Part of the early spectacle of the circus featured a person on horseback serenading the audience in the sawdust ring. Spirituals were frequently sung, and this tradition was adopted in the later minstrel format. The organizational structure of the minstrel show was established between 1843 and 1850. Edwin P. Christy made his name synonymous with this type of theater as the white-faced master of ceremonies, known as Mr. Interlocutor, who directed the three distinct parts of the production: the formal opening, with an introduction; the second section (the olio), which featured a collection of variety acts, including at least one long speech and a man dressed in women's clothing acting in a so-called wench segment; and the finale, later known as the walk around, that showed the actors promenading around the stage, reminding the audience of their part in the variety portion of the show. The finale of the longer productions incorporated a short play, usually depicting plantation life, or a watered-down version of a well-known Shakespearean tragedy.

The music was an important feature of minstrel shows. To the audience's right was a banjo or tambourine player, whom the master of ceremonies referred to as Mr. Tambo (and later as Mr. Lean). The left side of the stage featured a man, Mr. Bones or Mr. Fat, who played rhythm with wooden spoons or bone clappers. In the center rear stage was a group of singers and dancers, given names such as Congo Melodists or New Orleans Serenaders, who added variety to the performance in between acts. Additional instrumentation was also located to the rear of the stage and included bass, drums, and fiddles. The early minstrel bands were the precursors to the modern jazz band in formation and the types of instruments used. The stage became an oval of talent, with the guests performing in the middle facing the audience. The repartee and interaction was fast, and the humor was under the direction of a competent Mr. Interlocutor. People from all social classes and religions attended minstrel shows; unlike burlesque and later vaudeville performances, most ministers did not speak from the pulpit against attendance at minstrelsy. Minstrels' popularity lasted until the 1870s, when African American actors and performers began to be used with white actors in performances and theater construction became more widespread.[6]

Burlesque used the minstrel show format but expanded the type of performances to include more leg. In an age when the uncovered ankle or wrist would bring more than a raised eyebrow, the appearance of legs (even seen through thick tights) was shocking to moralists. The most popular burlesque first arrived from Europe, and the best-known actress was Lydia Thompson, who led a troupe of British Blondes that filled theaters in the late 1870s and the early 1880s. Burlesque, too, developed its own unique format. The first section of the show featured only singing and dancing women (a rarity in early theater) and male comedians. The second section followed the format of the minstrel shows with variety acts, and the third part offered the walk around, or grand finale, with finely dressed but scantily clad women parading on the stage. This walk was later taken on a long lighted runway that extended out into the audience. The early burlesque shocked sensibilities with the fact that female performers were included in usual entertainment fare, but the farther west the theater genre moved, the rowdier and rawer the burlesque became.[7]

The Ziegfeld Follies, the brainchild of Florenz Ziegfeld, proved that sex did sell. Ziegfeld used the French Folies Bergère as inspiration for his annual extravaganza that included modeling, posing, and female formations by his famous Ziegfeld girls. He claimed his productions "glorified the American girl," though the earliest featured the European actress Anna Held. In his production *Miss Innocence* (1908), each female was dressed elegantly, often in an elaborate headdress. Held and Ziegfeld split in 1913, but he continued to produce large-scale musicals with other stars. Singer Eddie Cantor, comedians W. C. Fields, Will Rogers, and Fanny Brice, and paired dancers featuring the latest dance steps were featured in the vaudeville-type Follies shows. Irving Berlin was a regular composer for the troupe, and Joseph Urban laid out the artistic design for the elaborate staging and set decoration. The Follies began in 1907 and ended in 1928, and then Ziegfeld transferred his staging to the big screen in a series of films that included elaborately choreographed dance productions before he died in 1932.[8]

The Minsky Brothers (Morton, Billy, Abe, and Herbert) made burlesque into an art form from 1900 until 1935 from their chain of theaters in New York. Belly dancers were first introduced, and then lighted runways, and ultimately performances showcasing strip tease dancers wearing twirling tassels, a costume innovation introduced in 1921. Gypsy Rose Lee, Anne Corio, Willie Howard, Jackie Gleason, and Phil Silvers (who would later become family favorites on television) as well as Abbot and Costello (film comedians after their stint in burlesque) were well-known burlesque entertainers until 1942, when burlesque was banned. The remaining performers went into strip clubs and Las Vegas shows in the early 1950s, after the circuit was shut down by police enforcing pornography laws.[9]

Vaudeville was a variety show that developed from circus performances, the variety portion of minstrel, burlesque, and patent medicine shows. The term *vaudeville* was used early in the 1870s by Benjamin Franklin Keith, considered to be the Father of Vaudeville. Keith opened his own theater and museum in Boston in 1883, and from the profits, he then constructed the Bijou Theater. His productions followed strict standards of acceptable performance, allowing working-class Americans to attend in large numbers. Edward F. Albee later joined Keith as a partner, but the team had fierce competition. The two men were able to control the circuit until well after Keith's death through the establishment of booking agencies such as United Booking Artists and the Vaudeville Manager's Association; these limited the acts' participation in theaters that the team did not own. They pioneered the use of continuous shows lasting 12 hours, with performances by 7–10 live acts. Performers in upscale vaudeville and traditional theater houses had only two performances each day. Vaudeville never died, but rather faded away with the invention of radio and expanded construction of inexpensive movie palaces. Many popular actors of the 1920s through 1940 trained in vaudeville, including Bob Hope and Al Jolson. Over 25,000 performers graced the vaudeville stages from the 1880s through the 1920s.[10]

Theater fans make a clear distinction between regional theater and the rural theater of summer stock, even though summer stock usually attracted audiences from a specific region. The distinction between the two is that regional theater was considered highbrow and summer stock lowbrow. Regional theater had professional actors, playhouses, and productions, while summer stock frequently used amateur actors, some of whom even paid to be involved in the performances. This should not diminish the significance of summer stock in building culture in rural America. As the once-massive Chautauqua circuit faded, summer stock theater rose to popularity in the 1920s and 1930s in the Northeast. Professional and amateur actors, stage crews, production designers, and directors were hired each summer to put on a group of plays, or a new play each week, in independent theaters that attracted upper- and middle-class vacationers from nearby summer resorts. Some theater historians claim that summer stock is the only true regional theater in the United States. English and early American theaters had resident actor stocks, but summer stock did not operate year-round. English theater companies did not have a separate group to be involved exclusively in summer productions.

Summer stock theaters operated during the months of June to September, from Maine to Virginia to Pennsylvania in the west. By the 1930s, some houses offered touring companies, and most had a permanent playhouse. Summer stock venues ranged from converted barns to small theaters constructed specifically for the permanent summer company. Early playhouses used local talent, then shifted to the star system that employed a featured actor (often on hiatus from Broadway shows that were closed during the hot summer months of July and August), and finally used a combination of the two during the 1960s. Playwright Eugene O'Neill premiered his first work in summer stock at the Provincetown Wharf Theatre in Cape Cod, Massachusetts, in 1918. Summer stock's popularity first came with the automobile, which allowed escape from the summer heat of the city, and the new road system that made getting to rural resorts easy.[11]

American theater came into its own during World War I. European plays and actors were not visiting as frequently, and the influence from Europe on American staging and plays was minimal. The First International Exhibition of Modern Art, held in 1913 at the building that normally housed the 67th Regiment Armory in New York City, with its American and European paintings and sculpture, challenged the traditional definition of art and encouraged people working on the stage, and in set and costume design, to take greater artistic risks. The Broadway theaters in New York became the center of America's theater world at the turn of the century, routinely taking productions from Philadelphia and Chicago.

During the Depression years of the 1930s, theaters received funds from the Federal Theatre Project, a part of President Franklin Delano Roosevelt's Works Progress Administration (WPA) that provided salaries for unemployed designers, writers, actors, and stage workers. The program, under the direction of Hallie Flanagan, came under fire in the late 1930s for employing members of the Socialist and Communist parties and for producing works that attacked big business. *The Living Newspaper,* a short-lived experiment in theater design, was abandoned when federal funding was abruptly cut after elected officials objected to criticism from the quickly written plays that interpreted the economic, political, and social issues from the front pages of the news. The electric industry was mocked for the high prices for service in the play *Power.*[12]

The period from 1900 to 1932 saw theaters in New York City dwindle from 5,000 houses to only 132. Travel was limited during the Depression and World War II due to fuel shortages and restrictions on hard-to-find products such as natural rubber, which was used to manufacture automobile tires. After World War II, there was a resurgence in theater and summer stock productions. The decades between 1945 and 1965 are considered the brightest of the Broadway stage. The plays or musicals of Lerner and Loewe, Tennessee Williams, Rogers and Hammerstein, William Inge, and Arthur Miller were performed to small audiences in theaters that were built decades before, without expensive audio and lighting equipment: the play was the thing. Musicals starring Shirley MacLaine, dramas with headliners such as Geraldine Page and Marlon Brando, and plays and shows that remain on Broadway in revivals today—*West Side Story, Cat on a Hot Tin Roof,* and *A Streetcar Named Desire*—were first performed in this period.[13]

During their heyday, the summer theaters brought recent Broadway hits, comedies, and melodramas to new audiences. Between 1930 and 1960, summer stock employed more theater folk than any other venue in America, including Broadway. The Ford Foundation, under the direction of W. Mac-Neil Lowry, gave generously to the arts, but by the 1960s, the middle classes could travel by air to exotic locations, and attendance at summer stock venues and on Broadway fell. Many small Broadway theaters and summer stock venues could not attract enough revenue and were abandoned. A few regional theaters continue to perform historic dramas; Roanoke Island, North Carolina, Tamiment in the Pocono Mountains, and Green Mansions in the Adirondack Mountains remain in operation today.[14]

Funding has always been a concern for theater productions, and the federal government created assistance in the form of the National Endowment for the Arts, which provided nearly $3 million in grants in 1966 and increased the figure each year until it reached over $162 million in 1995. After a long period of increases, the legislature was motivated by constituent letters over funding for art that offended some sensibilities and took a red pen to the arts budget, reducing funding to $99 million. During the period from 2004 through 2007, the funding remained around $124 million for future years.[15]

American theater frequently experimented with avant-garde productions in the decades between 1920 and 1970, notably in theaters appealing to workers and union members. The Workers' Theater, Workers Drama League (later called the New Playwrights Theater), and the Theater Union put on performances to illustrate the struggles of the working class and promote a political transformation in America. The 1950s and the early 1960s saw little experimentation in the mainstream theater, but the late 1960s into the 1970s were much different. The Open Theater performances attempted to eliminate the invisible barrier between the actors and the audience and meld them together in plays such as *The Mutation Show* by Joseph Chaikin (produced off Broadway) and the Bread and Puppet Theater's *Fire*, which challenged America's position as aggressor in Vietnam. Sitting was not an option at *Fire*, as symbolic masked figures were allowed the freedom to move through the audience in a theater devoid of traditional seats.[16]

There were only 23 regional theaters in the United States in the early 1960s, but by 2007, the number had mushroomed to over 1,800. Many are new structures with state-of-the-art lighting and sound systems. The smaller venues offer new playwrights an opportunity to get produced without the large financial losses a Broadway production could incur. Some famous writers prefer to test a new play in a small venue before opening a Broadway play or touring production. The top five regional theaters year in and year out in the United States include the Old Globe Theatres in San Diego, California; the South Coast Repertory in Orange County, California; the Goodman Theater in Chicago; the American Repertory Theater in Cambridge, Massachusetts; and the Guthrie Theater of Minneapolis, Minnesota.

The Guthrie continues to lead all small theaters in the country, with 32,000 season ticket subscribers. Playwrights such as Arthur Miller have premiered works on this stage with the company's seasoned actors. Theater founder Sir Tyrone Guthrie directed the first production, Shakespeare's tragedy *Hamlet*. The project grew out of a plan that Guthrie made with Oliver Rea and Peter Zeisler to establish a resident acting company and a venue to stage the classics, far away from Broadway's glare and pressure for success. The group did not select Minneapolis; in fact, the city selected the Guthrie planners. A Drama Section appeal in the *New York Times* brought offers from seven cities, but Minneapolis brought more than interest: it brought funding and cooperation with the theater arts program at the University of Minnesota. The T. B. Walker Foundation donated land and a sizable fund to be put toward the theater's construction. With Ford and McKnight Foundation grants providing monies for construction and operation, the Guthrie opened in 1963. The focus of the Guthrie has changed with the appointment of each new artistic director, but over the decades, the theater has been given a Tony Award for outstanding contributions to American theater and is routinely included in lists of America's best regional theaters. It now includes a touring theater group and a lab theater that explores the works of contemporary playwrights.[17]

While regional and local theaters have gained audiences, Broadway fans have seen a decline in offerings since the mid-1960s. Stage productions have been transformed into films on a regular basis since the beginnings of the film industry, but playwrights have also taken films and transformed them into stage shows. The most notable series of successful plays adapted for screen are those of the Marx Brothers. Brothers Harpo, Chico, Groucho, Gummo, and Zeppo clowned their way to Broadway success in nearly a dozen shows. However, only two of the recreated stage plays, *Duck Soup* (1933) and *A Night at the Opera* (1935)—productions not usually noted as high art—are listed by the American Film Institute among the 100 most significant films in movie history.

The Wiz, a restaging of the 1939 classic movie *The Wizard of Oz*, won Tony awards for choreography and costume design in 1975. The stage version of the 1951 film *Sunset Boulevard* received critical acclaim when it was introduced in London and then toured the United States in the 1980s. More recently, modern films that are box office successes without critical acclaim have made their way to Broadway. *Legally Blonde* and *Hairspray* join remakes

The Broadway show *Rent* struck a chord with audiences in the 1990s. Courtesy of Photofest.

of Disney animated features and have drawn a new generation of theatergoers. Popular music from the 1960s is currently featured on Broadway in *Jersey Boys* (chronicling the life of the Four Seasons singing group) and *Dream Girls* (a fictionalized portrayal of Motown's Supremes). *High School Musical*, a popular Disney television movie with a plotline revolving around musical theater, has drawn teen and "tween" wannabes to Broadway in droves. Broadway shows are experiencing longer lives for productions and musicals. *Cats, Chicago, Beauty and the Beast,* and *Phantom of the Opera* are currently in contention for record-breaking runs on Broadway.[18]

SYMPHONIC MUSIC AND OPERA

The evolution of classical music performance in America has always suffered somewhat from what might be called a frontier mentality. Two and a half centuries ago, if someone in town owned a violin, there could be music for a village dance. However, if the village had to be defended in battle, or if everyone was needed to bring in the harvest, the violin was packed away in its case and stayed there until leisure time returned. American society has always viewed serious music as a luxury, not a necessity. When an economic recession looms in modern times, charitable giving to symphony orchestras falls off steeply; when school levies fail, the first programs to be cut are music and the other arts—that is, if they had not been discontinued in favor of the study of math or science years before.

What is remarkable is how far the performance of classical music in America has come. Folk music, church music, and any number of singing styles came over with the first immigrants. Parents who could afford instruments and music lessons had their children study the piano or the violin, and music was made in the home—voice and keyboard, soft-toned classical guitars, even a string quartet. Choirs could always be mustered even in small towns, and any talented singer drew an audience; but in times when concerts of orchestral or chamber music were exceedingly rare events, Americans' appreciation of instrumental music was honed by *playing* it, not listening to it.

The nation's first major symphony orchestra, the New York Philharmonic, was formed in 1842. Over a period of many years, a Big Five of symphony orchestras arose, comprising some of the oldest from the biggest cities. The Boston Symphony Orchestra (1885), the Philadelphia Orchestra (1900), the Chicago Symphony Orchestra (1891), and a relative newcomer, the Cleveland Orchestra (1918), joined the New York Philharmonic in an unbreachable clique that persists to the present day. Despite ascents to fame by other fine orchestras—those of St. Louis, Cincinnati, San Francisco, Baltimore, Pittsburgh, Minneapolis, and Los Angeles, just to name a few—the Big Five have always paid the highest salaries, received the most lavish financial endowments, attracted the top conductors and best players, made the most recordings, and retained their mystique even during periods of artistic decline. Opera houses also acquired a hierarchy. No American house will ever overtake the fame of the Metropolitan Opera in New York City, even if other superb companies, such as the Chicago Lyric Opera or those of Houston or San Francisco, occasionally mount better productions.[19]

It is no accident that the majority of America's most prestigious musical organizations are east of the Mississippi River: out West, music lovers had to wait longer while cow towns slowly morphed into civilized metropolises. Many millionaire American industrialists lavishly supported their home cities' cultural institutions, not only out of local pride, but also to attract executives and keep them in town. During the nineteenth century, as with theater productions, much of American art music was imported from Europe: famous composers, singers, violinists, pianists, and conductors toured the United States, and some of them stayed. One hundred years ago, when Vienna's master conductor Gustav Mahler rehearsed the New York Philharmonic, he spoke German to the musicians because so many of them were immigrants from Germany and Austria.

Only gradually did American musical education begin to produce musicians competitive with those of Europe, and as of a century ago, no American composer had made a true international reputation. On the other hand, in the early decades of the century, the top opera singers, such as Enrico Caruso, were as fascinating to the masses as rock stars are today. The twentieth century saw a remarkable rise in American musical prestige. Europeans, including conductors Arturo Toscanini and George Szell, tenor Caruso, pianist Arthur Rubinstein, and soprano Maria Callas, continued to dominate the American musical landscape. However, by the 1940s, the music of American composers, such as George Gershwin, Aaron Copland, and Samuel Barber, attracted international attention, African American singers Marian Anderson and Leontyne Price were major stars, and a young man from Boston, Leonard Bernstein, was entering the prime of a career that would outshine that of any other American musician.

Classical music performance in the United States in many ways reached its golden age in the late 1950s, with Bernstein—composer, pianist, educator, and the first American to be given the post of music director of the New York Philharmonic—becoming a popular television idol with his *Omnibus* and *Young People's Concerts*. Bugs Bunny sang Wagner, comic actor Danny Kaye conducted orchestras, and a great many young Americans learned instruments and played in school ensembles. The rise of the musicians' unions gave professional players protection from the long-held tyranny of conductors, and the top American orchestras began to be recognized as the most technically accomplished ensembles in the world.[20]

A gradual decline set in beginning in the 1960s. American composers, many now tenured on university faculties and safe from the whims of audience tastes, began writing cerebral music that left the public behind. Recordings, which had been beneficial in spreading classical music to the masses, also lessened the motivation for people to learn to play instruments themselves or to attend public performances. As the century waned, the nation's tastes changed. Televised sports dominated weekends, and attention spans grew shorter as TV shows, with commercial breaks every few minutes, took firm hold of the public. Classical music, long perceived as a pleasure mainly for the elite and educated, began to fall victim to the traditional American suspicion of anything highbrow. Rock 'n' roll, R&B, and country music, exploding in popularity, required no background musical knowledge to enjoy. As the world economy shifted, major American corporations were acquired by overseas concerns, and their sense of obligation to local American cultural institutions vanished. Rich families shifted their attention to the humanities, rather than the arts, and individual charitable giving faded as the baby boomer generation came to power.

Citing a lack of innovative and imaginative composers focusing on their audience, but instead writing with an eye toward the history of music and theory, one South African music scholar has suggested that classical music died as early as 1950, after making a slow decline from 1939: music scholars, university-trained theorists, and intellectuals made up more and more of the concert audience, and the public less and less.[21]

After 1970, most school systems cut their string orchestra programs entirely, and the remaining wind and brass students were busier with marching band than with concerts. Fewer and fewer youth wanted to learn the clarinet or trombone since playing guitar in a garage band was undeniably cooler. Many American classical music institutions, saddled with huge fixed costs and accustomed to being bailed out by deep-pocketed donors, began to languish in an era when even a nonprofit entity must pay its own way or vanish. The Tulsa (Oklahoma) Philharmonic, one example out of many orchestras that have suffered, faced a million-dollar deficit and was forced to cancel the remaining concerts in its 2002–2003 season.[22]

Classical radio stations changed format to sports, light rock, or talk. Most symphony orchestras felt they had to play more pops concerts to stay afloat, in the process further dumbing down the public taste, just as Broadway was reduced to adapting more popular movies and cartoons for stage productions. Most record companies had ceased to record classical music by the end of the twentieth century, with classical releases today averaging only about 100 new discs a year, compared to nearly 700 in the 1980s. A top classical artist such as cellist Yo-Yo Ma is far better known for a crossover CD with pop star James Taylor than for his recording of the Bach suites. The Three Tenors, Placido Domingo, Jose Carreras, and Luciano Pavarotti, helped accelerate these trends during their 1990 concert tour: operatic high points for which audiences used to happily wait an hour or more were now strung together in machine-gun fashion.[23]

Classical music exists in today's mainstream media only as endlessly repeated excerpts of four or five tired favorites, grotesquely compressed into background music for TV commercials. In the wake of September 11, 2001, American philanthropy in the performing arts dropped off grievously, while the painstakingly built endowment funds of opera companies and symphony orchestras dropped precipitously with the stock market. The marketing of many classical soloists and singers now depends more on their physical and photogenic appeal than their musical artistry. The high costs of tickets are another barrier to popularity: theater managers maintain that the price of a ticket covers less than half the cost of the production today. Ticket prices for the New York Philharmonic in 2007 rivaled those of top-rated rock acts, and most orchestras perform today with only 60–65 percent of audience seats filled.

Savvy symphony promoters realized, with the success of Little Einstein and tops of the charts classical music CDs for children, that if their organizations were to survive, they must hook parents on the idea that classical music provides children a head start on skills necessary for college and success in life. The Internet assisted in this project. The San Francisco Symphony and the Boston Symphony Orchestra developed kids' sites offering interactive games, images, music feeds, and downloads, but kids are not the only group who require education in the classical literature. Most orchestras now provide adult educational concerts and concert previews to educate the audience about how to appreciate the musical works and biographical background of the composer. For listeners who do not care to dress for a performance in formal wear or even long pants, many orchestras now offer casual dress concerts. Most symphonies now program with a hook, such as a meet-and-greet singles event. Orchestras have seen increases in attendance when a tie-in to television or popular culture is used, such as voting off a section of the orchestra or playing movie music while screening silent films. Opera companies have found some success in projecting supertitles (translations of opera texts) on a small screen above the stage. The Met reached some new audiences in 2006 with live closed-circuit high-definition television broadcasts (shown across the country in movie theaters) of Mozart's *The Magic Flute,* staged by the producer of *The Lion King,* with the music severely shortened to cater to modern attention spans.

Despite all efforts, classical music, never attractive to a major percentage of the public and now scantily funded, hovers on the edge of irrelevancy, while TV reality shows, NASCAR, *American Idol,* and ultimate fighting define the pop culture trend in American tastes. If the complete disappearance of classical music in America seems unlikely, so does a significant comeback.

DANCE

American dance did not break away from the European influence until the introduction of modern dance in the early 1920s. Dance became a hot topic in America and garnered major press coverage when the first belly dance was performed at the World's Columbian Exposition in 1893. Early dance performances catered to specific ethnic groups, featuring wooden shoes or clogs. Clog dancers were frequently used as comic relief in variety shows and performed the clown dances. Modern clowning, or *krumping,* shares similar moves with break dancing. Military clogging and clog dances were often part of local variety shows, and a novel form of the dance became popular with the minstrel and vaudeville shows. Clog shoes and acrobatics were featured in a bizarre performance that required the dancer to do steps atop a pedestal. The smaller the tap area, the larger the audience the performer would draw.

American classical dance performances relied heavily on European ballet, and until choreographer Vaslav Nijinsky and composer Igor Stravinsky premiered *Le Sacre du Printemps (The Rite of Spring)* in Paris in 1913, all ballet followed strict conventions for performances. *The Rite* flew in the face of the classical traditions of both music and dance, and police were called to restore order in the audience after fighting broke out between supporters and detractors of the new forms. Russian promoter Sergei Diaghilev was quite pleased with the open controversy. American ballets were inspired by this creative impulse in ballet and began to interpret dance in their unique way. Portions of *The Rite of Spring* today remain standard repertory for many professional companies.[24]

America developed a rich ballet and modern dance tradition. American dancer Isadora Duncan inspired modern dance with her so-called free dance performance in 1899. Her light, free-form costumes, bare feet, and long, flowing hair shocked the dance and theater world in United States, but audiences in Paris loved her. Duncan returned to the United States with dancers Loie Fuller and Ruth St. Denis to set the stage for a transformation of the way in which dance was perceived. Formal dance, hard-toed shoes, and strict interpretation gave way to open, interpretative dance performed in flowing costumes. Duncan was killed in a freak car incident when her scarf became tangled in the wheel of her sports car in 1927 at the age of 49, but Ruth St. Denis and her husband, dancer Ted Shawn, carried on the modern dance tradition in their school that opened in 1914. This group of dancers, including Duncan, Shawn, and St. Denis, are now called the first generation of American modern dancers.

Doris Humphrey, Charles Weidman, Martha Graham, and Edna Guy, students at the Denishawn School, became the second generation. Martha Graham danced at Denishawn until 1923, when she became a principal soloist in the *Greenwich Village Follies* three years later. Graham continued choreographing and started her own modern dance company, overseeing it until her death in 1991. The company carries on her vision today in performances around the world.[25]

Ted Shawn was instrumental in developing the role of the male dancer beyond partnering the female in lifts and turns. Ted Shawn and his Men Dancers gave their first performance in Boston in 1933 and changed the world of dance. Shawn revolutionized dance performance, both in his methods and in the promotion of the art form. His students would become the future leaders of dance in America. Merce Cunningham, Alvin Ailey, Robert Joffrey, Agnes de Mille, and Pearl Lang all benefited from his instruction, mentoring, and promotion. Shawn's festival Jacob's Pillow, established in 1932 as a home for American dance and a center for his company, is America's longest continuously running dance festival. It offers dance workshops, professional performances, and training, with over 80,000 visitors attending classes and performances each summer. Shawn died in 1972 at the age of 81, but Jacob's Pillow, named for the farm in the Berkshires in western Massachusetts where the festival is held, continues to share "Papa's" spirit of the dance.[26]

Since the organization of the Ballet Negre, founded by Katherine Dunham in 1930, detractors of African American dancers as professionals claimed that they were not suited to perform classical ballet owing to differences in the European and African body styles. African American dancers were required to overcome both racial and artistic discrimination. Edna Guy and Hemsley Winfield danced *First Negro Dance Recital in America* in 1931, and by 1937, Eugene Von Grona created the American Negro Ballet with dancer James Weldon Johnson, garnering favorable reviews from major white news sources. The Negro Dance Company, created by Felicia Sorel and Wilson Williams, danced the choreography of Ann Sokolow, a dancer trained by Martha Graham. African American dancer Katherine Dunham, appointed the director of ballet for the Federal Theatre Project in 1938, performed in *Tropics and Le Jazz Hot* in New York in 1940, which established her as a sought-after star. That same year, her dance troupe joined the Broadway musical *Cabin in the Sky,* an all–African American production. Despite the discrimination the group faced, white audiences regularly attended performances. The creation of the Dance Theater of Harlem, under the direction of dancers Arthur Mitchell (a principal dancer in the New York City Ballet) and Karel Shook (Mitchell's dance teacher), took the debate head-on in 1969 by creating a ballet school. The company first met in the basement of a Harlem church and now is known throughout the world for its efforts in educational programming and dance performance. Today, contemporary dance companies routinely feature African American dancers such as Carmen de Lavallade, Dudley Williams, and Gus Solomon, and African Americans direct important dance troupes, including Judith Jamison, who has taken over the position of artist director of the American Dance Theater from the late Alvin Ailey.[27]

The 1960s and 1970s saw a boom in dance, reflected in the number of dance schools and new companies founded. The story of the Ohio Ballet (OB) is a textbook illustration of the highs and lows of a dance company. OB was founded in 1968 by artistic director Heinz Poll and associate director Thomas R. Skelton (also an award-winning lighting designer). The company toured the United States, South America, and Europe to good reviews. Union dancers were paid for 36 weeks per year, but by the late 1980s, pay cuts were necessary. Beginning in 1975, the company established a tradition of putting on a six-week summer program of free shows on outdoor stages in northeast Ohio. OB's National Endowment for the Arts (NEA) funding was reduced in the 1980s, and revenues for its more cutting-edge repertory were not as high as those of ballet companies performing classical story works such as *Swan Lake*. With Skelton's death in 1994 and Poll's retirement in 1999, the company took stock. Reorganization efforts resulted in a permanent home (and a 15-year contract) at the University of Akron in 2003, with the state of Ohio and a group of foundations offering funding for the new Center for Dance and Music. The plan was for the company to work with the university in creating a higher profile for fine arts on the campus. OB also performed in residence at the Cleveland Playhouse Square Center, but financial difficulties and lack of attendance at their performances forced the company to incorporate with the Cleveland Ballet.[28]

Cleveland and San Jose appear unlikely partners for a ballet company, but because of funding difficulties, the two companies attempted to work together, giving the first position in the ballet's title to the city where they were performing. Office staff was in place in both cities, and the dancers lived and trained in Cleveland but performed in both places. A formal announcement ended the company's 25th season and split the partnership. Half of the dancers joined the reconfigured company, Ballet San Jose Silicon Valley (popularly known as Ballet San Jose), and the other group of dancers joined small companies in the Cleveland area. Performances for the San Jose company today include *The Nutcracker, Carmina Burana, Swan Lake,* several Balanchine ballets, and Stravinsky's *The Firebird*.

While Cleveland topped the list in 2005 and 2007 of major U.S. cities with the highest percentage of the population living in poverty, sponsors for the new Ballet San Jose are plentiful and include Fry's Electronics, SanDisk, eBay Foundation, Linear Technology, and the William and Flora Hewlett Foundation (part of the Hewlett and Packard partnership), proving that location is an important component for a dance company. Dancers from four regional ballets with rights to perform Poll's choreography today, along with a group of dancers who studied with Poll, continue the tradition of putting on free summer performances in Akron public parks, but the formal dance company no longer performs. The series is called the Heinz Poll Summer Dance Festival, in honor of the artistic director and founder of the Ohio Ballet.[29]

Like symphony performances or operas, classical dance is not a big money-maker. Traditionally, performances in the arts have been dependent on a patron, and ballet has followed that pattern to modern times. A handful of national companies, usually banking and financial institutions with local branches, sponsor many regional or large local dance companies. Many other countries provide backing for national dance companies, but that has never

been the case in the United States. Some states offer competitive grant funding for the arts, and many ballets use these renewable funds for operating
expenses. Most funds have strings that require companies to do outreach
concerts to rural areas. Federal funds are available in the form of specialized
grants, many from the NEA. Congressional support (in terms of the amount
of money budgeted for the NEA) periodically wavers, and some decades
have found high-priority public issues pressuring elected representatives to
reduce cutting-edge performance funding. Strings currently attached to federal grants almost uniformly require the recipients to offer low-cost or free
performances for the public and at elementary, middle, and high schools.
Grant applications must outline a regional need and a unique proposal to
address that need.

During the years when NEA and state funding is tight, avant-garde and
controversial projects are rarely funded. This forces many companies to go for
attendance money and perform only holiday and story ballets, further widen-
ing the gap in dance education and creating situations in which audiences
come to stereotype ballet as "women as swans." Large dance companies have
a grant writer on staff who works year-round to obtain funding. Smaller companies have staff members that take on the grant writing duties in between
their own assignments or ask community members to volunteer for the task,
with mixed results. A professional grant writer usually has an advantage over
volunteer efforts. Success attracts the successful, and the companies with international reputations attract the largest amount of capital. Even with ongoing
funding difficulties, a number of American dance companies have international reputations.

Tap Dancing

Dance had a revival in the 1960s and 1970s, and interest in tap dancing
also increased. Tap is one of the pure American cultural innovations, and a
long line of dancers have developed the art. European clog and jigs, mixed
with African immigrant rhythms and improvisations, form the basic elements
of tap. Early saloon dancers Uncle Jim Lowe and William Henry "Juba"
Lane were documented step dancers who toured the country before the Civil
War, often appearing in racially integrated shows. Lane traveled to London
to perform and challenged noted Irish step dancer Jack Diamond to a dance-
off. Although a clear winner was never established, Lane billed himself as the
"King of Dance." Whites adopted tap dancing, notably Thomas Dartmouth
"Daddy" Rice, who tapped in his productions in 1828. Rice, a minstrelsy per-
former, used blackface to portray the stereotypes of the dandy and the clown.
Black dancer William Henry "Juba" Lane gained fame with his dancing in
1840. Several schools of tap developed, with one group using wooden shoes

(sometimes called "buck and wing" style) and the other a smooth-sole shoe style, where the dancer would shuffle, rather than loudly pound, the shoe on the stage. These two styles integrated by the 1920s to utilize a smooth shoe with metal plates affixed to the toe and heel.

The Floradora Sextet, turn-of-the-century female dancers, tapped out a synchronized routine that the Ziegfeld Follies chorus line adapted into a regular performance feature. Eubie Blake and Noble Sissle created a show called *Shuffle Along* that played on Broadway in 1921, creating national interest in tap. Personal innovation in tap led to a group of dancers called Nerve Tappers, who would tap as many beats with the foot as a loose ankle would allow. All vaudeville performers from the 1920s onward were expected to perform some form of tap as well as the black bottom and the Charleston, made popular in Broadway shows.[30]

Two levels of touring tap performers developed: flash and class acts. The flash acts included attention-getting tap steps and acrobatic moves to awe audiences, while the class acts frequently used a story line that focused on their smooth steps and graceful movements. Honi Coles and Cholly Atkins were a noted class acts duo, and Bill "Bojangles" Robinson would later join child star Shirley Temple to popularize the class act for movie audiences. Children growing up in the 1930s frequently took tap lessons to tap just like Miss Temple. Some groups developed a style that allowed them to play both the flash and class venues. The Nicholas and Condos brothers are the best-known duos of this type.

The 1930s and 1940s saw Fred Astaire, Ginger Rogers, and Ray Bolger bring tap to the movies, and both tap and popular dance schools sprang up across America to teach adults the buck and wing and shuffles. Residents in large cities and small towns alike wanted to learn to dance. Americans in the Midwest attended weekly lessons in a studio, while many city dwellers tapped informally on street corners. Top tap acts routinely borrowed and adapted steps from street tappers. Actors and hoofers Buddy Ebsen and Gene Kelly carried on the tap legacy into the 1950s on the big screen and Broadway. In the 1970s and 1980s, tapping was again the rage with Broadway hits such as *On the Twentieth Century* and a remake of the 1920 stage hit *The Girlfriend.* Tommy Tune choreographed tap dances for a new group of Broadway hits and families of tappers, such as Gregory and Maurice Hines, who followed in the steps of the brothers Harold and Fayard Nicholas and the Covan Brothers.[31]

Actors from earliest times were trained in dancing and singing, in addition to acting. Although not popularly known for their dance prowess, actors James Dean and Marlon Brando were students at the Dunham School of Dance in New York City. Dramatic actor Christopher Walken, known for his

Gregory Hines, right, danced his way into fame through the 1970s and 1980s with movies such as *History of the World: Part I* and Broadway shows such as *Jelly's Last Jam.* Courtesy of Photofest.

roles in films such as *The Deer Hunter* and *Pulp Fiction,* is a trained tap dancer who starred both in Broadway and on film in the musical hit *Chicago.*

POPULAR MUSIC

Popular music performance, once centered on the parlor piano and family entertainment at the community school auditorium, underwent a metamorphosis with the invention of the radio. Radio featured professional performers and moved music from a personal event to a regional, national, and even international experience. With the invention of the television, listeners no longer had to imagine the appearance of the performer. Sound and music records, made at 78 rpm and 45 rpm, and then long-play records of 33 1/3 rpm, were popular for decades (along with tape cassettes from the 1960s onward), but these were swept away by CDs in the 1980s. Music videos, which exploded on the scene in the 1980s on MTV, had an indelible effect on the public's perception of musicians. After 2000, the Internet moved popular music into the future, offering downloading capabilities in both sound and the capture of visual images. Despite the availability of entertainers on the

Internet, live concerts remain popular in the United States. Rock concerts are the most popular and bring in the highest revenues.

The legacy of culture-changing rock performances began with Elvis Presley and the first American tour of the British band the Beatles, but bands touring the United States had their origin in the early jazz orchestras that traveled from city to city during the period 1914–1919. Restrictions were placed on African American musicians near New Orleans that made it difficult for them to obtain work permits, so many left the area and began touring. The original Creole Orchestra is a typical example. Organized in Los Angeles by Bill Johnson in 1909, the group of displaced New Orleans jazzers, including Freddie Keppard, James Palao, and George Baquet, toured from 1914 through 1918 (ignoring requests to make recordings of their music). Their dance music was not well received due to the basic difference in audiences: northern audiences expected to listen to the music, but New Orleans audiences expected to dance to it. The music became known as ratty because of the improvisational style used when the five-instrument band played. The Creole Orchestra dissolved in 1918, but this period established a touring tradition that future rock bands would emulate to earn a living.[32]

Musical tours prior to the 1950s usually included dancing by audience members. Religious, classical, and country performers developed circuits that they would tour each year, but the guitar-playing vocalist Elvis Presley would change this pattern. Presley performed live in Shreveport, Louisiana, on the *Louisiana Hayride* radio program (a competitor to the Grand Ole Opry) and was an instant hit. He signed a contract committing him to a weekly show for one year, and it was during this work that he met and signed with promoter Colonel Tom Parker, manager to stars Eddy Arnold and Hank Snow. From this partnership, Presley was able to cross over from country music to the new rock 'n' roll, a musical format that had similarities to early jazz in that it encouraged dancing. Elvis recorded, made movies, and toured, garnering top rankings on the hit parade and in performance tours until the early 1960s and the introduction of English groups to the American musical market. He continued to perform developing into a Las Vegas headliner for showrooms until his death on August 16, 1977.[33]

The British Invasion of the 1960s brought the Beatles, the Rolling Stones, the Animals, Herman's Hermits, the Zombies, and the Kinks. The Beatles, one of the first groups to write all their own songs, were also the first to play at large venues once reserved only for sporting events. Shea Stadium hosted the Beatles and nearly 60,000 screaming fans on August 15, 1965. The concert was so successful that the stadium agreed to host many more rock concerts, including the Police, Elton John, and a 1970 Summer Festival for Peace with Jimi Hendrix and Janis Joplin.[34]

Large-scale rock outdoor music concerts were pioneered in the 1960s, and the largest was in New York State. The Woodstock Music and Art Festival holds a unique place in the history of popular music. The first event took place from August 15 to 17, 1969, on land rented from farmer Max Yasgur near the towns of Bethel, Woodstock, and Wallkill. The young concert promoters, Michael Lang, Artie Kornfeld, Joel Rosenman, and John Roberts, planned for attendance of nearly 200,000, but by the time the event concluded, estimates put the weekend crowd in excess of 400,000. Fans trampled fences and declared Woodstock a free event, denying concert promoters any profits and opening the organizers to a host of lawsuits from vendors and local residents for damages. Word of mouth and radio disc jockeys hyped the event, and crowds swelled, blocking the roadways into and out of the grounds.

Singer-songwriter Richie Havens played for hours before any of the other performers were able to reach the stage. His song "Freedom," entirely improvised while on stage, is remembered as an anthem of the festival. The rock group the Who played a 24-song set. The Grateful Dead; Crosby, Stills, Nash, and Young; Santana; Jefferson Airplane; Janis Joplin; and a host of others,

A Woodstock '99 concertgoer hammers a pay phone off of a burned out Bell Atlantic phone truck. Rioting broke out after the three-day festival ended. © AP Photo/ Stephen Chernin.

some arriving by helicopter to reach the stage, played to crowds left for an entire summer weekend without food, shelter from the rains, and sanitation. Woodstock was a failure for its promoters, but it created music history, immortalized in a record and film that carried the music to millions. An attempt at a Woodstock revival in 1994 was peaceful but failed to capture the spirit of the first concert. Woodstock '99, promoted again by Michael Lang, ended with a riot by several hundred fans, who torched vendor trailers, claiming they were angered by prices of $4 for a bottle of water.[35]

Rock groups gave titles to their tours in the 1970s, many named for recently released albums. Large arena rock tours in the 1980s began the evolution of concert themes. David Bowie performed as Ziggy Stardust with the Spiders from Mars, and rock group KISS and Alice Cooper morphed into ghoulish figures with costumes and full-face makeup. Ozzy Osbourne bit off a bat's head in one performance and used this as a theme for later tours, biting heads from plastic bats in each city the tour played.

Performers today make more from touring than from music sales, and some groups tour year-round to earn income and keep tour crews working. The Grateful Dead was formed in the San Francisco Bay area in 1965, while the members lived at 710 Ashbury Street. The group and the Haight-Ashbury district became part of a music scene that would make both famous. The international media in 1967 drew national attention to what is now called the "Summer of Love," and hippies from the world came to San Francisco to hear live music, wearing flowers in their hair as gestures of peace in the time of the Vietnam War. The Grateful Dead, along with other oddly named musical groups called Jefferson Airplane, Quicksilver Messenger Service, and Moby Grape, gave free concerts in parks. The Dead added to their legend in performances with author Ken Kesey.

The group continued to tour regularly for decades and became legendary for shows featuring space music, incorporating hours of improvised music solos fans called *The X-Factor*. Illegally recorded bootleg albums and tapes, encouraged by the group, were feverishly traded among diehard fans, angering record executives, who felt the practice denied profits to the record company. The Grateful Dead performed 85 concerts in one year, even though the group failed to have a hit song on the charts or to be included in a regular rotation on any syndicated radio programming. Even after the death of group leader Jerry Garcia in 1995 at the age of 53, the remaining members, known simply as The Dead, were still a top act on the college music circuit. Group members sold merchandising rights to T-shirts, bumper stickers, and hats to build their personal fortunes.[36]

The top touring acts in the country in 2007 included rock music groups that have been in the industry for decades, including Pearl Jam, Rush, the

Rolling Stones, Genesis, Guns N' Roses, Bob Dylan, Bon Jovi, the Who, and Aerosmith as well as the Police, returning after a 23-year hiatus. Industry insiders speculate that the revival tours earn top dollar because of the age of the audience, many of whom have established careers with a large amount of disposable income. Fans spent an average of $130 to be serenaded by former Beatle Paul McCartney on his tour in 2002, while new acts such as Nickel-back set concertgoers back less than $30. Rumors claimed that ticket scalpers received over $3,000 for front row seats to Sir Paul.[37]

Outdoor amphitheaters were the top live music rock concert draws in the 1980s, but today, many have closed. Arena concert venues allow larger crowds, and now that groups and record labels market their own T-shirts and posters, there is less profit to be made in owning a venue that features a large amount of land. The dramatic increase in land values, especially in states with moderate climates, has made home building far more lucrative.

Hip hop and rap music performances began to develop in large metropolitan areas such as New York City and Los Angeles in the 1970s. Local performers developed styles that integrated regional characteristics and combined with exotic influences that included Jamaican "toasting." Toasts were done by disc jockeys playing records (usually American R&B) at live dances to encourage the dancers. Toasting evolved to encompass a practice known as "dubbing," where the DJ would select short phrases (samples) from the record. Samples would be manipulated using the turntable to create individual styles. Competitions, or "battles," took place between competing DJs. These performance styles came to the United States in the mid-1960s and were integrated into musical forms called "rapping" and "hip hop" that began to grow to popularity in the 1970s. Dance forms, such as locking, popping, clowning, and flow, were an integral part of live performances and audience participation, and each performer developed a style and a fan following. Some noted live performance DJs were: Theodor, inventor of "scratching," a process that influences the speed of the record; Grandmaster Flash (George Saddler) who developed "punch phasing" (adding percussion from one record to highlight the beat of the main recording); and The Fat Boys, a group that perfected using human sounds to create percussion (a "Human Beat Box"). Afrika Bombaataa and the Zulu Nation were an early hip hop act that focused on dance and music, rather than on the gang aspect of performance music. Regional Zulu Nation clubs were established around the country.

Early rap music was associated with gang activity and, as the music style became more mainstream, rappers began touring the United States. Violence broke out at some concert venues and communities passed laws banning rap performances. There is debate as to whether rap and hip hop appealed to white and black audiences alike at first, but record companies and concert promoters began to target white audiences. The three-member rap group Run D.M.C. sold out concert venues across the country in the 1980s. Females, targets of abuse in early rap records and live stage performances, began earning top honors for rap music in groups such as Salt 'N' Pepa. By the mid-1980s, hip hop evolved into more than just music and dance: the hip hop culture included dress, hairstyles, and a unique slang vocabulary. By the 1990s, spontaneously arranged dance parties called "raves" featured all types of music but featured hip hop performers.

Latin, Salsa, Tex-Mex, and Tejano music are now also a major component of American performance culture. Latin influences were first found in the folk music performed in the southwestern United States from the earliest U.S. history, and popular music in the United States has been influenced by Latin culture since before the turn of the nineteenth century. Couples danced the rumba and tango to orchestra music of the 1920s and dancers added the mambo and conga line to the popular dances in the 1940s and 1950s. Once confined to areas of the country with large Latin populations, performers such as Gloria Estefan's Miami Sound Machine and Carlos Santana brought Latin influences to the pop charts in the 1970s. Jennifer Lopez, Ricky Martin, Christina Aguilera, and Tex-Mex singer Selena attracted sellout audiences to performances in the 1990s. Latin music today is considered to be a mainstream musical offering.

REGIONAL PERFORMANCES

French observer Alexis de Tocqueville noted the regional differences of the American landscape and culture when he toured the country in 1831, and those unique characteristics remain at the heart of American performance today. Each region offers unique performance opportunities and has developed a culture of music theater and dance performances.

The North

British tastes established the criteria for performance for the first colonies that would later become the United States. As the colonists constructed theaters, they became aware of the differences between French and British performances versus American offerings. The symphony orchestras in Boston, New York, and Philadelphia first set the bar for American classical music, and the public still looks to these cities to uphold the standards of performance. Theater productions may rehearse and offer trial runs in other parts of the country, but the ultimate objective is to fill theaters on

Broadway. Other important performance traditions have developed in the American North.

Upstate New York is the home of the Chautauqua Institution. The Chautauqua movement grew out of a public desire to experience the performances written about in magazines and newspapers that were held at the Chautauqua Institution at the lake in southwestern New York State. The summer sessions originated in 1874 with Lewis Miller of Ohio and John Heyl Vincent of New Jersey as a Sunday school camp and quickly expanded into performances and instruction that included art, music, and physical education courses for teachers. The program grew with the creation of the Chautauqua Literary Scientific Circle, which encouraged reading and, beginning in 1878, gave rise to tens of thousands of reading circles through the country.

Lectures were well established by 1880 and featured speakers on a wide range of topics, including politics, literature, philosophy, and international relations. Educator John Dewey directed the preschool classes at the institution, and both the Boys' and Girls' Clubs had constructed buildings on the grounds by 1902. Melvil Dewey began training librarians in 1900. The Chautauqua Institution for Lifelong Study was officially chartered in 1902. Ironically, the country's least capable president, Ulysses S. Grant, was the first U.S. president to attend classes and lectures at the institution, putting the camp on the wealthy class's list of *the* place to be in the summer. Among the most popular speakers were women's rights advocate Susan B. Anthony, aviatrix Amelia Earhart, First Lady Eleanor Roosevelt, composer and conductor John Philip Sousa, and (decades later) Supreme Court Justice Sandra Day O'Connor.

Magazine reading was a popular pastime at the turn of the century, and residents of rural towns and villages across the country wished to expand their knowledge, but they were unable to travel to the institution or were shut out by competition for tickets to the choice performances each summer. The traveling Chautauqua experience was created to bring the institution to these families. At the height of the movement, 21 troupes traveled 93 circuits throughout the United States, performing for and teaching more than 35 million people each year. A typical night at a tent performance in the Midwest might include speeches by a Populist Party member explaining the difference between the silver and gold economic platforms, a union leader from the Knights of Labor listing reasons why labor unions should be legal in all industries, musical performances of hymns or a selection from an opera, and a dramatic interpretation of a piece of classical literature or scripture reading from the Bible. The Chautauqua's aim was education, but the crowds clearly viewed the performances as entertainment.

For a time traveler from today, the Chautauqua circuit would have resembled a live presentation of the History Channel, mixed liberally with a large dose of the Public Broadcasting Service. Something at the two- or three-day program was bound to capture the interest of every member of the family. A full music program was offered at the New York summer camp, beginning in 1929, with the establishment of the Chautauqua Symphony Orchestra. The group continues to perform each summer at the 5,000-seat Victorian-style outdoor stage. An opera and ballet company and a conservatory theater were added to perform in halls built on the grounds for their exclusive use. Despite financial ups and downs, including a bankruptcy in 1933, the institution continues to put on a full summer session, attracting an average of 150,000 people to the picturesque village on the lake each year.[38]

The Tanglewood Festival, located in the Berkshire Mountains of western Massachusetts, is the summer musical venue for the Boston Symphony Orchestra (BSO; and its offshoot, the Boston Pops) as well as a group of select music students. The place that earlier inspired Nathaniel Hawthorne's children's stories *The Tanglewood Tales* has hosted the BSO since 1937. After a disastrous inaugural performance, during which the audience, musicians, and instruments were soaked in a summer rainstorm, a pavilion designed by Finnish architect Eero Saarinen was constructed. In the 1950s, Tanglewood banned women in shorts from sitting in the pavilion, claiming that uncovered legs were indecent. Bare-legged female visitors were forced to rent skirts at the festival entrance or sit on the lawn to listen to the performance. Bowing to recent public pressure to incorporate a visual element, Tanglewood has added a film night. On these special nights, the conductor and orchestra play original film scores, while movies are projected on a screen above the stage. Over 5,000 music fans today can be seated under the open-air shed, women in shorts are now allowed admission to any seat they wish, and an additional 10,000 music fans can picnic and take in the performance under the stars. Since 1990, Tanglewood on Parade has become a tradition that includes a finale with Tchaikovsky's *1812 Overture* and concludes with a fireworks display. Tickets to the event are always sold out, and television stations broadcast the performance across the country.[39]

The Newport Music Festival began in Rhode Island in 1969 as a summer performance location for New York's Metropolitan Opera. The location turned out to be unsuitable for opera, but the festival has continued with a series of more than 60 chamber music performances over 17 days each July, many of which use members of the Met Opera Orchestra. Among the festival's notable performances have been recitals by award-winning violinist Andrei Gavrilov and pianist Bella Davidovich. The Newport Jazz Festival (also in Rhode Island) began in 1954. This August, outdoor, exclusively jazz festival is considered the first of its kind in the world; most of the world's great jazz artists have passed through Newport during the summers. Singer

Dave Brubeck performs during the Newport JVC Jazz Festival in Rhode Island. © AP Photo/Joe Giblin.

Mahalia Jackson brought gospel to a new audience after performing at the venue in 1958. The festival closed down in 1971 but was revived again in 1981 by the original founders, jazz club impresario George Wein and financial backers Louis and Elaine Lorillard. The current management team, JVC Family of Jazz Festivals, now produces 117 jazz festivals across the United States and claims attendance of over 40,000 musicians and live audiences of nearly 4 million people since the group took over production in 1990. Dave Brubeck, Etta James, Dizzy Gillespie, Jack DeJohnette, and Branford Marsalis are but a few of the top musicians who have headlined at this granddaddy of jazz festivals.[40]

The Midwest

At the close of World War I, African American musicians toured or relocated from the South to midwestern and northern cities in search of work. New Orleans bassist and bandleader Bill Johnson settled in Chicago after touring failed to bring in the profits he had hoped for. He invited his friend Joe Oliver to join him since Chicago's economy was booming and music venues were opening around the city. Jazz was still a tough sell for most audiences until 1917, when jazz recordings began to educate audiences on the improvisational nature of the music. Mississippi riverboats began to hire jazz musicians to play for dance party excursions, and the jazz age was born. Rooftop dining and dancing became the rage, and Chicago became the place to be for jazz in the 1920s.

When the Storyville brothels and clubs were closed during this period, additional musicians went looking for work in music in the Windy City. Joe Oliver headed his King Oliver's Creole Jazz Band, with a young newcomer named Louis Armstrong on trumpet. Despite societal discrimination, white patrons hired African American orchestras to play for events. The 1930s saw jazz bands expand from five pieces to larger numbers. The orchestras also featured soloists. Duke Ellington, Paul Whiteman, and Fletcher Henderson headlined the top jazz clubs and hotel ballrooms in Chicago and around the country. Bluesmen from the South also came to Chicago. Little Walter, Sonny Boy Williams II, and Big Walter Horton were regulars on the local club circuit.

Blues and jazz went through a series of changes, splintering into diverse styles, and by the 1960s, Thelonius Monk and Miles Davis rose to be the top jazzers. Chicago Blues developed its own identifiable style, featuring a small string band with amplified instruments, percussion from a piano or drums, and a harmonica; some groups added a saxophone to the mix. Chicago blues usually has a single person on vocals. Important Chicago bluesmen Willie Dixon, Carey Bell, and Freddie King became known throughout the world for their individualistic styles. Jazz and blues clubs can still be found throughout Chicago today, and fans claim that districts specialize, with separate venues for bebop, big band, swing, fusion, experimental, delta, jump, and Chicago styles.[41]

The South

The Grand Ole Opry in Nashville, Tennessee, is the capital of country and bluegrass music. The first performance hall, built by the National Life and Accident Insurance Company, was home to live stage shows featuring banjo pickers and fiddle players, singers, and comedians who were broadcast to radio stations across the country under the call letters WSM (We Shield Millions). The Opry changed homes many times to allow for increasing audiences, and Hank Williams, Pete Seeger, Woody Guthrie, Flat and Scruggs, Patsy Cline, Dolly Parton, Porter Wagoner, and the Sons of the Pioneers appeared at the various early venues. Early Opry acts performed for the weekend broadcasts and toured the country in tent shows and auditoriums across the country during the week. The Opry continues to tour, but not at the frenetic pace of its pioneers.

Performances at the Opry today can be heard on a two-hour weekend radio program broadcast to over 200 markets as well as on satellite radio, the

The Grand Ole Opry is the longest continuously running radio show in the world.
© AP Photo/Mark Humphrey.

Internet, and the Armed Forces Network. Performers have been featured on television since 1955 and are now seen on the Great American Country cable channel. The solid oak center stage of the Ryan Auditorium, which has housed the Opry since 1943, was moved to a new Opry house in 1974 and continues to host fans to live music performances each year, with broadcasts on both radio and television. Ambassadors, members of the Academy of Country Music with sponsorship of the Opry, have toured since the 1930s, bringing country, western, and bluegrass music to the world.[42]

The city of New Orleans is a street performer's dream. Tap dancers, singers, horn players, and bucket drummers occupy city street corners each day and into the night. Carnivals are cultural events in the Big Easy. The influences of French costume balls and parades, masked Caribbean carnivals, and African music rhythms and melodic curves are evident each year at the Mardi Gras celebrations. Named for Mardi Gras Day in 1699, when a camp at Point du Mardi Gras was constructed near the present-day city, the first documented parade took place in 1837, but most historians cite 1857 as the inaugural Mardi Gras—the first with a parade and ball organized with a unifying theme. The Mystic Krewe of Comus, Merrie Monarchs of Mirth carried torches to light the parade path in an organized and nonviolent parade. The entire city, however, joined the revelry in 1872 and expanded the party with the selection of the king, an official flag, and an anthem adapted from a popular burlesque show. Burlesque sensation Lydia Thompson was, in fact, a guest for the parade. Mardi Gras began as a religious celebration and has expanded over the decades to include multiple types of performance art. Rebuilding after Hurricane Katrina has been slow, but the residents stood together and offered small parades and celebrations only a few months after the devastating storm. Attendance at Mardi Gras increases each year, as additional hotels and restaurants open in the city.[43]

New Orleans's Preservation Hall in the heart of the French Quarter draws crowds from around the world to hear jazz musicians play. The hall is old and surprisingly small. The audience sits on worn wooden chairs and benches, while the band plays the improvised jazz that music historians claim as an American innovation. Thousands visit the hall, and the associated jazz festival held each year in April attracted a crowd of over 600,000 in 2001.[44]

Grassroots music festivals such as the Southwest Louisiana Zydeco Music Festival have been organized in an attempt to maintain the history of a specific musical genre or performance style. Fearful of the disappearance of the Creole tradition of the La La (house dance), where homemade gumbo and a *bouchere* (hog roast) are enjoyed, a group of Louisiana residents formed the Treasure of Opelousas and organized a festival in 1982 to celebrate Creole and zydeco music and customs. Groups performing at this venue regularly use *frottiers* (washboards), spoons, and a fiddle to play dance music. The festival puts on a month of events that include an old-fashioned ball, where the king and queen of zydeco are crowned; a jam session; a breakfast; and dances, culminating in a one-day musical extravaganza near the first of September each year in Plaisance, Louisiana.[45]

The Bonnaroo Music and Arts Festival, begun in 2002, is held each June in Manchester, Tennessee (60 miles south of Nashville) on a 700-acre farm. It became the world's most profitable music festival in 2007. The event features performances on eight stages, with jam bands, such as Cat Power and Death Cab for Cutie, to more traditional bands, such as that of Phil Lesh (an original member of the Grateful Dead) and Blues Traveler.

The West

The Monterey Pop International Pop Festival was conceived by Alan Pariser after he attended the Monterey Jazz Festival. Pariser felt that pop music had matured as an art and that a pop festival would showcase talent in the same way that the jazz festival did. Record executive Benny Shapiro and rock producer Lou Adler joined the planning and recruited one music group, the Mamas and the Papas, who eventually bought out the promoters and turned the festival into a nonprofit event. A foundation was created, with a board of directors that included Paul McCartney, Mick Jagger, Paul Simon, Smokey Robinson, original Beach Boy Brian Wilson, and others. After extensive planning, over 30 acts were booked to perform at the first festival in 1967, including the Who, the Jimi Hendrix Experience, Buffalo Springfield, the Byrds, Johnny Rivers, Otis Redding, and Janis Joplin with Big Brother and the Holding Company. The Whitney Museum in New York featured a four-month exhibit in 2007, "The Summer of Love: Art of the Psychedelic Era," commemorating the 40th anniversary of the festival that many cultural observers view as a watershed event in the history of pop music.[46]

Colorado has made a concerted effort since 1960 to encourage the creation of festivals offering live performances throughout the state. Since the late 1940s, Aspen has held an annual classical music festival that now runs from June through August and is the only rival to Tanglewood as the top American summer experience for classical music students and performers. Bowing to the waning of audience members for the classical performances, the festival merges seamlessly into Jazz Aspen Snowmass (which has featured more cross-over rock than pure jazz in its most recent seasons). Former Colorado mining town Telluride has offered its own set of musical celebrations since the 1970s; classical music fans can enjoy nine days of performances there. For those whose tastes run to bluegrass or country, since the early 1970s, the summer solstice has been brought in at the Telluride Bluegrass Festival. Originally conceived in hard-core bluegrass style, the event now sees rock and jazz musicians joining pickers on stage for concerts.[47]

While New York City is the U.S. birthplace of the Poetry Slam, the West is home to a unique form of spoken word performance termed *cowboy poetry*. When most Americans think of cowboys, they probably visualize a man in jeans, western shirt, and boots who is driving a pickup truck, but both male and female ranch hands still ride the trails on horseback in many parts of the West. Even more surprising, many also celebrate their trade through poetry.

In celebration of their western heritage, cowboy poets, including the Gauchos of the Pampas, Fisher Poets, Badger Clark, Baxter Black, and Paul Zarzyski, interpret their poems at public gatherings. One of these, the National Poetry Gathering, has been held since 1983 at the beginning of each year at the Western Folklife Center in Elko, Nevada. The American national cowboy poet spirit has grown to the point that contests are also held in Heber City and Moab, Utah (including a Buckaroo Fair); Monterey, Big Bear Lake, and Santa Clarita, California; and Sierra Vista, Arizona. All of the venues have held contests for nearly a decade or more. The events range from simple spoken word presentations and weekend contests to more fully staged poetry events that include guitar and banjo picking to accompany the poems. Some poets do more than just read; they yodel and call the little dogies on the trail. Many events have separate judged contests in tall tale spinning, storytelling, and a challenge to find the best bold-faced liar. Some of these poets and pickers have become so well known that their programming at the National Cowboy Poetry Gathering in Elko has attracted major sponsors and Nevada Humanities Council funding. National Public Radio regularly broadcasts the poetry performances.[48]

The western states are known for rodeos, but the term "rodeo" was not generally used until after 1920. Rodeo began as informal contests between herders, wranglers, and ranch hands and developed into a circuit of competitions and performances throughout the United States, many in states outside the West. Each ranch would send one of its best hands in each category to compete in early rodeos, usually after the cattle were brought to market. Some accounts trace the first documented rodeo to Arizona in 1864, although it did not offer

A competitor in the bull-riding event of the ninth annual Idaho Women's Pro Rodeo. © AP Photo/Ted S. Warren.

award money or prizes. The first contests included challenges in riding and roping and featured two professionals who rode the cattle trail that ran beef from Abilene, Kansas, to an area northwest of Pecos, Texas. Trav Windham and Morg Livingston were the main challengers at the first contest held on July 14, 1883, but other cowboys, including a few females, joined the competitions. The contest jumped to another class with the move to its present location in 1936 and the construction of a professional arena and audience viewing stands.

Eastern rodeos have their roots in the Wild West shows that toured the nation since the Civil War. The elaborate productions that included drama, panoramic displays, and animals were a natural addition. Many western cities added rodeos to town heritage celebrations. Some of these events, with rodeos, are still held today, including the Pendleton (Oregon) Roundup and the Cheyenne (Wyoming) and Prescott (Arizona) Frontier Days. Modern rodeo is organized into timed and roughstock events. Bronc-riding and bull-riding contests are termed *roughstock,* owing to the wild nature of animals ridden in the ring. The rider must touch, or spur, the animal to gain points. Timed events include roping, wrestling (sometimes called *dogging*), and barrel racing. The first official rodeo circuit was created in 1934, with competitions in large cities, including the eastern and midwestern metropolitan areas of Detroit, Philadelphia, Indianapolis, Boston, and New York. The current headquarters for professional rodeo is located in Colorado, has over 7,000 members, and sanctions nearly 700 rodeos, with purses totaling over $35 million. There are currently 12 regional rodeo circuits. Rodeo continues to draw crowds of nearly 20,000 to the national finals, with the largest crowds in the western states. Canada and Australia also hold rodeos.[49]

Las Vegas, Nevada, once viewed as simply a place to gamble, has developed into a performance center attracting national and world visitors. Cirque du Soleil is the modern-day recreation of the traditional circus. The company was created in the early 1980s by a collection of street performers who soon added one tent and, since 1993, have been in permanent residence in a showroom on the Las Vegas strip. Other casinos feature live entertainment, including magic, music, and modern follies, but the largest entertainment draw for the city is the legalized gambling.[50]

The Northwest

The Britt Festivals, held since 1962 in the picturesque historic town of Jacksonville, Oregon, on the estate of the late photographer Peter Britt, have attracted audiences to classical, folk, rock, new age, and country performances and an education program that includes camps and music instruction. Founder John Trudeau turned the direction of the festival over to others after several decades of service. The three weeks of performances in August include the Martha Graham Dance Company, who perform and give dance master classes, and a symphony orchestra that draws 90 professional musicians from orchestras throughout the country. Many of the Britt Festival's classic rock acts also appear on the stages of the Bonnaroo Festival in Tennessee.[51]

Although there are other Shakespeare celebrations in the United States, notably in San Diego and New York City, the Oregon Shakespeare Festival is the largest and oldest in the United States. The festival hosts plays on three stages, with numerous off-festival sites, for eight months beginning in February. Nearly 360,000 theater fans attend the 770 performances given every year. One of the stages, the Elizabethan Theatre, is a restored structure from the turn of the nineteenth century. The grounds were originally used in 1893 as a Chautauqua circuit site for performers such as William Jennings Bryan and bandleader John Phillip Sousa and were enlarged over the years to accommodate more visitors. As the Chautauqua movement lost popularity in the 1920s, the first structure was abandoned. Angus L. Bowmer, an instructor at Southern Oregon Normal School (Southern Oregon University), proposed that a three-play July Shakespeare festival be held during the Depression in 1935, using a stage that was constructed by the State Emergency Relief Administration. The festival covered the costs of the production and made a bit of a profit, and two years later, the Oregon Shakespeare Festival Association was incorporated. The festival was dark during World War II but returned with a new stage in 1947 and a full-time paid general manager in 1953. Additional new construction followed, opening up additional theaters and halls in the 1970s, and by 1978, the festival had completed a second traversal of the complete plays of the bard. By the 1990s, the group had an outreach program in Portland and a new state-of-the-art Elizabethan stage. The festival, named by *Time* magazine as one of the top regional theaters in America in 2003, draws near sellout crowds to dramatic productions and chamber and symphonic music performances.[52]

Perhaps the biggest change over the centuries of American performance, besides the steady and monumental increase in the sheer number of cultural events across the country, is the newfound capability to publicize even the smallest and most remote venues and performances from coast to coast. Regional and geographic isolation once gave rise to distinctly individual styles in many areas, but the proliferation of recordings, radio, and television has made it possible for almost any American to see and hear performances that he or she might never have the chance to experience live. Finally, the Internet

An actor in the Oregon Shakespeare Festival performs in an all-male cast of "Henry IV Part 2." © AP Photo/Oregon Shakespeare Festival, David Coope.

and the rise of downloading have instituted a universal availability of cultural product for anyone in the world who can afford to purchase it.

The generations of today can scarcely imagine the physical, practical, and economic obstacles to experiencing exotic performances that confronted their grandparents. If there is a price to be paid today in lost authenticity, disparate styles blending together, and diminished appreciation for the effort of mounting a live performance, this is counterbalanced somewhat by the fact that Americans can now see, hear, or experience virtually any performance that has ever been recorded, in the privacy of their homes, on the moment.

Notes

1. Don B. Wilmeth and Tice L. Miller, eds., "Introduction: Survey from the Beginning to the Present," in *Cambridge Guide to American Theater* (New York: Cambridge University Press, 1996), 1–20.

2. Ibid.

3. Ibid.

4. Ibid., 493.

5. "History of the Ringling Brothers & Barnum Bailey Circus," http://www.ringling. com.

6. See Isaac Goldberg and Edward Jablonski, *Tin Pan Alley: A Chronicle of American Popular Music with a Supplement from Sweet and Swing to Rock 'N' Roll* (New York: Frederick Ungar, 1961), chap. 1.

7. John Kenrick, "A History of the Musical Burlesque," http://www.musicals 101.com/burlesque.htm.

8. Library of Congress, American Memory Collection, "This Day in History—March 21," http://memory.loc.gov.

9. Wilmeth and Miller, *Cambridge Guide,* 90–91.

10. Alan Trachtenberg, *The Incorporation of America: Culture and Society in the Gilded Age,* hypertext extension by Rick Easton, http://xroads.virginia.edu/~MA02/ easton/vaudeville/vaudevillemain.html; U.S. Library of Congress Information Bulletin, "Thanks for the Memory," June 20, 2000, http://www.loc.gov; "Vaudeville," Public Broadcasting American Masters, http://www.pbs.org.

11. Martha Schmoyer, *Summer Stock! An American Theatrical Phenomenon* (New York: Palgrave Macmillan, 2004), 1–13.

12. New Deal Network, "Power: A Living Newspaper," http://newdeal.feri.org.

13. Wilmeth and Miller, *Cambridge Guide,* 8–13.

14. William Arnold, "Homage to Broadway's Heyday Hits High Points," *Seattle Post-Intelligencer,* September 24, 2004, http://seattlepi.nwsource.com.

15. National Endowment for the Arts, "History," http://www.nea.gov.

16. Victoria Ann Lewis, "Radical Wallflowers: Disability and the People's Theater," *Radical History Review* 94 (2006): 84–110.

17. Richard Zoglin, "Bigger Than Broadway!" *Time,* May 27, 2003, http://www. time.com; Guthrie Theater, http://www.guthrietheater.org.

18. American Film Institute, "100 Years...100 Movies," http://www.afi.com; "The Wiz," http://www.ibdb.com; Ernio Hernandez, "Long Runs on Broadway," http://www.playbill.com.

19. "The Top U.S. Orchestras," *Time,* February 22, 1963, http://www.time.com; Opera Company Web sites, http://opera.stanford.edu.

20. John H. Mueller, *The American Symphony Orchestra: A Social History of Musical Taste* (Westport, CT: Greenwood Press, 1976), 17.

21. See Peter Van der Merwe, *Roots of the Classical: The Popular Origins of Western Music* (Oxford, UK: Oxford University Press, 2007).

22. Michael Tsai, "Symphony Finances a Problem across U.S.," *Honolulu Advertiser,* October 15, 2003, http://the.honoluluadvertiser.com.

23. Martin Kettle, "Vanishing Act," *Manchester Guardian,* April 3, 2007, http:// music.guardian.co.uk/classical/story/0,2048916,00.html; Allan Kozinn, "Check the Numbers: Rumors of Classical Music's Demise Are Dead Wrong," *New York Times,* May 28, 2006, http://www.nytimes.com.

24. "Culture Shock: Music and Dance," http://www.pbs.org.

25. Martha Graham Center for Contemporary Dance, "About Martha Graham," http://www.marthagraham.org.

26. Jacob's Pillow Web site, http://www.jacobspillow.org.

27. Alvin Ailey American Dance Theater Web site, http://www.alvinailey.org.

28. Octavio Roca, "Ballet San Jose Emerges from Cleveland Collapse," *Dance Magazine* 75 (2001): 38.

29. Wilma Salisbury, "Two Companies in Transition—Cleveland San Jose Ballet and Ohio Ballet Companies Survive Financial Strife," *Dance Magazine* 72 (1998): 70.

30. Maryland Historical Society, "Shuffle Along: The Eubie Blake Collection," http://www.mdhs.org.

31. Paul Corr and Tony Curtis, "History of Tap Dance," http://www.offjazz.com.

32. U.S. National Parks Service, "New Orleans Jazz History, 1895–1927," http://www.nps.gov.

33. "Biography," http://www.elvis.com.

34. Barbara McHugh, "History of Shea Stadium," http://newyork.mets.mlb.com.

35. Steve Morse, "Destruction at Woodstock '99 Shakes Promoter's Faith," *Milwaukee Journal Sentinel,* July 27, 1999, B8; Richie Unterberger, *Eight Miles High: Folk-Rock's Flight from Haight-Ashbury to Woodstock* (San Francisco: Backbeat Books, 2003), 265–87.

36. Herb Hendler, *Year by Year in the Rock Era: Events and Conditions Shaping the Rock Generations That Reshaped America* (Westport, CT: Greenwood Press, 1983), 101–7; William F. Buckley Jr., "Jerry Garcia, RIP, Obituary and Editorial," *National Review* 47 (1995): 102–3.

37. Fred Goodman, "Trouble for the Tour Biz," *Rolling Stone,* August 2, 2002, http://www.rollingstone.com; Princeton University, "Economist Alan Kruegar Examines Pricing of Concert Tickets," http://www.princeton.edu/main/news/archive/S01/18/72I40/index.xml.

38. The Chautauqua Institution, "History," http://www.ciweb.org.

39. Boston Symphony Orchestra, "History of Tanglewood," http://www.tanglewood.org.

40. JVC Jazz Festival Web site, http://www.festivalproductions.net.

41. PBS, "Jazz," http://www.pbs.org.

42. Grand Ole Opry Web site, http://www.opry.com.

43. See National Park Service, "New Orleans," http://www.nps.gov.

44. New Orleans Jazz and Heritage Festival Web site, http://www.nojazzfest.com.

45. Southwest Louisiana Zydeco Music Festival Web site, http://www.zydeco.org.

46. Unterberger, *Eight Miles,* 271–73.

47. Aspen Music Festival and School Web site, http://www.aspenmusicfestival.com; Telluride Bluegrass Festival Web site, http://www.bluegrass.com.

48. Western Folk Life Museum Web site, http://cybercast.westernfolklife.org.

49. Bonnie Cearly, "The History of the World's First Rodeo," http://www.pecosrodeo.com; Ralph Clark, "Rodeo History," http://www.prorodeoonline.net.

50. Cirque du Soleil official Web site, http://www.cirquedusoleil.com.

51. Britt Festival Web site, http://www.bemf.org.

52. Oregon Shakespeare Festival Web site, http://www.orshakes.org.

BIBLIOGRAPHY

Anderson, Jack. *Ballet and Modern Dance: A Concise History.* New York: Princeton Book Company, 1992.

Bayles, Martha. *Hole in Our Soul: The Loss of Beauty and Meaning in American Popular Music.* Chicago: University of Chicago Press, 1996.

Bloom, Ken. *Broadway: An Encyclopedia Guide to the History, People and Places of Times Square.* New York: Zeisler Group, 1991.

Bordman, Gerald. *American Theater: A Chronicle of Comedy and Drama, 1914–1930.* Oxford, UK: Oxford University Press, 1995.

Chang, Jeff. *Can't Stop, Won't Stop: A History of the Hip Hop Generation.* New York: St. Martin's Press, 2005.

Clarke, Donald, ed. *The Penguin Encyclopedia of Popular Music.* London: Penguin, 1990.

Csida, Joseph, and June Bundy Csida. *American Entertainment: A Unique History of Popular Show Business.* New York: Billboard-Watson Guptill, 1978.

Frank, Rusty. *Tap! The Greatest Tap Dance Stars and Their Stories.* New York: William Morrow, 1990.

Gillett, Charlie. *The Sound of the City: The Rise of Rock and Roll.* New York: Da Capo Press, 1995.

Glatt, John. *Rage and Roll: Bill Graham and the Selling of Rock.* New York: Carol, 1993.

Goldberg, Isaac, and Edward Jablonski. *Tin Pan Alley: A Chronicle of American Popular Music with a Supplement from Sweet and Swing to Rock 'N' Roll.* New York: Frederick Ungar, 1961.

Hendler, Herb. *Year by Year in the Rock Era: Events and Conditions Shaping the Rock Generations That Reshaped America.* Westport, CT: Greenwood Press, 1983.

Hicks, Michael. *Sixties Rock: Garage, Psychedelic, and Other Satisfactions.* Chicago: University of Illinois Press, 1999.

Horowitz, Joseph. *Classical Music in America: A History of Its Rise and Fall.* New York: W. W. Norton, 2005.

Lebrecht, Norman. *Who Killed Classical Music? Maestros, Managers, and Corporate Politics.* Secaucus, NJ: Carol, 1997.

Levine, Lawrence W. *Highbrow Lowbrow: The Emergence of Cultural Hierarchy in America.* Cambridge, MA: Harvard University Press, 1988.

LoMonaco, Martha Schmoyer. *Summer Stock! An American Theatrical Phenomenon.* New York: Palgrave Macmillan, 2004.

Long, Richard A. *Hot Jazz and Jazz Dance.* New York: Oxford University Press, 1995.

Morales, Ed. *The Latin Beat: The Rhythms and Roots of Latin Music, from Bossa Nova to Salsa and Beyond.* Cambridge, MA: Da Capo Press, 2003.

Mueller, John H. *The American Symphony Orchestra: A Social History of Musical Taste.* Westport, CT: Greenwood Press, 1976.

Taylor, Karen Malpede. *People's Theatre in Amerika*. New York: Drama Book, 1972.

Unterberger, Richie. *Eight Miles High: Folk-Rock's Flight from Haight-Ashbury to Woodstock*. San Francisco: Backbeat Books, 2003.

Van der Merwe, Peter. *Roots of the Classical: The Popular Origins of Western Music*. Oxford, UK: Oxford University Press, 2007.

Wilmeth, Don B., and Tice L. Miller. *Cambridge Guide to American Theatre*. New York: Cambridge University Press, 1993.

Zeidman, Irving. *The American Burlesque Show*. New York: Hawthorn Books, 1967.

9

Art, Architecture, and Housing

Benjamin F. Shearer

ART

> If art is to nourish the roots of our culture, society must set the artist free to follow his vision wherever it takes him. We must never forget that art is not a form of propaganda; it is a form of truth.
>
> —President John F. Kennedy

AMERICAN FINE ART today has no single style, method, subject matter, or medium. This eclecticism draws from the reworking of past movements, the adoption of new technologies, and the imagination of each artist. Regionalism, defined primarily by its local subject matter, remains an important force in American art. Folk art also remains an important expression of American life. Government support for the arts developed only lately in the United States, and even at that, it was halting and niggardly. The early public art that it supported tended to be propagandistic, thus President Kennedy's admonition in 1963 quoted above. Likewise, most of America's great art museums came into being through the largess of those who had made immense fortunes, rather than through government funding. As a young America of mostly European immigrants looked back to Europe for the best of art as well as fashion and architecture, truly American art took a long time to emerge, and when it did, it changed the focus of the art world.

Art and Artists in America

Fine art and those who create it have a struggling existence in the everyday life of America. Jobs for artists in general are scarce. In 2004, there were only 208,000 of them. Of those, 94,000 were for multimedia artists and animators. Art directors held another 71,000 jobs; 8,500 jobs fell in all the other categories. That left fine artists, including sculptors, painters, and illustrators, at only 29,000 and craft artists at only 6,100 for the entire nation. The median annual income for fine artists was $38,060 and for craft artists, $23,520, as of May 2004.[1]

Pragmatic Americans find it difficult to value things that are neither necessary nor useful. In 2002, for example, only 29.5 percent of Americans 18 years old or older purchased an artwork at least once. The greater the person's educational attainment, the greater the chances of buying an artwork.[2] Americans are also notorious for avoiding confrontation, preferring businesslike compromise and accommodation so that they can go on with their personal beliefs hidden and intact. American art, however, became purposely confrontational, seeming to delight in iconoclasm. The art that Americans are now accustomed to experiencing has even delved overtly into the realms of religion, race, sex, and politics, the most avoided subjects by American social convention. Contemporary American art, at least much of what is considered avant-garde, is uncomfortable.

The comfortable art, often the romantic realism that Americans seem to prefer, can be found in their homes, where it is decoration. Furniture stores use art on the walls of their displays as props, which set the tone. The display with the big dark wooden desk, green leather chairs, and sofa for the wood-paneled den is complemented by prints of riders attired appropriately in red, black, and white while hunting foxes through a green countryside on chestnut horses. A painting of fluffy white clouds hanging in the deep blue sky illumined by the fainting sunlight with stars twinkling around them adorns the wall above the headboard in the child's bedroom display. There are generic seascapes in the wicker patio furniture display, paintings of bright baskets of flowers for the eating area display, paintings of romantic cottages in idyllic forests for the family room display that say this is home sweet home. Americans are just as likely to buy a painting or print because its colors go with the colors of their walls and furniture as they are to purchase art with a message they enjoy and do not have to figure out.

Great American artists at one time chronicled the nation's history. With artistic license, Benjamin West (1738–1820) depicted death in the French and Indian War and William Penn signing the treaty with Native Americans that would found Pennsylvania. John Trumbull (1856–1843) produced major paintings of the Revolutionary War. Every child in America knows George Washington from the portraits by Gilbert Stuart (1755–1828). Thomas Cole (d. 1848), Frederic Church (1826–1900), and Albert Bierstadt (1830–1902) painted the beauty of the American landscape. George Catlin

(1796–1872) captured the life of Native Americans as it was quickly dissipating into eventual assimilation. What Catlin did with a brush for natives, Mathew Brady (c1823–1896) did with a camera for the Civil War. George Caleb Bingham (1811–1879) captured fur traders and riverboat life in the west on the Mississippi and Missouri rivers. Charles Russell (1864–1926) chronicled the passing of the Old West in his paintings.

As the twentieth century opened with America becoming ever more urbanized, Robert Henri (1865–1921), George Luks (1867–1933), Edward Hopper (1882–1967), and the other members of the Ashcan school realistically portrayed life in New York City. Yet as American artists had always taken their cues from old Europe, indeed many had studied at least briefly there, that trend would continue. Modernism came to America before World War I in the various forms of abstract art represented in the paintings of Morgan Russell (1886–1963) and Max Weber (1881–1961), and many others. Modern art and its progeny would come to play a new role in American society that was no longer as historical or natural chronicle. Furthermore, American modernists succeeded in creating an American art. By the end of World War II, many American artists set out to loose themselves from the conventions of representational art and express themselves in new ways alien to many Americans. While all this was going on, however, Norman Rockwell (1894–1978) was still celebrating small-town America in his paintings for the covers of the *Saturday Evening Post.* By the end of the twentieth century, art had appropriated new media and new technologies that proliferated new styles, new messages, and not a little controversy.

During the 1950s, abstract expressionism separated American from European modern art. Jackson Pollock (1912–1956) had forsaken representational art for the art of self-expression in the 1940s. His so-called action paintings were abstracts made by pouring and dripping paint on canvases lying on the floor in a nearly unconscious state of activity and revolutionized American art. He would even claim that he himself did not know what would evolve on canvas as the paint layered. He did believe, however, that the action itself was important because it revealed an inner self, an inner truth. The new age called for a new art, and the new age was American. Mark Rothko's (1903–1970) chromatic studies, Willem De Kooning's (1904–1997) layering of paints to bring birth to emerging forms, Robert Motherwell's (1915–1991) introduction of meaning to abstract forms, and Lee Krasner's (1908–1984) full abstract gestural canvases were all part of abstract expressionism.

Abstract expressionism began taking many turns in the turbulent but artistically innovative 1960s and 1970s. Agnes Martin (1912–) painted grids, and Frank Stella (1936–) did a series of formalized black paintings as well as pinstripes. These minimalists believed that form and content were one;

they were trying to make sense of the 1960s without using symbols and sending messages—pure art for art's sake. Robert Rauschenberg (1925–) and Jasper Johns (1930–) turned to neo-Dadaism, mixing known objects and symbols in their works along with their paint and effectively ending the reign of abstract expressionism. In 1959, Allen Kaprow (1927–2006) started doing happenings, which brought a new vitality and creativity to art in a very nontraditional way. In 1961, Claes Oldenburg (1929–) opened the Store, a happening in which his sculpted objects provided the atmosphere of a variety store, where they were bought and sold. Oldenburg also employed hamburgers and French fries as subjects for his art. Pop art, based solidly and happily on America's mass consumer culture, also emerged in the early 1960s in the works of Roy Lichtenstein (1923–1997), Andy Warhol (1928–1987), Tom Wesselmann (1931–2004), and James Rosenquist (1933–). Campbell's soup cans, Del Monte fruit cans, Coke bottles, Marilyn Monroe, Jackie Kennedy, Elizabeth Taylor, Volkswagen Beetles, and comic books were only some of the subjects for these pop artists.

If the art of abstract expressionism could be criticized as the product of its creator's self-centered egotism, conceptual artists took it a step further, claiming to be arbiters of ideas to the people as they questioned social norms. Thus the concept or idea held greater importance than the art piece itself, as Joseph Kosuth's (1945–) 1967 *Art as Idea as Idea* epitomized. This was the perfect medium for political protest during the Vietnam War era. Its basis was in linguistic theory, and thus it branched rather quickly into performance art, again with the artist-performer as arbiter. Body art came into vogue. Chris Burden (1946–) crawled naked through broken glass on Main Street in Los Angeles in his 1973 performance *Through the Night Softly.* In his 1970 performance of *Trademarks,* Vito Acconci (1940–) bit his body wherever he could, inked the bites, and applied his so-called trademark to different places. Among the feminist artists who were attempting to reclaim women's bodies from a history of use (and abuse, they would argue) by male artists, Carolee Schneemann (1939–) performed *Interior Scroll* in 1975, in which her otherwise nude body was painted, and she read from a scroll she pulled out of her vagina. Photographer Cindy Sherman (1954–) began her series of so-called self-portraits in 1977 with *Untitled Film Still,* which explored stereotypes of women in film. Her later series continue to investigate the development of self-image.

As feminist artists were trying to reappropriate the female body and feminine symbols of art for themselves, African Americans, Native Americans, and Hispanics also sought to send a message. Betye Saar (1926–) sought to debunk a familiar stereotype in her 1972 *The Liberation of Aunt Jemima.* Faith Ringgold (1930–) employed the American flag to make her point. Her 1967 *The Flag Is Bleeding* depicted three figures, one black, trapped inside the U.S. flag, its red stripes bleeding. Her 1969 *Flag for the Moon: Die Nigger Black Light #10* depicted the word *die* in red inside the white stars on the flag's blue field and the word *nigger* formed by the flag's white stripes. This was powerful protest. Fritz Scholder (1937–2005) used his art to try to rid people of the notion of Native Americans as noble savages, preferring to depict his subjects as real people without stereotyping, such as in his 1969 *Indian with a Beer Can.* R. C. Gorman (1931–2005) redefined Indian painting styles with his abstracts. Judith Baca's (1946–) *Great Wall of Los Angeles,* a gigantic, half-mile collaborative effort that was completed over the years 1976–1983, sought an integrative approach to the inclusion of all the cultures that inform Los Angeles life.

The 1960s and 1970s also birthed other artistic experiments. Lynda Benglis's (1941–) *For Carl Andre,* created in 1970, was a scatological example of process art (also called antiform art) in plopping layers of brown polyurethane foam. In this art, the process was clear. As artists continued to try to escape cultural and institutional boundaries, some artists created earthworks in the western deserts. Nancy Holt (1938–) completed *Sun Tunnels* in 1976 in the Great Basin Desert, which consisted of placing four large concrete pipes in an *X* with holes drilled in the sides to reflect constellations. The pipes were placed to view the rising and setting sun through them. Robert Smithson's (1928–1973) *The Spiral Jetty* at the Great Salt Lake is perhaps the best known of the earthworks. It was completed in 1970.

By the mid-1970s, modernism was history. Postmodern art tolerated a diversity of styles that were not necessarily dependent on particular artists. The neoexpressionists brought painting back to large canvases with a style that was recognizable and sellable. Julian Schnabel (1951–) and David Salle (1952–) ushered in this new style that borrowed heavily and liberally from the past to the extent that their work could not be placed in any particular style. Appropriation artists took their cues from America's mass consumer culture. Vacuums, lava lamps, pots and pans, magazine pictures—anything could become art with a message. Installation art, which defines the setting for a piece, and video art were coming of age, too, along with a new generation of artists who made identity politics their cause. Gender, sexuality, and AIDS became the subject matter for artists like Kiki Smith (1954–), Robert Gober (1954–), and Janine Antoni (1964–).

American artists have never been shy in adopting new technologies to their art. Adrian Piper (1948–) took a hidden tape recorder that played belching noises with her to a library for her Catalysis series (1970–1971). Bill Viola (1951–) used video in his installation *Stations* (1994) to project naked human figures onto five hanging screens, which produces the experience of bodies freed of the forces of nature. Tony Oursler (1957–) projected video to make the faces on inanimate objects come alive. He used this technique in his *Crying Doll* (1993), in which the face of the doll is a moving video, and in his *We Have No Free Will* (1995), with talking puppets. His 1997 *Eye in the Sky* is a video sculpture featuring a fiberglass sphere on which is projected an eye watching television.

The Internet and computer technologies are ripe for artistic exploration. Mark Napier (1961–) mixed up text and images from various Web sites to create his 1999 *Riot* to an arresting effect. New York artist Cory Arcangel (1978–) developed a Web site that juxtaposed singer Kurt Cobain's suicide letter with Google AdSense in 2006. He called his 2005 performance of *I Heart Garfunkel* a "messy lecture/performance involving my slide from the Nintendo iPod to my current obsession with Art Garfunkel." In 2004, Arcangel took the group Iron Maiden's song "The Number of the Beast" and compressed it 666 times as an MP3. Also in 2004, he erased all the invaders but one from the Atari Space Invaders video game, thus creating *Space Invader,* and he did a "mash-up" called *Beach Boys/Geto Boys* of the songs "Little Surfer Girl," by the Beach Boys, and "6 Feet Deep," by Gravediggaz. In Arcangel's *Super Mario Clouds—2005 Rewrite,* he erased everything but the clouds from a Super Mario Brothers Nintendo game and provided the source code and instructions for those who wanted to do it themselves.[3]

Public Art

The federal government had established a precedent in 1927 to devote a percentage of construction costs to art when the Post Office Department and Department of Justice were built at Federal Triangle in Washington, D.C., and for the National Archives building, which opened in 1935. It had long been the government's practice to adorn public buildings with appropriate art and decoration, even though there was no legislative mandate to do so. In 1934, however, a federal percent-for-art program was established that allowed for approximately 1 percent of construction costs to be set aside for art, with the idea that patriotic, democratic, realistic art with local, recognizable cues would inspire Americans otherwise untouched by art to experience good art in federal buildings. Murals and monuments were then the stuff of public art. While the percent-for-art program suffered through shortages during World War II and squabbles about who or what committee should actually hire the artists, by 1973, it was up and running again on a firm footing as the Art in Architecture Program, with experts in charge of commissioning the artists. The installation of Alexander Calder's mobile *Flamingo* in Chicago's Federal Center in that year proved to be a success.[4]

The notion that government buildings should be showcases for relevant, site-specific art was picked up outside of Washington first by Philadelphia in 1959, by Baltimore in 1964, and by San Francisco in 1967. Later, state governments adopted percent-for-art programs based on the construction costs of state public buildings. The movement spread across the nation. For example, Oregon began its program in 1977; Nebraska in 1978; Maine and New Hampshire in 1979; Wisconsin in 1980; Montana in 1983; Ohio in 1990; and Louisiana in 1999. More than 30 states now have percent-for-art programs.

Public art, bolstered by these federal, state, and municipal percent-for-art programs, began picking up steam in the 1960s. Corporations, private foundations, and other large institutions joined the movement, and in fact, most public art today is not government funded. Public art was to be the socially relevant art that defined public places—plazas, playgrounds, parks and subway stations, walls and building façades. Public art allowed artists to bring their messages to the people; art could be an agent for change. Artists could become the arbiters of public opinion. This idyll was put to the test after the General Services Administration, the federal agency that oversees federal construction projects, commissioned minimalist sculptor Richard Serra (1939–) in 1979 to create a site-specific piece for the Federal Plaza at Fogarty Square in New York City. In 1981, Serra's *Tilted Arc* was dedicated. It was a 120-foot-long, 12-foot-high, 2.5-inch-thick slightly tilted wall of rusted steel. Workers in the federal buildings began complaining about it and petitioned for its removal, and in 1989, the General Services Administration removed *Tilted Arc* from the plaza after a series of court cases and splenetic rhetoric on all sides.

While some couched this public debacle in the terms of ignorant people and politicians who do not understand modern art against an enlightened and misunderstood artist, it did bring forward a fundamental question: What if the public do not want or like the public art their tax money paid for? Throughout the 1980s, public artists wanted to make social statements to advance the people, the public, convincing themselves that they were creating the art of the public. Making public art was doing good for the people. In the 1990s, many public artists began to question their own personal cultural superiority and started creating art in collaboration with the public. With the public actually involved in art making, and with the artist immersed in the culture of the site through the people, American art will have achieved true democracy.

WaterFire, in Providence, Rhode Island, is a stunning example of public art that involves the public directly as volunteers and engages from 40,000 to 60,000 people each performance in exploring the relationship between human existence and the primal elements of water, fire, earth, and air. *WaterFire,* the concept of artist Barnaby Evans, is a site-specific sculpture

Crowds gather along the riverfront to watch Waterfire, an art illustration by Barnaby Evans. The work centers on a series of 100 bonfires that blaze just above the surface of the three rivers that pass through the middle of downtown Providence. © AP Photo/Stew Milne.

and performance. The site is the three rivers that run through downtown Providence. Metal braziers are strategically placed in the water, filled with aromatic oak, cedar, and pine, and set afire at twilight. Volunteers dressed in black tend the fires. Torch-lit boats travel the rivers. An eclectic assortment of music accompanies the performance. *WaterFire* was scheduled for 17 performances in 2006. Evans began his work in Providence in 1994 with an installation called *FirstFire,* and another called *SecondFire* in 1996. These performances were so successful that in 1997, WaterFire was set up as an ongoing nonprofit arts organization.[5]

The National Endowment for the Arts

The U.S. government did not directly support the arts outside of the federal building programs until the establishment of the National Endowment for the Arts (NEA) in 1965, save for the emergency arts programs established by President Franklin Roosevelt to provide jobs during the Great

Depression. The NEA began awarding the National Medal of Art in 1985. Several of America's most noted artists have been honored with that award, including Georgia O'Keefe (1985), Willem De Kooning (1986), Robert Motherwell (1989), Jasper Johns (1990), Robert Rauschenberg (1993), Roy Lichtenstein (1995), Agnes Martin (1998), and Claes Oldenburg (2000).

Initial support for the arts was quite meager in the NEA's first year, however, amounting to less than $3 million. NEA appropriations grew steadily, however, reaching nearly $176 million in fiscal year 1992. In the 1970s, the NEA also pursued public art with its Art in Architecture program. Appropriations decreased steadily from that 1992 peak through fiscal year 2000, bottoming at $97.6 million. Since then, funding has increased to nearly $121 million in fiscal year 2004. Although the NEA does support art mostly through grants to mount exhibitions, its national initiatives include supporting jazz presentations, bringing Shakespeare performances to American cities and towns, and supporting arts journalism institutes in opera, theater, classical music, and dance. Its objectives now have to do with access to and learning in the arts.[6] To put the place of arts in the perspective of federal spending, one B2 Spirit bomber costs over $1 billion.

Funds for the NEA, which must be appropriated by the U.S. Congress, nearly came to an end in 1989 when some congressmen and senators found out that NEA funds were used to support exhibitions of so-called obscene art, namely, of the works of Robert Mapplethorpe (1946–1989) and Andres Serrano (1950–). The traveling Mapplethorpe exhibit, which the Corcoran Gallery cancelled owing to political considerations, included homoerotic photographs as well as photographs of nude children. The Serrano photograph that inspired congressional ire was titled "Piss Christ," a photograph of a crucifix emerged in a clear container of the artist's urine. The NEA was using federal tax dollars to exhibit obscene, pornographic, sexually perverted, and sacrilegious material around the country in the view of several members of Congress, and they were outraged. Congress amended the NEA legislation in 1990, instructing the NEA chair to consider "general standards of respect and decency for the diverse beliefs and values of the American public" as grants are awarded.[7]

Federally funded art projects were to be filtered through this so-called decency clause, and four artists, soon dubbed the "NEA 4," challenged this new provision when the NEA yanked away their grants. They claimed that their First Amendment freedom of speech rights had been violated, and they went to court. Karen Finley (1956–), among other things a performance artist, dealt with women's issues sometimes scatologically in such performances as *We Keep Our Victims Ready,* a series of monologues in which she smeared chocolate over her body, which was naked, save for boots and panties. Holly Hughes (1955–), a lesbian performance artist, used explicit sexual and religious imagery in her show *World without End*. Tim Miller (1958–) explored aspects of his gay identity in such performances as *Some Golden States* in 1987 and *Stretch Marks* in 1989. In *Blessed Are All the Little Fishes*, performance artist and later actor John Fleck (1951–) urinated on stage and simulated masturbation.

The NEA 4's case meandered through the courts and was finally decided by the Supreme Court in 1998. The Court found that because the NEA's decency clause asked only that general standards be considered in awarding grants, the artists' First Amendment privileges were not violated, nor would lack of government funding prevent the artists from performing their art. In short, the NEA 4 lost, and the NEA ceased to award individual grants for avant-garde categories. The American government would not subsidize art that questioned basic American values.

Museums

The Founding Fathers of the United States did not envision the collection of art to be in the purview of government. For one thing, the United States began its existence completely broke and heavily in debt. For another, patronizing the arts surely must have smacked to them to be the stuff of popes, monarchs, and noblemen, all anathema in the new republic. Furthermore, they understood government to have a very small role in domestic life. In 1841, the National Institute was created in the Patent Office to oversee art and historical items the government had come to own. John Varden, its first curator, had begun collecting art privately, and his collection was added to what the government already had. The institute was disbanded in 1862 and its collections sent to the Smithsonian Institution, which was founded in 1846. After a fire at the Smithsonian Castle in 1865, most of the art was loaned out to other museums well into the twentieth century. A 1906 court case caused the Smithsonian's art collection to be named a National Gallery of Art, a heightened status that encouraged donations of new artworks.

The federal government's entrance into art collecting and museums had been, for the most part, accidental to this point, and certainly unenthusiastic. There was no proper federal art museum until financier Andrew W. Mellon donated his European art collection to the United States in 1937, the year he died, and his foundation paid for the building, designed by Eliel Saarinen, to house it. In 1941, the National Gallery of Art opened on the mall in the nation's capital. The Mellon family and foundation also donated funds for the gallery's East Building, designed by I. M. Pei. It opened in 1978. Varden's original collection, greatly enlarged, is housed in the newly renovated Old Patent Office Building and is known as the Smithsonian American Art

Museum. The collection includes the works of more than 7,000 American artists.[8]

The National Gallery of Art was not the first federal art museum. The Smithsonian's first fine art museum was the Freer Gallery. Charles Lang Freer (1854–1919) made a fortune as a railroad car manufacturer in Detroit. He was an avid collector of Asian art and Buddhist sculpture. He gave his collection to the nation along with the money to build a museum. The Freer Gallery opened in 1923. The Arthur M. Sackler Gallery of Asian Art is connected to the Freer and was opened in 1987 to house Dr. Sackler's (1913–1987) gift to the country.[9]

There was one case, however, in which the U.S. government aggressively pursued a new collection and museum. President Lyndon Johnson, not known as an art aficionado, sealed the deal with financier Joseph H. Hirshhorn to donate his collection of sculpture, American modernists, and French Impressionists to the American people. Hirshhorn, born in Latvia in 1899, made his fortune in the uranium mining business and considered it an honor to donate his art to the people of the United States. Although Hirshhorn also donated $1 million toward the Gordon Bunshaft–designed Hirschhorn Museum and Sculpture Garden of the Smithsonian Institution, government funds made it happen. Ground was broken for the Hirshhorn in 1969, and it opened in 1974. Joseph Hirshhorn, who died in 1981, left substantially all his art to the museum.[10] With the establishment of the National Endowment for the Arts in 1965, it may have seemed that the federal government was about to embark on a continuing program to support the arts.

America's great art museums were founded and nurtured not by government, but by the initiatives of citizens, particularly wealthy citizens. New York City's Metropolitan Museum of Art, arguably one of the world's great museums, was founded in 1870 by wealthy art patrons and artists seeking to further the democratic ideal of getting art out of private collections and to the people. It took nearly 100 years after the American Revolution before museums began to be established—bringing art to the American people was, therefore, a noble ideal. Banker and financier William Wilson Corcoran (1798–1888), one of America's few collectors of American art, donated his collection and the building that housed it to a board of trustees, who ran the congressionally chartered, tax-exempt Corcoran Gallery of Art. The Corcoran in Washington, D.C., opened in 1874. The Philadelphia Museum of Art was chartered in 1876 as the Pennsylvania Museum and School of Industrial Art. Again, local business leaders, who wanted a school to support local art and textile industries, and artists, notably Thomas Eakins (1844–1916), got together to see that the City of Brotherly Love would have an art museum. The genesis for the movement was Philadelphia's Centennial Exposition of 1876.

The permanent building, called Memorial Hall, was to be the exposition's art museum. The success of the Centennial Exposition was, in turn, the genesis of citizens of Cincinnati, Ohio, deciding to found an art museum, which opened in 1886. The Art Institute of Chicago was founded in 1879 as the Chicago Academy of Fine Arts, both a school and museum, as Philadelphia's had been, and Mrs. Henry Field was its first major donor.

The movement to establish art museums went all over the country. The Los Angeles County Museum of Art, now with extensive and diverse collections, was established in 1910 without a collection. The Museum of Fine Arts in Houston, Texas, opened in 1924, the result of 24 years of work by the Houston Public School Art League. Today, America has more than 1,700 art museums, and some of its most significant ones were founded in the twentieth century. Wealthy art collectors and patrons Mary Sullivan, Abby Aldrich Rockefeller, and Lillie P. Bliss founded the Museum of Modern Art in 1929 in New York City because the large museums were reluctant to collect modern and contemporary art. Thus was established one of the world's premier art museums. Major Duncan Phillips and his wife, Marjorie, left their Washington, D.C., home in 1930 for another residence, turning their old home into an art museum. The Phillips Collection is a major institution of modern art and its origins. Gertrude Vanderbilt Whitney founded the Whitney Museum in 1931, with her own collection of twentieth-century American art as its foundation. The Frick Collection was created and endowed by Henry Clay Frick, the Pittsburgh steel magnate. When he died in 1919, he requested that his New York City residence become a museum to house his hundreds of artworks, including old masters, after the death of his wife. The museum opened to the public in 1935.

Oilman J. Paul Getty opened the J. Paul Getty Museum at his Malibu, California, ranch in 1954. Since 1984, the trustees of his estate have sought to promote Getty's belief in art as a humanizing influence by expanding the museum's programs beyond the original campus with the Getty Center in Los Angeles, designed by Richard Meier and Partners and opened in 1997. The collections have been greatly enhanced beyond Getty's collection of antiquities and European paintings and furniture. In 1937, industrialist Solomon R. Guggenheim established his eponymous foundation to operate museums based on his collections of nonobjective art. While Solomon's artworks were put into traveling shows and his niece Peggy Guggenheim was making her own name in the art world as a dealer and patron, the first permanent home for the Guggenheim opened in Frank Lloyd Wright's famous New York City landmark in 1959. The Kimbell Art Museum in Fort Worth, Texas, opened in a Louis I. Kahn–designed building in 1972. It was established through a foundation by entrepreneur Kay Kimbell, his wife, and his wife's sister and her husband. The museum houses a diverse collection reaching back to antiquity.

Traveling museum exhibits take important art throughout the country. The Museum of Contemporary Art (MoCA) in Cleveland, Ohio, recently exhibited some of the paintings of Dana Schutz (1976–) completed between 2002 and 2006. Schutz tried to extend reality into the imaginary in her paintings. These included selections from her series Self-Eaters. MoCA also exhibited two shows of Catherine Opie's (1961–) photographs, "1999" and "In and Around the House." The "1999" photographs were taken on a trip around the country in 1999; the photographs of the other show depict a close look at American life at home, with Opie's family as subjects. In an exhibit called Sarah Kabot: On the Flip Side, emerging Cleveland artist Sarah Kabot (1976–) had the opportunity to show her interest in the relationship between form and content through her art, which included transforming a spiral notebook into a new meaning.[11]

In Houston, Texas, the Contemporary Arts Museum presented its patrons with the traveling exhibit Kiki Smith: A Gathering, 1980–2005. Smith's exploration of humanity and spirituality could be discovered in about 250 works in diverse media. In its Perspectives series, the museum gives artists their first opportunities for museum exhibition. Artists who have lately exhibited in this series include Michael Bise, who draws domestic scenes; Soody Sharifi, who photographs communities; Janaki Lennie, who paints cityscapes; and Demetrius Oliver, who is a Houston conceptual artist engaged in performance, sculpture, and photography. The Houston museum also mounted a traveling retrospective of Sam Gilliam's (1933–) draped paintings. Gilliam took canvases off stretchers and walls, turning them into three-dimensional installations.[12]

The Contemporary Art Center of Virginia in Virginia Beach featured Watering, an exhibition of 24 photographs by Elijah Gowin (1967–). Gowin used composite photos from the Internet that he built digitally into montages, and which he then, as negatives, put through a scanning and printing process to invoke contemporary meaning for the act of baptizing. The Butler Institute of American Art in Youngstown, Ohio, showed Lightboxes and Melts. Artist Ray Howlett (1940–) produced light sculptures using LED technology. The San Francisco Museum of Modern Art featured a nearly three-month run of the Drawing Restraint series, an ongoing work of art by Matthew Barney (1967–). It is a performance-based project that employs film, photography, drawing, sculpture, and video to investigate the idea that form comes out of struggle against resistance.[13]

The attendance rate for art museums across the United States is 34.9 percent, which means that only about one in three Americans visits an art museum in a given year. There are regional variations, however, in attendance rates. New England (42.4%), the Mid-Atlantic (38.7%), and the Pacific Northwest with Hawaii (39.7%) exceed the national average. The attendance rate in the south Atlantic region is bolstered by Florida (35.5%), but its overall rate is only 30.5 percent. (This region includes the states of Florida, Georgia, South Carolina, North Carolina, Virginia, West Virginia, Maryland, and Delaware.) The west south central region outside of Texas, which exactly meets the national rate, has an attendance rate of only 26.5 percent. This region includes Texas as well as Oklahoma, Louisiana, and Arkansas. Art museum attendance in the mountain states (Montana, Idaho, Wyoming, Utah, Nevada, Arizona, Colorado, and New Mexico) at 40 percent exceeds the national average. In the east south central region, including Kentucky, Tennessee, Mississippi, and Alabama, the attendance rate at art museums is a meager 24.8 percent. The Midwest generally meets the national rate. When participation rates in art experiences through television are considered, however, most regions come near or above the national rate of 45.1 percent. The east south central region is the notable exception at only 36.5 percent.[14] The American Association of Museums reported in 2003 that median annual attendance for art museums totaled 61,312, whereas zoos had 520,935; science and technology museums had 183,417; arboretums and botanical gardens had 119,575; children's/youth museums had 85,088; and natural history museums had 64,768.[15]

The Contemporary Art Scene

The Whitney Biennial is an important event that showcases contemporary American art and may therefore be considered representative of what is happening in the American art scene. Among the artists whose works were chosen for inclusion in the 2006 Biennial, called Day for Night, was Los Angeles artist Lisa Lapinski (1967–), whose installation *Nightstand* was inspired by the contradiction between simple Shaker furniture and the religious ecstasy depicted in Shaker gift drawings. In this sculpture, the basic wooden nightstand adorned with curious decorations seems to have exploded in all directions. Trisha Donnelly (1974–) is a conceptual/performance artist from San Francisco. Her demonstrations rely on unpredictability to transcend the time and place of exhibition. For her, art is ephemeral, but it can be the vehicle to a brief transcendent experience. Lucas Degiulio (1977–), also working out of San Francisco, likes to make small sculptures out of things he finds and transform them into a sort of otherness. His *Can Barnacles* in the Biennial is a barnacle-encrusted aluminum can.

Four Houston, Texas, artists, all members of Otabenga Jones & Associates, an artists' collective founded in 2002 and dedicated to educate young

African Americans about the fullness of the African Americans experience, were picked for individual works in the Biennial. Jamal Cyrus (1973–) invented a mythical record company of the 1970s, and his collage, on a Cream album, depicts in a cutout a group of African American militants marching with fists raised and carrying a coffin. His 2005 piece is called *The Dowling Street Martyr Brigade, "Towards a Walk in the Sun."* Robert A. Pruitt (1975–) sought to comment on the African Americans struggle in his 2005 *This Do in Remembrance of Me.* Hair, iPods, a mixer, wine, and other offerings lay on a communion table. Kenya A. Evans (1974–) employed texts to diminish and bolster the importance of history books, while a slave on the ground attempts to defend himself helplessly from a robotic slave master. Her canvas is titled *Untitled (Overseer).* A drawing by Dawolu Jabari Anderson (1973–) is titled *Frederick Douglass Self-Defense Manual Series, Infinite Step Escape Technique #1: Hand Seeks Cotton* is an ink and acrylic on paper that the artist treated to give it an historical look.

The 2006 Whitney Biennial, if nothing else, exposed the great diversity of American art today. Los Angeles–based Mark Grotjahn (1968–) showed his debt to the conceptual art of an earlier era in his *Untitled (White Butterfly).* Matthew Monahan (1972–), also based in Los Angeles, explored the human body inside and outside in his drawings and sculptures. Another Los Angeles–based artist, Mark Bradford (1961–), is famous for his mixed media collages, installations, and videos that may include string, magazine pages, and ads found on city lampposts.

Angela Strassheim (1969–), who divides her time between New York City and Minneapolis, Minnesota, employed her training as a forensic photographer to create extremely crisp color photographs of the grotesque and the ordinary. Anthony Burdin of California, who insists on being ageless, made his fame singing along with tunes as he photographed the passing scenery from his 1973 Chevy Nova, in which he claims to have lived. New Yorker Kelley Walker (1969–) used a computer, scanner, and photo software along with such things as smeared and dabbled chocolate and toothpaste on archival images to create digitally printed two-dimensional abstracts. In Austin, Texas, Troy Brauntich (1954–), working from photographs, has managed to veil representational art to make it something other than itself. His 2005 *Untitled (Shirts2)* in the Biennial, a 63 by 51 inch conté crayon on black cotton depiction of folded shirts in a rack, is almost ethereal. There is nothing ethereal, however, about Dash Snow's (1981–) photographs of his life in New York City, including a dog eating garbage.

Inventive American artists can turn about anything into art, as the Biennial demonstrated. New York City's Dan Colen (1979–) used wood, steel, oil paint, papier-mâché, felt, and Styrofoam to create *Untitled.* This 96 by 108 by 96 inch sculpture appears to be a poorly constructed, graffiti-encrusted wooden fence, the kind of fence the little rascals may have built around their clubhouse. Los Angeles sculptor Liz Larner (1960–), who uses color to draw attention to her works, rather than form, used aluminum tubing, fabric and ribbons, batting, wire rope, padlocks, and keys to create her 82 by 117 by 117 inch *RWBs* in the Whitney show. It appears to be a completely formless but colorful pile of stiffened spaghetti.[16]

While the Whitney Biennial shows may be said to be mounted within the tradition of avant-garde American art in the spirit of art for art's sake, the U.S. government uses American art for politics' sake, thus revealing another side of American art. The embassies of the United States around the world act in part as art museums to show American art. The U.S. Department of State established its ART in Embassies Program in 1964 to mount exhibitions of original American art in the public rooms of diplomatic installations at some 180 international locations. The purpose of the program is to "provide international audiences with a sense of the quality, scope, and diversity of American art and culture" through the work of American artists.[17] In 2004, the ART in Embassies Program, working with the Bureau of International Information Programs, showcased 17 of the younger program artists in the hope of increasing "international understanding" and in the belief that experiencing their art would also be to experience the fundamental American values of "innovation, diversity, freedom, individualism [and] competitive excellence." Their works were chosen because they reflect "the great imaginative variety of the current American art scene."[18]

Among the artists whose works are shown around the world is Philip Argent (1962–), who lives in Santa Barbara, California. He is influenced by the layering of visual effects in the way that Windows software presents information. He uses that technique and puts together seen objects with imagined ones to produce various optical effects. His acrylic and diamond dust on canvas called *Window Drop #1* (2000) is a primary example of his technique. Graham Caldwell (1973–) of Washington, D.C., sculpts in glass. His 2002 work *Elizabeth's Tears* illustrates in glass, steel, water, and wood his exploration of connection and interdependence. New Mexico artist Lauren Camp (1966–) designs colorful threadworks about jazz because she claims to be able to hear colors and shapes in the music. New York City photographer Gregory Crewdson (1962–) attempts to involve viewers of his work in a narrative from a frozen moment in time. In his Natural Wonders series, he uses the beauty of nature to engage the viewer. New York City native Hillary Steel (1959–) is a textile artist. Her use of color is ordinarily quite bright, but her *Current Events* (2001) is made of hand-woven newspaper and cotton, making her point that the cloth or fabric itself has a structure and a history that allows it to deliver messages. Will Cotton (1964–), who lives in New York City, does oil paintings of confections on linen. His paintings, such as *Brittle House* (2000), a miniature, idyllic cottage made of peanut brittle, and *Flanpond* (2002), four flans that appear to be floating on flowery water, look good enough to eat and evoke a perfect world of unfettered consumption. Nicole Cohen (1970–) of Los Angeles is a video installation artist. Pictures of rooms become the stages (a digital print) on which a performance video is projected. Santiago Cucullu (1969–) was born in Argentina but raised in the United States. He is interested in large wall pieces, which include *Lunchtime, the Best of Times* (2002), a high shelf of folded plastic tablecloths, and *Come to Me* (2002), a wall of colorful plastic table skirting.

Benjamin Edwards (1970–) of Washington, D.C., chooses his subject matter out of the consumer society he inhabits to create new syntheses from unorganized realities, as in his *Starbucks, Seattle: Compression* (1998). Kiev-born Valerie Demianchuk, now of New York City, intensifies the essence of her subject matter in detailed graphite drawings on plain drawing paper; her 2001 *Terra Firma (Dry Land)* is but one example. Jason Falchook of Washington, D.C., is a photographer who explores life within the boundaries of communities and sometimes uses inkjet printers to produce his pieces. Trenton Doyle Hancock's (1974–) mixed media pieces are inspired by the discarded things (garbage) he finds, which, he believes, have their own stories to tell. Dante Marioni (1964–) is a glassblower who creates his colorful and fanciful pieces in homage to the history of the craft. Stacy Levy (1960–) of Philadelphia uses her art, rather than science, to evoke a heightened sense of nature. Her *Mold Garden* (1999–2002) is made of sandblasted glass, agar, and mold spores.[19]

Folk Art

American folk art, more pejoratively known as primitive art or naïve art, is the product of unschooled artists and arguably an unvarnished insight into American life. This is outsider art—outside the academic tradition. America's best-known folk artist was probably Anna Mary Robertson Moses, or Grandma Moses (1860–1961). A farmer's wife and mother of five children who lived in rural eastern New York State, she did not take up painting until she was in her seventies. With a bright palette, she depicted the simple life and the natural beauty around her. Her paintings are of a happy America. Earl Cunningham (1893–1977) was born in Maine but eventually settled in St. Augustine, Florida. He had been a tinker, a seaman who worked up and down the Atlantic coast, and a chicken farmer before he opened his curio shop in Florida in 1949. Even before moving to Florida, however, he had begun to paint vividly colored fanciful landscapes of the places he had visited.

These, too, are happy paintings. Cunningham's works are the foundation of the Mennello Museum of American Art in Orlando, Florida.[20]

The essence of folk art is self-expression. While some early American folk artists like Joshua Johnson (1763–1824) and Ammi Phillips (1788–1865) were portrait painters, Pennsylvania artist Edward Hicks (1780–1849), a Quaker and a preacher, used many of his paintings to deliver moral and religious lessons. Bill Traylor (1854–1949) was born a slave in Alabama. For 82 years, he remained at the place where he was born, and then he moved to nearby Montgomery, Alabama, where he began drawing the scenes around him. Henry Darger (1892–1973), who stole himself out of a deplorable children's home for the so-called feeble-minded to become a janitor in Chicago, created an entire unreal life in his small apartment, written and illustrated by himself. The American Folk Art Museum in New York City celebrates Outsider Art Week in January.

ARCHITECTURE AND HOUSING

> The mother art is architecture. Without an architecture of our own we have no soul of our own civilization.
>
> —Frank Lloyd Wright

It is curious that no one anywhere would identify a photograph of any street in any American city as a street in Johannesburg, Paris, Istanbul, or Rio de Janeiro because it looks American. Yet for all the efforts of architects at one time to create an American architecture, none emerged. Likewise, American residential neighborhoods look American, but here again, houses, too, appear to be copies of historical relics built with locally available materials. American buildings, having gone through a history of derivative European architecture, are now said to be eclectic and regional. A walk through any city or residential neighborhood proves the point. Banks in central cities may demonstrate their financial strength through Ionic columns, Romanesque stonework, or towering heights in glass and steel. In many suburban neighborhoods, faux Spanish colonial, French provincial, Tudor revival, Dutch colonial, and Greek revival houses may share the same block.

This is not to say that the potpourri of styles that constitutes American architecture, public and residential, are not without American values. George Washington and Thomas Jefferson spent decades building their homes, Mount Vernon and Monticello, to make statements that endure. Washington, the consummate practical farmer, military hero, and father of the nation, found a way to wed the grand style befitting a public man with the comforts of private life. His final rendering of Mount Vernon, garnered from his perusal of the pedestrian English building guides available to him, suggested with Palladian and neoclassical accents that this home was a temple of democracy. Calling to mind the ancient Roman republic, Mount Vernon became a symbol of the strength of democracy, an American castle, a sacrosanct place in which the occupants were safe, a place replicated to this day all over America.

For Jefferson, Monticello was as much a home as it was an idea and an ideal. He famously denigrated architecture in colonial America. Jefferson sought perfection in classical architecture, borrowing liberally from English and French architectural studies of classical buildings. The disciplines of art and architecture blurred in Jefferson's works. He believed America needed architecture to express its unique place in the world, and it was he who would proffer the reworked Roman temple as the exemplar of American democratic architecture: bold, pure, solid. In fact, Jefferson's design for the Virginia statehouse, widely copied in the South for libraries and other public buildings, was squarely based on a Roman temple. What made Jefferson's architecture American, however, was the freedom he felt to blend and marry differing classical styles together. It was Jefferson who would set the tone for America's aspirations and public architecture for years to come.

American Cities

American cities look young and orderly. They express a kind of hopefulness and vitality. Most of them were laid out on grids, with straight streets and broad avenues. While sections of cities developed over time around entrepreneurial visions punctuated by freestanding, single architectural statements, the grid maintains a certain civic unity. It also defines the footprints of the buildings and the public spaces where commerce can take place.

The rapid expansion of the United States was all about the successful entrepreneurial commerce that took place on Main Street America. For a century from the 1850s, these small-town and city commercial centers provided one-stop shopping for burgeoning populations and businesses. Grocery stores, drugstores, hardware stores, furniture stores, clothing stores, emporiums, shoe stores, jewelry stores, banks, hotels, theaters, restaurants, doctors' and lawyers' offices, repair shops, candy stores, billiard halls, bars and grills—all these and more came together in commercial buildings remarkably alike across the country. America's commercial Main Street architecture was dominated by the supremacy of street-level trade; that is, access to first-floor businesses from wide sidewalks that invited business activity was easy, and parking for horses and buggies and cars was immediately available off the sidewalks. One-story businesses, in detached buildings and rows, popped up everywhere. The popular two- and three-story buildings were clearly defined into two zones: the commercial, public spaces on the first floor and more private spaces on upper floors. Thus doctors' offices might be above drugstores or hotel rooms or apartments above shoe stores. Some twentieth-century buildings began to feature framed large windows for displays, and as land values increased, buildings began getting taller, but five stories was considered a maximum, until passenger elevators and structural steel made the sky the limit.[21]

No matter the style of the façades, which were often designed in the style prevalent at the time, Main Street America still has a familiar feel for Americans, even though it has fallen on hard times. With the shift of population to suburbs and the development of shopping malls to serve it, large central city commercial districts fell into disuse and disrepair. Likewise, the thousands of Main Streets in small towns across the country experienced a similar demise because small mom-and-pop businesses could not compete against big chain stores with more variety and better prices. In American memory, however, Main Street is the real America—a safe place with a bustling friendliness and hardworking, honest merchants who treat their customers as kings and queens. Happily, urban renewal and historic preservation programs have brought some Main Streets back, reincarnated as specialty shops and boutiques that may make their revenues more from Internet sales than foot trade. The big crowds are at the shopping malls. That old Main Street America feeling, replete with penny candy and ice cream sodas, is now mostly the stuff of theme park–induced imagination.

The only thing that could be more idyllic than visiting Walt Disney World's Main Street would be to live in it, or at least a version of it. Seaside, an 80-acre development on Florida's northern Gulf Coast, hatched a movement called the *new urbanism.* Begun in 1981, its pastel-painted wooden cottages with front porches catch the Gulf breezes. White picket fences both define properties and invite conversation with passers-by. Everything is within walking distance: the small stores and the town square where community events take place. The streets are narrower than Americans are accustomed to; cars do not dominate the streets, and garages do not dominate the front of the homes. In fact, the entire development is scaled down from normal size to give it the feel of a manageable urban environment. Critics may have called Seaside a la-la land with strict rules, but it sparked a revolution.

The primary architects of Seaside, Andres Duany and Elizabeth Plater-Zyberk, were among the founders of the Congress for the New Urbanism in 1993. It now claims some 2,000 members worldwide. The congress's charter takes a stand in favor of restoring urban centers, rationalizing suburban sprawl "into communities of real neighborhoods," conserving the environment, and preserving what is already built. Furthermore, it declares that land development policies and practices should further diversity "in use and population"; support the automobile as well as mass transit and pedestrian traffic; shape urban areas by the use of "accessible public spaces and community institutions"; and employ architecture and landscape design based on "local history, climate, ecology, and building practice" to frame urban areas. Finally, the group's charter commits to "reestablishing the relationship between the art of building and the making of community." This would occur only when citizens participate in planning and designing their communities.[22] Idealism is not dead in American architecture; looking back to an idealized past is always comfortable.

America's efforts to revitalize urban centers began in the 1960s and continues. In the largest cities, urban malls, some of them spectacular, like Liberty Place in Philadelphia, were built around subway and train stops. The value of waterfront property was realized in New York City's South Street Seaport and Baltimore's Inner Harbor. In Boston, a dilapidated old Faneuil Hall was renovated and reborn as a modern marketplace. In Washington, D.C., the Old Post Office was reclaimed as a tourist attraction featuring small shops and food, and the magnificent train station near the Capitol was restored as a busy tourist center, with a number of retail establishments and still with arriving and departing trains as well as a subway stop. With developments like San Francisco's Embarcadero Center and Chicago's Water Tower Place, American cities have taken on a new look. The new Main Street of America's big cities is spacious, tall, glass and steel–encased retail, office, eating, and drinking establishments and living quarters that are not necessarily dependent on the automobile. They are safe places.

American Architects

Benjamin Latrobe (1764–1820), who designed the U.S. Capitol, was British, having come to America in 1796. Even the first U.S.-born American architect, Charles Bullfinch (1763–1844), traveled to Europe for inspiration. His Massachusetts State House, completed in 1798, demonstrated his debt to the classicism then current in England.[23] America had no professional architecture program, until the first was established in 1865 at the Massachusetts Institute of Technology. There were 13 professional programs by 1900, but they were all modeled after the Ecole des Beaux-Arts in Paris, where many American architects had studied.[24] America's affair with English classical architecture was therefore reinforced by Beaux-Arts classicism. Indeed, architects chose classical buildings to make the statement to the world that the United States was no longer a second-rate power in any respect at the 1893 World's Columbian Exposition in Chicago.

Skyscrapers were the chance for American architects to shine. In 1875, a skyscraper was a 10-story building. When architect Cass Gilbert's New York

City Woolworth Building was completed in 1913, it stacked 60 tall stories to a height of 792 feet. In 1931, what was long America's tallest building, the Empire State Building, was built to 102 stories and a total height of 1,252 feet, dwarfing the 1930 Chrysler Building at only 1,046 feet. These three skyscrapers defined and redefined the New York City skyline, yet they remain period pieces. The Woolworth Building is swept with Gothic ornament. The verticality of Gothic architecture seemed to lend itself to skyscrapers for there were no other precedents for what these tall buildings might look like. The Chrysler Building is full-blown art deco, with decoration relating to automobiles, Chrysler's livelihood. The Empire State Building is in a muted art deco style.

Operating out of Chicago, architect Louis Sullivan (1856–1924) had some ideas about tall buildings. He believed that they should embrace their tallness in new ways and that their forms should follow the buildings' functions. The Wainwright Building in downtown St. Louis, which was completed in 1892, is on the National Register of Historic Places because Sullivan and his partner, Dankmar Adler, dealt with steel and glass and brick and terra cotta for a tall building in an entirely new way.

The 10-story Wainwright Building respected the urban tradition of differentiating public from office functions in the façade. The first two stories are defined as retail and public space—this was form following function. However, in no other respect was this building traditional. The brick piers of the façade that extend from above the second floor to the terra cotta cornice that caps the building suggest the strength of the structural steel they hide, but more significantly, they suggest the tallness of the building itself. Likewise, the larger corner posts, although not structurally functional, suggest the strength of the steel that is really the structure of the building in terms recognizable to the uninitiated. Terra cotta spandrels or panels between the windows lend horizontal cues to the building. Sullivan varied the organic designs of the spandrels above each floor, thus solving the issue of ornament in this new architecture. These terra cotta panels as well as the cornice were not the work of artisans, but they could be produced mechanically. While Sullivan's design of the Wainwright Building predated the modern skyscraper, it was decidedly an American contribution to the tall building.

The United States now has nine skyscrapers that hover above 1,000 feet. Among the top five are the Sears Tower in Chicago, with 110 stories, which is the tallest at 1,450 feet. The Empire State Building is 102 stories at 1,250 feet. The Aon Centre in Chicago, although only 80 stories, rises to a height of 1,136 feet. Chicago also has America's fourth tallest building, the John Hancock Center, which has 100 stories at 1,127 feet. New York City's Chrysler Building, with 77 stories, rises to 1,046 feet.

Another original American architect worked for Adler and Sullivan from 1888 until 1903. Frank Lloyd Wright (1867–1959) always claimed Sullivan as his mentor, even though his influences were quite diverse and even included Japanese architecture. Wright's enduring legacy to American architecture would be his liberation of the house from a rabbit warren to an open space, but his final work, the Solomon R. Guggenheim Museum in New York City, gave America one of its signature buildings. If Wright was a member of any particular school, it was his own. His cantilevered buildings and houses suggested an organic architecture springing from nature like branches unfolding from trees. Nature and technology could be complementary. In the Guggenheim, however, technology and modern materials—molded concrete and steel—are formed into a plastic sculpture. The form of the sculpture was defined by the function of a museum: to view art, in this case, on spiraling ramps. The museum was completed in 1959, shortly after Wright's death.

In 1932, American architecture was awakened from its classical slumber by a show at the Museum of Modern Art in New York that was called Modern Architecture: International Exhibition. The show went on the road,

The Solomon R. Guggenheim Museum in New York City, designed by Frank Lloyd Wright, stands out architecturally. Corbis.

and a book called *The International Style: Architecture Since 1922* by Henry Russell Hitchcock and Philip Johnson was based on it.[25] Johnson would later attend architecture school and prove one of its most famous practitioners. The international style—modern architecture—opened a new avenue of expression for American architecture because it condemned historical decoration, classical symmetry, and mass, all the stuff of traditional American architecture. As fate would have it, two of Europe's greatest modernist architects ended up as citizens of the United States. Walter Gropius, who founded the Bauhaus in Germany in 1919, came to the United States to direct Harvard's Graduate School of Design in 1937, retiring in 1952. In that same year, Ludwig Mies van der Rohe came to the United States and was ensconced in the Armour Institute of Technology as head of its architecture program from 1938 until 1958. Mies's Seagram Building in New York City, completed in 1958, is considered the height of his work and spawned glass and steel towers of simple elegance in many of America's largest cities. To Mies, less was more.

It was Philip Johnson (1906–2005) who first brought Mies to America, and he collaborated with him on the Seagram Building. The pure lines of international-style glass and steel towers became so ubiquitous across America's cities (America was not alone in this experience) that they attained a kind of anonymity, save for the color of the glass. Most Americans found them sterile and bereft of meaning. Johnson's famous glass house, an homage to Mies, which he built in 1949 in New Canaan, Connecticut, is a case in point. This glass and steel box looked more like an architectural statement than home sweet home to the American eye, but Johnson lived in it. In the dominant architectural circles, however, modernism represented the perfect mingling of materials, technology, precision, and art—the essence of modern architecture. The form and the materials were themselves the decoration.

Johnson, however, began to crawl out of the box, as it were. In 1967, he joined with architect John Burgee. In their design for the IDS Center in Minneapolis, Minnesota, completed in 1973, modern architecture appeared sleek, but with human spaces—a glass atrium and elevated walkways. Their 1976 Pennzoil Place in Houston was another innovation—modern architecture truly out of the box and now shaped to dramatic effect. Johnson then began wedding historicism to modern architecture methods. His 1984 Republicbank Center in Houston was topped with ever-taller three-stepped pyramids. His AT&T Building (now Sony) in New York City, also in 1984, was controversial—it was apparently inspired by furniture, a Chippendale highboy. While controversial, it was another architectural statement by Johnson, namely, that the European modernism he helped to introduce to

America and that dominated American architecture for 50 years was nearly dead.

The Pritzker Architecture Prize was inaugurated in 1979 to recognize the world's most significant architects. Often referred to as architecture's Nobel Prize, Philip Johnson was its first recipient. In accepting the prize, Johnson noted that "new understandings are sweeping the art." He hoped that architects might, as they had in the past, "join painting and sculpture once more to enhance our lives."[26]

Modernist architects were employing technology to build forms other than boxes. One of America's most recognizable buildings, William Pereira Associates' 1972 Transamerica Pyramid in San Francisco, defines both the corporation (it appears in all its advertisements) and the cityscape. Kevin Roche and John Dinkeloo completed the sculptures that had been designed under Eero Saarinen after his death. Two of the buildings are quite familiar to travelers: the old TWA terminal at New York's JFK International Airport and Washington, D.C.'s, Dulles International Airport. Roche was awarded the Pritzker Architecture Prize in 1982, a year after Dinkeloo's death. Ieoh Ming Pei, born in China in 1917, came to America from China in 1935. He became the master of geometrical shapes in architecture. His well-known designs include the John Fitzgerald Kennedy Library and Museum outside Boston; the East Building of the National Gallery of Art in the nation's capital; and the Jacob K. Javits Center in New York City. Cleveland, Ohio, is home to the Rock and Roll Hall of Fame and Museum, opened in 1995 and designed by Pei. His famous pyramid at the Louvre is known throughout the world.

Modern architecture was taking shape in many different ways as architects grew restive under orthodox international style. Robert Venturi received the Pritzker Architecture Prize in 1991. The jury's citation noted that his 1966 book *Complexity and Contradiction in Architecture* "is generally acknowledged to have diverted the mainstream of architecture away from modernism."[27] Venturi argued essentially that modern architecture had lost context in its struggle for simplicity and clarity. Buildings were being designed to mythic architectural ideals, rather than to the site or historical cues. The contradiction and complexity that can be observed in the architecture of any city should be part and parcel of the new architecture. There should not be one school of architecture, but many. Buildings should have meaning. Thus none of Venturi's buildings look alike. The Seattle Art Museum looks nothing like Oberlin College's Allen Memorial Art Museum.

The symbolic end of modern architecture in America occurred in 1972 when the main buildings of the modernist Pruitt-Igoe housing project in

St. Louis were dynamited. Opened in 1955 and designed by American architect Minoru Yamasaki, who also designed New York City's ill-fated World Trade Center twin towers, Pruitt-Igoe represented high-rise housing for the poor in a new age. By the time it was demolished, it had become a drug-infested, crime-ridden, hellish place. Modern architecture, contrary to its hopes and beliefs, proved not to be ennobling.

Frank Gehry won the Pritzker Architecture Prize in 1989, and he was the last American to receive that award until Thom Mayne was named the laureate for 2005. Both operating out of California, they typify where American architecture is now. Gehry gained notice in 1979 when he renovated his 1920s Santa Monica bungalow into a deconstructed expression of architecturally curious materials (plywood, chain-link fencing) and unexpected planes. In his later and larger works, Gehry successfully used new technologies to create voluminous space in various forms that came together in buildings whose interiors were solidly functional. His Frederick R. Weisman Art and Teaching Museum at the University of Minnesota, completed in 1993, is one such example. His Guggenheim Museum in Bilbao, Spain, finished in 1997, is an exquisite example that rivals and even vaguely recalls Frank Lloyd Wright's Guggenheim in New York. Clearly architecture for him is art, and his buildings are sculptures. The Pritzker jury complimented Gehry's risk taking and forward vision at a time when most were looking backward. The jury also noted that Gehry's work is "refreshingly original and totally American, proceeding as it does from his populist Southern California perspective."[28]

Thom Mayne founded his firm Morphosis in 1972 in Los Angeles. He and his firm have designed buildings all around the world. However, as the Pritzker jury pointed out, Mayne's approach to architecture "is not derived from European modernism, Asian influences, or even from American precedents of the last century." Indeed, his work is original and "representative of the unique...culture of Southern California."[29] Mayne's works defy labels, but they are absolutely marriages of art, technology, and engineering that are at one with their environments and attentive to clients' program objectives. Mayne and his colleagues have designed a number of innovative schools, including the celebrated Diamond Ranch High School in Pomona (1999) and the Science Center School (2004), as well as office buildings and residential complexes in the Los Angeles area, but their most interesting designs may be yet to come. Morphosis won the competition for the Olympic Village in New York City and the state of Alaska's new capitol. This new capitol building would incorporate a dome—the symbol of most state capitols, fashioned after the U.S. Capitol—but not in classical form. This would be an elliptical, translucent dome that would be lit as a beacon of democracy in a thoroughly contemporary setting that could dominate the city of Juneau.

Housing

There are 119,117,000 housing units in the United States of America. Excluding seasonal housing units, there are 116,038,000 that may be occupied year-round. The American dream is to own a home, and when most Americans think of owning a home, they usually think of a detached single-family house, that is, a house whose walls stand alone and do not touch the neighbor's. More than 71.5 million of America's housing units are those dream houses. There are also some 8.2 million manufactured or mobile home residential units; 670,000 units in cooperatives; and 5.6 million condominium units. The remainder of the housing units are composed of attached structures such as apartment buildings, row houses, and townhouses. Half of all American housing units were built before 1969.[30]

Only a little over 24.1 million housing units lie outside of metropolitan statistical areas (MSAs), which are federally defined areas in and around large population centers (cities) that are socioeconomically interdependent. MSAs are, then, urban areas that include dependent suburbs. Almost 92 million housing units lie inside MSAs, but of them, only about 35 million are in central cities, whereas 57 million are in the suburbs of those cities. Thus nearly half of America's housing stock is in the suburbs.[31]

American year-round residences are not primitive by any standard. Virtually 100 percent have all plumbing facilities and heating equipment, with natural gas favored to electricity 59 percent to 37 percent. Over 10.5 percent of residential units use heating oil. The vast majority are tied into public sewer and water systems. Of the housing units, 114 million of them have full kitchens (sink, refrigerator, stove or range), and 67 million have dishwashers; 52.6 million have garbage disposals installed in the kitchen sink, 90 million have washing machines, and over 67 million also have clothes dryers. Over 65 million have central air-conditioning, but another 25 million units have window units.

Builders continue to build the homes Americans want. In 2005, they started 2.06 million new housing projects, of which 1.72 million, about 85 percent, were single-family houses. The American dream comes, however, at a price. In 1980, the average price of a new home was $76,400. In 2005, it was $295,100. The prices of existing single-family homes likewise have risen, much to the pleasure of those who stayed in them, but they were slightly less expensive to purchase than new homes. They averaged $257,500 in 2005, and the median was $207,300. In 2005, new home sales totaled 1.28 million units, and existing single-family home sales came to 6.18 million.

Affordable housing has become an issue: 1.3 million American households are in public housing units operated by 3,300 local housing agencies, to which the U.S. Department of Housing and Urban Development administers federal aid.[32] Housing is also a racial issue that is reflected in home ownership when considering the race of the householder. Sixty-nine percent of all Americans own their own home. Non-Hispanic whites exceed the national norm at 76 percent, but no minority group even meets the norm. African American home ownership stands at 49.1 percent; Hispanic home ownership at 46.7 percent; and Asian home ownership at 59.8 percent. One ongoing survey of housing prices found that in the first quarter of 2006, only 41.3 percent of the new and existing homes sold that quarter could be afforded by families whose income was at the national median of $59,000. Among large MSAs, Indianapolis, Detroit, Youngstown, Rochester, and Buffalo were found to be the most affordable.[33] These areas are not, however, where housing is expanding. The hottest housing markets in the United States in 2005 in terms of single-family housing permits were the MSAs of Atlanta, Phoenix, Houston, Dallas, and Riverside, California.

Most of America's homes built before 1969—half of all homes, as noted earlier—survive. Comparing some of the features of new 1950 homes, built during the boom of babies and houses that followed World War II, to new 2004 homes helps to understand how American houses have changed. The new home of 1950 had, on average, 983 square feet of finished area. In fact, 62 percent of them had less than 1,200 square feet; 19 percent had 1,200–1,599 square feet; and only 17 percent had between 1,600 and 1,999 square feet. None was larger than 2,000 square feet. The new home of 2004, however, averaged 2,349 square feet, even though the size of American families has dwindled since 1950. Fully 57 percent of these homes had 2,000 square feet or more—39 percent had 2,400 square feet or more. Americans want a lot of space, and with easy credit and innovative mortgage packaging (interest-only mortgages, for example), some can get it.[34]

The typical new home of 1950 was one story (86%), had two or fewer bedrooms (66%), one and a half bathrooms or fewer (96%), no fireplace (78%), and no garage or carport (53%). The typical new home of 2004 was two stories (52%), had three bedrooms (51%) or four bedrooms (37%), and only 5 percent had one and a half or fewer bathrooms (39% had two, 33% had two and a half, and 24% had three). Most new homes had at least one fireplace (55%) and a two-car garage (64%)—19 percent had three-car garages. Ninety percent of the new 2004 homes were built with central air-conditioning, which did not exist in 1950.[35] June is national homeownership month in America.

Americans by and large want traditional houses, rather than radically innovative houses that look like they came out of a *Jetsons* cartoon. What is traditional varies by region, but that does not mean that today, a Cape Cod cottage would not appear as a traditional house in a Chicago suburb. Contemporary reiterations of traditional American houses continue to be built all over the country. The English brought medieval architecture to America in New England in the form of one- and two-room simple, heavy timber cottages. Until about 1700, the two-and-a-half-story versions of these clapboard-sided cottages, including saltboxes and Garrison houses, were built there. The saltbox was typified by a rear extension along the length of the house. Garrison houses had overhanging second stories, often decorated with pendants. Both were only one room deep, had steep roofs on which snow would be less likely to accumulate, and central chimneys and fireplaces that could warm the home in winter. The symmetrical two-and-a-half-story New England farmhouse, popular throughout the eighteenth century and the first half of the nineteenth, was framed and sided with wood and had the steep, gabled roof and central chimney of the saltboxes, but it was larger and two rooms deep. The Cape Cod cottage of the eighteenth century was a very basic, almost square, one-and-a-half-story house with a centered chimney, steep roof, and the front door centered between four windows. Cedar shingles are its distinguishing characteristic. At the other end of the spectrum, New England imported Georgian architecture during the eighteenth century before the Revolution. These large, two-story, symmetrical homes were the choice of well-to-do, urban New Englanders, who embellished them in various ways.

In the Mid-Atlantic region, much of the eighteenth-century residential architecture was quite substantial. Quakers, Swedes, and Germans built small, two-story stone houses at first, and eventually larger stone farmhouses that, with time, took on Georgian themes. Greatly prized today, these houses were being built from the middle of the eighteenth century until nearly the end of the nineteenth century. The Dutch in New York were also building stone farmhouses, noted for their stepped gable roofs. The gambrel roof was not, however, the sine qua non of a Dutch house, as it seems to be for so-called Dutch colonial houses today.

Two houses originating in the Mid-Atlantic region were to become ubiquitous in westward-expanding America. One was the tall, two-story, long and narrow Mid-Atlantic *I* house, brought to America by the English. These symmetrical houses were built for more than two centuries into the twentieth century. They were made of stone, wood, bricks, and even logs. Most were quite plain, but decoration like a Greek temple entrance was not unheard of in the early nineteenth century. They are the old midwestern farmhouses that pepper the cornfields. Log houses, favored by Germans and Scandinavians, also spread across the country with new settlers. The claim to have been born in a log cabin became a valuable political commodity in the nineteenth century—it was proof of being a man of the people. Contemporary log houses now have the opposite connotation.

Plantation houses from the Virginia tidewater southward were, of course, the homes of wealthy people, mostly of English extraction. The simple structures of the first settlers were eventually replaced by villas, often in the classical tradition, as interpreted by Andrea Palladio, often through English enthusiasts. Many of these great, historical American homes came right out of architectural books and lent little to development of an American vernacular.

The seaports of Charleston, South Carolina, and New Orleans, on the other hand, developed architectures unique in America. Charleston's single houses, which appear to be sitting sideways on their narrow lots, could rise to three stories. Piazzas or porches stretch along the sides of the houses on the first and second floors. Around New Orleans, Creole cottages on posts with their surrounding porches almost invite a crawfish boil. The same look appeared in much larger plantation houses. Cajun houses, with a single front porch, were like the Creole cottages, built on piers. In New Orleans itself, an indigenous architecture grew up from French, Spanish, and other influences when the city was rebuilt after fires in 1788 and 1794. The one-and-a-half-story Creole cottage went urban (no front porch at street side) and was expanded to a townhouse, often with a balcony. Shotgun houses, built for a century after 1830 to house Haitians, are another specialty of New Orleans. They are only one-story dwellings that are one room wide but may extend back to two or more rooms. Anglo influences were quick to invade New Orleans when it became U.S. territory, and many of New Orleans's grand homes, and even the fronts of shotgun houses, took on the highly prized classical design elements prevalent around the country.

Although Spain owned a large part of the United States at one time, from Florida to California, it had little influence on the development of American architecture outside of New Orleans, the Southwest, and California. Spanish Florida was essentially a disconnected backwater of the Spanish Empire that was not heavily colonized. Texas, New Mexico, and points north and west of them were, however, very connected. The early Spanish houses in New Mexico were single-level adobe structures that could take various shapes and even enclose a courtyard. New Mexico's later territorial architecture of the mid-nineteenth century wedded the adobe construction with modern American window treatments and classical decoration. The Spanish California houses, often *U* shaped, with porches along the inside of the *U* and clay tile roofs, were also made of adobe bricks.

While regional architectures have persisted and been revived, America's search for a national style began after the Revolution with classical revivalism

An example of a Native American adobe home. Getty Images/DAJ.

in the form of the rather elegant Federal style, Jeffersonian classicism based on Roman forms, and Greek revival. By the mid-nineteenth century, however, architects were looking elsewhere for inspiration. Tellingly for American architecture, these new styles were generally named for the British queen Victoria. Gothic style came into vogue with a liberating verticality, in comparison to the composed block of Greek temples. Furthermore, Gothic was a Christian, religious architecture. Gothic cues appeared in residential architecture as tremendously articulated, large homes and also even in small, white, wood-frame homes as wood cutout gingerbread nailed to very steep gables. For large homes, Italian villa and Italianate styles became popular.

In the second half of the nineteenth century, the revitalization of Paris drew architectural interest and brought mansard roofs to America in the Second Empire style. Architect Henry H. Richardson went back into Christian history to rediscover Romanesque architecture, building massive stone houses with turrets and sweeping arches. Before architects tired of looking across the sea for new ideas, the Queen Anne style briefly flourished, the style that most Americans would call quintessential Victorian. These houses had turrets and towers and gables and porches popping out from everywhere. They were showy homes, but a bit too much for people of simple taste. Shingle-style homes, which were very large houses with smooth lines of shingles and eyebrow dormers, did emerge, also thanks to Henry H. Richardson, as an indigenous American style late in the century, but these were country and shore houses not suitable for urban environments. By the end of the nineteenth century, and throughout much of the twentieth, the architecture of American homes returned to where it had started. The colonial revival brought back all the old styles, but in larger versions. The Georgian colonial is America's favored home.

The twentieth century dawned on another revival of classical residential architecture, American style. Architects also looked to the Italian Renaissance, France, and England. English revival houses were built all over the nation before World War II. They are known popularly as Tudor houses. In California and the Southwest, mission, Spanish colonial, and pueblo styles were revived. Meanwhile, however, Frank Lloyd Wright and his compatriots in the midwestern prairie school were designing houses with modern materials that would take their occupants out of the box by opening spaces and integrating the site with the environment. Famous as Wright's homes have become, the prairie school was a complete failure. In California, craftsman-style houses, characterized by built-in wooden structures, large hearths, informal spaces, and inviting front porches that transitioned from outside in, were popular for a brief period of about 25 years, until 1930.

While the prairie- and craftsman-style homes had limited appeal, the bungalow, first popularized in California, had wide appeal. These one-and-a-half-story unassuming, rather small houses with spacious front porches and gently sloping roofs became and remain the homes of middle America. Whether gabled in front or on the side, most Americans are quite familiar with the layout either because they grew up in one or because it was grandma's house. The front door opens into the living room, which flows into the dining room into a small, square hall. A door to the rear enters the kitchen, where there is a back door. To the right of the hall there is a bathroom with two bedrooms front and rear siding the kitchen and dining room. A steep set of stairs off the hall leads to the upper half story, where there is storage space that many families finished into another bedroom. Sears, Roebuck & Company as well as others sold tens of thousands of bungalows all over the country. They were delivered on railroad flatcars to be assembled at the building site.

The twentieth century also gave rise to two seemingly very different architectural expressions. Art Moderne, with its round, smooth stucco lines and protruding features, had the look of a 1956 Oldsmobile. The use of glass brick is a giveaway to this style, not to mention that it looks like no other style. The international style that came out of Germany in the 1930s produced, and still produces, houses that were, like Art Moderne houses, not particularly popular with Americans. Called contemporary houses by most people, these rather stark houses (devoid of period decoration and consciously nonhistorical) opened spaces and celebrated pure structure. To many Americans, they looked like sculptures or museums, rather than comfortable homes.

Americans' concepts of traditional homes have changed with new family and social circumstances and their increasing desire for bigger, better, and more innovative spaces as housing prices have risen. They want more than a series of boxy rooms in a boxy house laid out on a boxy grid, and they want their dwellings to meet their personal needs. The U.S. housing stock has therefore become more diverse to serve the needs of singles and older people who do not want yard work or extra bedrooms for children. Owner-occupied condominiums fit that bill. Condominiums and townhouses began taking new shapes. Even though attached like row houses, staggering the units or building them to differing elevations gave each unit a definition, as if it were a detached house. As with detached houses, decks and small backyards took activity to the rear of the house. Whole retirement communities have sprung up, such as Sun City and its progeny in Arizona and the Villages in Florida, along with many others, that promise to make retirement socially active in smaller but traditional houses surrounded by shuffleboard courts and golf courses. Attractive assisted living complexes have been built with central amenities—libraries, dining facilities, social areas, courtyards—in which residents have their own living quarters.

Before World War II, the single-family detached house was the rule outside of urban row houses. Long and rather narrow housing lots were set on rigorous grids. Houses sported front porches that promoted communal welcoming, with detached garages, if any, in the rear at the end of driveways along the side of the lot that led into them. After World War II, Americans began to want open interior spaces, as if the failed prairie school had actually succeeded in getting at least this point across. While kitchens were opened to eating areas, stairways were no longer enclosed, skylights began to be used, and sloped, elevated ceilings became popular, Americans still wanted interior spaciousness, with a traditional exterior look.

By the 1960s, however, the entire orientation of houses had changed. Front porches went out of style, and garages were attached to the house, with front or side entrances and shorter driveways in favor of opened backyard patios and decks. The front yards became more formal settings for the houses, whereas backyards became places for entertainment, relaxation, swing sets, pools, and, of course, cookouts. Lots were now being drawn into more square than rectangular plots to accommodate larger backyards. Inside, master bedrooms and baths were enlarged and considerably fancied up to provide parents of teenage baby boomers a respite and some privacy. A new addition, often at the expense of formal living rooms, was added to the American home: the family room. The gathered family had always been a cherished American ideal, but in the 1960s, any pretense of formality in home life was gone for good.

There were also other forces helping to change American housing. The growth of planned unit developments allowed flexibility for developers to break away from grids and aggregate differing kinds of housing in large developments with open spaces. These kinds of developments proliferated all over the country and resulted in new settings for homes on cul-de-sacs, winding roads, loops, and circles. It would be unusual today to find a large suburb laid out on a square grid. As land suitable for building has become scarce and more expensive, however, the preservation, renovation, and restoration of some of America's older structures for use as housing has occurred. Old warehouses, schools, factories, apartment buildings, and single homes have been preserved and rehabilitated as new housing. The United States was slow to recognize the value of its older and historical buildings, but the hope to preserve one of America's classic homes helped to get the ball rolling. The Mount Vernon Ladies' Association, founded in 1853, is often given credit for begetting a new

A bird's eye view of American suburbia. Getty Images/PhotoDisc.

awareness of America's historic architecture. The secondary effect of having federal grants available for historic preservation was the rebirth of craftsmanship long lost to modern construction.

American residential building of the twenty-first century, largely the province of real estate developers, has taken a new twist. As already noted, houses have, as a matter of fact, become bigger, and they are made to look bigger by expanded articulation and, in large two-story houses, by a severe verticality. Window extensions and dormers abound—they add value and spaciousness. New materials have often replaced traditional wood and brick façades. Vinyl and aluminum sidings and brick veneers attached to wooden studs give the appearance of solidity. Even contemporary exteriors that appear from a distance to be stucco are often veneers that, when gently pressed against, give way. More interestingly, however, many new houses are impossible to place into the historical spectrum. There are suggestions of known styles—Palladian windows frequently are used in structures anything but classical. Suggestions of Greek revival porticoes may be found on one-story ranch houses. An oddly placed round window hints of colonial revival. So confused is residential architecture that developers do not call their houses Georgian, Tudor, or Italianate, but rather names like the Pearl, Millstone, Avalon, Chestnut, and Prescott—names that rightly evoke no architectural style at all.

It is a sad fact that security has become an important element in the design of new communities of homes. High-end homes can now be found in gated developments and even on limited-access islands. Entrances to housing developments have long been defined by the suggestion of entry gates, but there was open access to the streets inside. Today, the gates are operative and limit access to residents and those they permit to enter. Protected inner courts in multiunit buildings allow safety out of doors for their residents. Playgrounds have been designed on the roofs of schools for the safety of the children.

In fact, however, a home, no matter its value or location, means owning a real piece of America. Homeowners—property owners—pay taxes and protect their investment. They are good citizens living the American dream. In turn, the government guarantees the principle that personal property is sacrosanct. The Founding Fathers understood this well, allowing only male property owners to vote in federal elections. While this, of course, changed with time, the federal government has remained instrumental in expanding home ownership through governmental agencies like the Federal Housing Administration and quasi-governmental organizations like the Federal National Mortgage Association, which creates a secondary mortgage market. The Government National Mortgage Association guarantees prompt payment of housing loans issued by government agencies like the Federal Housing Administration, the Rural Housing Service, the Veterans Administration, and the Office of Public and Indian Housing. Federal bankruptcy law excludes $125,000 of the value of a home, while the states of Texas and Florida have unlimited exclusions. Home ownership is an elemental American value.

NOTES

1. U.S. Department of Labor, Bureau of Labor Statistics, *Occupational Outlook Handbook,* 2006–2007 ed., http://www.bls.gov. Note that these data do not include fine and craft artists who may be practicing their art in their leisure time but making their livings by other means.

2. *Statistical Abstract of the United States, 2006,* http://www.census.gov.

3. Cory Arcangel, "Cory's Web Log," http://www.beigerecords.com.

4. John Wetenhall, "A Brief History of Percent-for-Art in America," *Public Art Review* 9 (1993), http://www.publicartreview.org.

5. See the *WaterFire* Web site at http://www.waterfire.org.

6. National Endowment for the Arts, "2004 Annual Report," http://www.nea.gov.

7. First Amendment Center, "Case Summary for National Endowment for the Arts vs. Finley," http://www.firstamendmentcenter.org.

8. Smithsonian American Art Museum, "About the Museum," http://americanart.si.edu; National Gallery of Art, "About the National Gallery of Art," http://www.nga.gov.

9. Smithsonian Institution, "History of the Galleries: Freer and Sackler Gallery," http://www.asia.si.edu.

10. Smithsonian Institution, "The Hirshhorn Story," http://hirshhorn.si.edu.

11. MoCA, "Exhibitions," http://www.mocacleveland.org.

12. Contemporary Arts Museum, Houston, "Exhibits," http://www.camh.org.

13. Contemporary Art Center of Virginia, "Exhibitions," http://www.cacv.org; The Butler Institute of American Art, "Current Exhibitions," http://www.butlerart.com; San Francisco Museum of Modern Art, "Exhibition Overview: Matthew Barney," http://www.sfmoma.org.

14. National Endowment for the Arts, Research Division, "Arts Participation by Region, State, and Metropolitan Area," note no. 72, January 1999, http://www.nea.gov.

15. American Association of Museums, "Museums FAQ," http://www.aam-us.org.

16. See "Whitney Biennial: Day for Night," http://www.whitneybiennial.org.

17. U.S. Department of State, ART in Embassies Program, "Mission," http://aiep.state.gov.

18. U.S. Department of State, Bureau of International Information Programs, "Art on the Edge: 17 Contemporary American Artists: Preface," http://usinfo.state.gov.

19. Ibid.

20. The Mennello Museum of American Art, "Earl Cunningham," http://www.mennellomuseum.org.

21. See Richard Longstreth, *The Buildings of Main Street: A Guide to American Commercial Architecture,* updated ed. (New York: Alta Mira Press, 2000).

22. Congress for the New Urbanism, "Charter of the New Urbanism," http://cnu.org.

23. Carter Wiseman, *Shaping a Nation* (New York: W. W. Norton, 1998), 22–24.

24. Ibid., 36–37.

25. See Henry Russell Hitchcock and Philip Johnson, *The International Style: Architecture Since 1922* (New York: W. W. Norton, 1932).

26. Pritzker Architecture Prize, "Philip Johnson: Pritzker Architecture Prize Laureate, 1979," http://www.pritzkerprize.com.

27. Pritzker Architecture Prize, "Robert Venturi: Pritzker Architecture Prize Laureate, 1991," http://www.pritzkerprize.com.

28. Pritzker Architecture Prize, "Frank Gehry: Pritzker Architecture Prize Laureate, 1989," http://www.pritzkerprize.com.

29. Pritzker Architecture Prize, "California Architect Thom Mayne Becomes the 2005 Pritzker Architecture Prize Laureate," http://www.pritzkerprize.com.

30. U.S. Census Bureau, "American Housing Survey for the United States: 2001," http://www.census.gov.

31. Ibid.

32. U.S. Department of Housing and Urban Development, "Homes & Communities: HUD's Public Housing Program," http://www.hud.gov.

33. National Association of Home Builders, "Indianapolis Remains Nation's Most Affordable Major Housing Market for Third Consecutive Quarter," May 17, 2006, http://www.nahb.org.

34. NAHB Public Affairs and NAHB Economics, "Housing Facts, Figures and Trends," March 2006, http://www.nahb.org.

35. Ibid.

BIBLIOGRAPHY

Attoe, Wayne, and Donn Logan. *American Urban Architecture: Catalysts in the Design of Cities.* Berkeley: University of California Press, 1989.

Burchard, John, and Albert Bush-Brown. *The Architecture of America: A Social and Cultural History.* Boston: Little, Brown, 1961.

Causey, Andrew. *Sculpture Since 1945.* Oxford History of Art. New York: Oxford University Press, 1998.

Doss, Erika. *Twentieth-century American Art.* Oxford History of Art. New York: Oxford University Press, 2002.

Doubilet, Susan, and Daralice Boles. *American House Now.* Contemporary Architectural Direction. New York: Universe, 1997.

Foster, Gerald. *American Houses: A Field Guide to the Architecture of the Home.* New York: Houghton Mifflin, 2004.

Gelernter, Mark. *A History of American Architecture: Buildings in Their Cultural and Technological Context.* Hanover, NH: University Press of New England, 1999.

Handlin, David P. *American Architecture.* 2nd ed. Thames and Hudson World of Art. London: Thames and Hudson, 2004.

Hopkins, David. *After Modern Art, 1945–2000.* Oxford History of Art. New York: Oxford University Press, 2000.

Joselit, David. *American Art Since 1945.* Thames and Hudson World of Art. London: Thames and Hudson, 2003.

Langdon, Philip. *American Houses.* New York: Stewart, Tabori and Chang, 1987.

Lippard, Lucy R. *Mixed Blessings: New Art in a Multicultural America.* New York: Pantheon Books, 1990.

Pohl, Frances K. *Framing America: A Social History of American Art.* New York: Thames and Hudson, 2002.

Pokinski, Deborah Frances. *The Development of the American Modern Style.* Ann Arbor, MI: UMI Research Press, 1984.

Rifkind, Carole. *A Field Guide to American Architecture.* New York: New American Library, 1980.

Rifkind, Carole. *A Field Guide to Contemporary American Architecture.* New York: Dutton, 1999.

Upton, Dell. *Architecture in the United States.* Oxford History of Art. New York: Oxford University Press, 1998.

Wentling, James. *Designing a Place Called Home: Reordering the Suburbs.* New York: Chapman and Hall, 1995.

Selected Bibliography

Althen, Gary, Amanda R. Doran, and Susan J. Szmania. *American Ways*. 2nd ed. Yarmouth, ME: Intercultural Press, 2003.

American Social History Project, City University of New York. *Who Built America?: Working People and the Nation's Economy, Politics, Culture, and Society*. 2nd ed. 2 vols. New York: Worth, 2000.

Ashbee, Edward. *American Society Today*. New York: Manchester University Press, 2002.

Ashby, LeRoy. *With Amusement for All: A History of American Popular Culture Since 1830*. Lexington: University Press of Kentucky, 2006.

Baker, Wayne E. *America's Crisis of Values: Reality and Perception*. Princeton, NJ: Princeton University Press, 2005.

Buenker, John D., and Lorman A. Ratner, eds. *Multiculturalism in the United States: A Comparative Guide to Acculturation and Ethnicity*. Rev. and expanded ed. Westport, CT: Greenwood Press, 2005.

Carnes, Mark C., ed. *A History of American Life*. Rev. and abridged ed. Edited by Arthur M. Schlesinger Jr. New York: Scribner, 1996.

Filene, Peter G. *Him/Her/self: Gender Identities in Modern America*. 3rd ed. Foreword by Elaine Tyler May. Baltimore: Johns Hopkins University Press, 1998.

Fischer, William C., ed. *Identity, Community, and Pluralism in American Life*. New York: Oxford University Press, 1997.

Gellert, Michael. *The Fate of America: An Inquiry into National Character*. Washington, DC: Brassey's, 2001.

Gutfeld, Arnon. *American Exceptionalism: The Effects of Plenty on the American Experience*. Portland, OR: Sussex Academic Press, 2002.

Healey, Joseph F. *Diversity and Society: Race, Ethnicity, and Gender.* 2nd ed. Thousand Oaks, CA: Pine Forge Press, 2007.

Hughes, Richard T. *Myths America Lives By.* Foreword by Robert N. Bellah. Urbana: University of Illinois, 2003.

Jones, Jacqueline, ed. *Created Equal: A Social and Political History of the United States.* 2nd ed. New York: Pearson/Longman, 2006.

Kennedy, Sheila Suess. *God and Country: America in Red and Blue.* Waco, TX: Baylor University Press, 2007.

Miyares, Ines M., and Christopher A. Airriess, eds. *Contemporary Ethnic Geographies in America.* Lanham, MD: Rowman and Littlefield, 2006.

Nostrand, Richard L., and Lawrence E. Estaville, eds. *Homelands: A Geography of Culture and Place Across America.* Baltimore: Johns Hopkins University Press, 2001.

Shumsky, Neil Larry, and Timothy J. Crimmins, comps. *American Life, American People.* 2 vols. San Diego, CA: Harcourt Brace Jovanovich, 1988.

Wilson, Leslie, ed. *Americana: Readings in Popular Culture.* Hollywood, CA: Press Americana, 2006.

Woods, Randall B., and Willard B. Gatewood. *The American Experience: A Concise History.* 2 vols. Fort Worth, TX: Harcourt College, 2000.

Index

About the Editor and Contributors

BENJAMIN F. SHEARER received his PhD in the history of ideas from St. Louis University and his MSLS from the University of Illinois at Urbana-Champaign. He has written and edited several reference books, including *Home Front Heroes* (Greenwood Press, 2007), *The Uniting States* (Greenwood Press, 2004), and *State Names, Seals, Flags and Symbols* (3rd ed., Greenwood Press, 2002).

ELLEN BAIER is an independent scholar and writer who is active in theater and national tour productions. In 2004, Franklin & Marshall College awarded her its Williamson Medal. She is also a major contributor to *Home Front Heroes: A Biographical Dictionary of Americans during Wartime* (Greenwood Press, 2007).

WENDE VYBORNEY FELLER, PhD, is a corporate consultant and freelance writer. A graduate of the University of Minnesota, she has taught at a variety of universities, including, most recently, in the executive MBA program at the College of St. Mary in Moraga, California. Among her academic presentations are papers in Japanese and American war rhetoric at the conclusion of World War II. She lives in Phoenix, Arizona, and is working on her first novel.

AGNES HOOPER GOTTLIEB is the dean of Freshman Studies and Special Academic Programs at Seton Hall University. She also holds the rank of professor in the Communication Department. She is the coauthor of *1,000 Years, 1,000 People: Ranking the Men and Women Who Shaped the Millennium* and the author of *Women Journalists and the Municipal Housekeeping Movement, 1868–1914,* from the Edwin Mellen Press. She has written dozens of articles and book chapters on journalism history. She also writes a monthly advice column for the parents of Seton Hall University students.

PAMELA LEE GRAY is an independent scholar who holds a PhD in American history from the University of Southern California. Her written work includes over 100 academic articles and several books on local history. Her curriculum design work teaches history using ethnography and historical visual images.

WILLIAM P. TOTH teaches writing at Heidelberg College and has been published in both the United States and England. His historical and literary writing has appeared in *African American National Biography, Back Home in Kentucky, Bend in the River, Chronicles of the Old West, Encyclopedia of African American History, SuperReal: The British Journal of Surrealism,* and others.